THE YOUNG PEOPLE'S THESAURUS DICTIONARY

THE YOUNG PEOPLE'S
THESAURUS DICTIONARY

HARRIET WITTELS
JOAN GREISMAN

Edited and with an Introduction by
WILLIAM MORRIS
Editor-in-Chief of the American Heritage Dictionary

GROSSET & DUNLAP • Publishers • New York
A NATIONAL GENERAL COMPANY

Library of Congress Catalog Card Number: 70-158760

ISBN: 0-448-02688-0 (Deluxe Edition)
ISBN: 0-448-02653-8 (Trade Edition)
ISBN: 0-448-04286-X (Library Edition)

THE YOUNG PEOPLE'S THESAURUS DICTIONARY

INTRODUCTION

"The difference between the right word and the almost right word is the difference between lightning and the lightning bug." — Mark Twain.

Mark Twain is, of course, the author of many of America's most popular books; in fact, some students of our literature consider him our greatest writer. If you haven't already read *Tom Sawyer, Huckleberry Finn, A Connecticut Yankee in King Arthur's Court,* and other Mark Twain novels and stories, then a wonderful treat is in store for you.

Mark Twain spent his life looking for the *right* word, and avoiding the *almost right* word. And that's what this book is all about.

In the pages that follow you will find hundreds of lists of words. Each word in each list means the same thing or nearly the same thing as the other words in that list. Why bother, you may ask, to gather such words together into lists like these? Simply to help you in two ways. First, to give you all the words which are similar in meaning, so that you can choose the word which seems just right for the thought you wish to convey. Second, to introduce to you words you may not already know. Since you know that all words in each group are synonyms (that's the technical name for words similar in meaning), you can easily guess the meanings of unfamiliar words and thereby greatly expand your vocabulary.

You may wonder why in the world the English language has so many words that mean practically the same thing. Wouldn't life be much simpler if we had only one word for each object or idea?

Well, let's look at a word we all use every day — "friend." We all have friends. If we're lucky, we have lots of them. But some of them are closer friends than others. Suppose you are writing a short essay or poem about friends and friendship. You will find it very helpful to look up the word "friend" in this book. There you will find: "acquaintance, intimate, companion, comrade, mate, associate, colleague, partner, crony, playmate," together with such informal or slang words as "chum, buddy, sidekick, pal."

From this group of more than a dozen words, you'll find it easy to pick the *right* word to express exactly the degree of friendship you want to express.

There's another way that this book can help you to choose the right word. Suppose you want to describe a friend who is usually very calm and quiet but suddenly, as the slang expression goes, "loses his cool." So you want a word that is just the opposite of "calm." Look up "calm" and at the very end of the list you will find a word in red type: "excited." That's the word you are looking for. It's what the word experts call an "antonym" — a word opposite in meaning to another word.

There aren't nearly as many antonyms in English as there are synonyms because one word, in most cases, will serve as the opposite to several other words. However, if "excited" doesn't seem to be exactly the right word to use, look up "excite" and you will find such words as "arouse, stir, stimulate, provoke." Perhaps a better way to describe your friend would be to say that he is "aroused," "stirred," "stimulated," or "provoked." And you don't need to stop here. If you go one step further, you will look up "arouse" and find more than a dozen synonyms there — and one of them may be the *right* word you have been looking for.

This brings us back to the question of why English has so many words that mean the same or nearly the same thing. The answer is that English is the only language which has borrowed words from every other language spoken on the face of the earth.

There are many reasons for this. Back in the times of the Caesars (43 B.C.), Roman legions invaded England and stayed for nearly four hundred years. They didn't contribute much to the development of English, though a few place names still reflect Roman influence. "Winchester," for instance, was once a Roman army camp, and the "chester" comes from the Latin "castra," the word for "camp."

The English language did acquire thousands of words of Latin and Greek origin when the Normans invaded England in 1066, taking over control of the country and, naturally, adding a great many words of French origin to the language. So we had the first examples of two words meaning almost the same thing — one originally French, the other originally English.

But this was just the beginning. The British proved to be masters of the sea for many centuries. As a small island nation, they had to trade with many other countries to get the food and other materials that they needed to live. And along with the supplies that they brought back to England, the traders brought words to enlarge and enrich their language. For example, many of you wear blue jeans, denims, or corduroy jackets and pants. Each of these names came originally to England — and later, of course, to America — from Britain's international trade. The first "jeans" were made of a fabric woven in Genoa, Italy. Originally woven for ships' sails, it is, as you know, a tough, sturdy fabric. Some sailors decided the fabric would make good, long-lasting pants — and blue jeans were born.

"Denim" also is named after the town in which the fabric was originally made — Nimes, a city in southern France. The original name was "serge de Nimes" (serge from Nimes), but it soon was shortened simply to "denim." And that rugged fabric we call "corduroy" was originally made to be used for hunting jackets worn by French kings. So "corduroy" was originally "corde du roi," or "cloth for the king."

But the British didn't only borrow from the French and the Italians. Everywhere their sailors went, they picked up native words and added them to English. The word "thug," for instance, sounds like something invented in New York City to describe the worst kind of gangsters or hoodlums. Actually, it was originally used in India to describe worshippers of the Indian goddess Kali.

In order to maintain the beautiful and elaborate shrines built in honor of Kali, her followers (the "thugs") would waylay, rob, and sometimes kill innocent travelers in India. So infamous were the thugs that the name came into English as a synonym for crook, ruffian, or hoodlum.

More recently, of course, Americans have contributed many thousands of synonyms to that brand of English sometimes called the American Language. We have invented many names for things and ideas that also exist in England but under very different names. For instance, what we call an "elevator," the British call a "lift." Our "cookies" are "biscuits" in England. A "run" in a stocking would be called a "ladder" by an English girl. Our "molasses" is their "treacle." Our "baby carriage" is their "perambulator," or "pram," for short. And so it goes.

In the pages that follow, you will find thousands of words to help you express yourself clearly, effectively, and imaginatively. Remember, you need not stop at the first list you look up. If you don't find precisely the right word, take any one of the other words in the list and look *it* up. That way, you will find the resources of the world's richest language at your fingertips. And always remember what Mark Twain said: make your goal the *right* word, not the *almost right* word.

William Morris

How to Use
The Young People's Thesaurus-Dictionary

Finding Entry Words

The words that have synonyms and antonyms are called entry words.

above   overhead, up, aloft, on, upon   below

The word **above,** in heavy black type, is the entry word. All entry words are listed in alphabetical order, just like words in a dictionary.

The word in smaller black type at the top of every page is called a guide word. It will help you to find an entry word quickly. The guide word at the top of the left-hand page is actually the first entry word. The guide word at the top of the right-hand page is the last entry word.

A Book of Synonyms and Antonyms

In the *Young People's Thesaurus-Dictionary* you will find synonyms and antonyms for words, *not* the definitions and explanations you can find in a dictionary. Synonyms are words that have the same meaning and can therefore be substituted for one another in a sentence.

expensive   costly, high-priced, dear   cheap
The bicycle was too *expensive* for him to buy.
The bicycle was too *costly* for him to buy.
The bicycle was too *high-priced* for him to buy.
The bicycle was too *dear* for him to buy.

If you cannot find a word, it simply does not have synonyms. Its definition will be found in a dictionary. For example, the word *accordion* has no synonyms, but a dictionary will give its meaning as "a musical instrument with keys, metal reeds, and a bellows."

Antonyms are words that have opposite meanings. Many words listed that have synonyms do not have antonyms.

> **army**   legion, forces, troops, military, militia
> **aroma**   fragrance, odor, perfume, scent

Entry Words With Groups of Synonyms

Sometimes an entry word will have synonyms grouped under different numbers. This means that the entry word has more than one meaning, and each meaning has its synonyms.

> **firm**   1. solid, fixed, secure, unyielding, inflexible, stationary, immovable, rigid, 2. company, business, enterprise

With this type of entry word, you must use judgment and common sense in choosing the appropriate group of synonyms. For example, if you wanted to substitute a synonym in the sentence, "His father's **firm** was closed for vacation," you would choose the group of synonyms following the number 2 for the word **firm**.

Entry Words With the Same Spelling

Sometimes an entry word has two different pronunciations, as well as different groups of synonyms. In that case, it will be entered twice, with numbers in front of the entry word itself.

> **1. minute**   instant, moment, twinkling (*Slang* — jiffy, sec, half a shake)
> **2. minute**   small, tiny, miniature, slight, negligible, insignificant

Placement of Antonyms

Antonyms will be listed immediately after the synonyms, in red. You will find antonyms for an entry word that has many groups of synonyms, right after each group, unless one antonym fits all the groups. In that case, the antonym will be listed on a separate line, under all the groups, in red.

> **due** 1. proper, rightful, fitting, just, fair, square, equitable unfair, 2. owed paid
> **bright** 1. shining, clear, vivid, 2. smart, alert, intelligent, 3. pleasant, cheerful, lively
> dull

Slang Terms

Occasional slang terms are given in parentheses, listed as synonyms for an entry word. Slang terms are used in common, everyday, informal talk, words that have developed from attempts to find fresh, colorful, or humorous expressions.

> **friend** acquaintance, intimate, companion, comrade, mate, associate, colleague, partner, crony, playmate, chum, buddy (*Slang* — sidekick, pal)

Adapting Forms of the Root Word

Many words are derived from one root word. Ordinarily, in this book, only one of those words will be listed with its synonyms. The other form of the word will simply be mentioned under the chosen entry word, in capital letters. Here again, judgment and common sense will be needed to adapt the synonyms to the form you need.

> **happy** contented, glad, joyful, blissful, cheerful, bright, radiant unhappy, sad
> HAPPILY, HAPPINESS

For example, in the sentence, "He found **happiness** in his work," you would change the synonym *contented* to *contentment* ("He found **contentment** in his work"), the synonym *glad* to *gladness* ("He found **gladness** in his work"), etc.

Adapting Parts of Speech

Similarly, if an entry word can possibly be considered as a verb, adjective, adverb, or noun, but is treated here as a verb, you might need to adapt it for use as one of the other parts of speech.

gag silence, muzzle, muffle, restrain

In this example, *gag* is treated as a verb, as are all of its synonyms. If you wanted to substitute synonyms for the noun *gag*, as in the sentence, "The robber put a **gag** on his victim's mouth," you would adapt the verb *gag* in this way:

gag silencer, muzzle, muffler, restraint

A

a   one, any

abandon   desert, forsake, leave, give up entirely, cease, depart, leave undone, discard, relinquish, surrender, discontinue, quit, evacuate, withdraw (*Slang* — throw up, turn one's back on, wash one's hands of, pull out on) keep, fulfill, stay with

abase   bring down, make lower, make humble, demote, degrade, reduce (*Slang* — bump, bust)

abashed   ashamed, embarrassed, confused, bewildered, humiliated, mortified

abate   reduce, lessen, put an end to, stop, do away with, decrease, curtail, moderate   increase

abbey   convent, monastery, nunnery, cloisters

abbot   monk, friar

abbreviate   shorten, curtail, condense, abridge, contract, reduce, cut, compress   lengthen, increase ABBREVIATION

abdicate   renounce, give up, resign, relinquish, abandon, quit, surrender, vacate   retain

abdomen   belly, paunch, stomach (*Slang* — breadbasket, pot, corporation)   ABDOMINAL

abhor   hate, dislike, detest, loathe, despise, feel disgust for love

abide   1. accept, obey, endure, tolerate, 2. stay, reside, dwell

ability   power, skill, talent, competence, capacity, capability, efficiency, aptitude (*Slang* — know-how)   inability

abject   wretched, miserable, deserving contempt

able   skillful, capable, having power, competent, efficient, qualified   incapable   ABLY

abnormal irregular, eccentric, odd, monstrous, insane, unnatural   normal, sane

aboard on board, on (or into) a ship, train or airplane

abode dwelling, residence, home, address, lodging place, quarters, housing (*Slang* — dump, joint, shack)

abolish cancel, exterminate, destroy, put an end to, do away with, wipe out   retain   ABOLITION

abominable hateful, disgusting, very unpleasant, dreadful, awful, horrible, atrocious, obnoxious, detestable   pleasant

abound plentiful, well supplied, filled, teem with, overflow scarce

about 1. concerning, of, upon, 2. nearly, almost, approximately, 3. around, 4. ready to, on the point of

above overhead, up, aloft, on, upon   below

abreast alongside, side by side, lined up, beside

abridge make shorter, abbreviate, curtail, condense, contract, reduce, cut, compress   lengthen, increase

abroad overseas, away, outside one's country

abrupt sudden, hasty, short, curt, unexpected

abscess sore, inflammation, pustule, wound

absent away, lacking, truant (*Slang* — playing hookey) ABSENCE, ABSENTEE

absolute complete, perfect, thorough, entire, total, essential, positive, supreme   partial   ABSOLUTELY

absolve forgive, cleanse, discharge, pardon, excuse, acquit blame

absorb take in, soak up, incorporate, integrate, engross, assimilate, sponge, suck up
ABSORBENT, ABSORPTION

abstain refrain, withhold, do without   pursue

abstract 1. unconcrete, apart from any real thing concrete, 2. difficult, hard to understand clear, 3. remove, take away, deduct add

absurd foolish, ridiculous, not true, unbelievable, impossible, ludicrous meaningful, sensible
ABSURDITY, ABSURDLY

abundance plenty, large amount, great quantity, profusion, (*Slang* — oodles, gobs, scads) insufficient, not enough
ABUNDANT, ABUNDANTLY

abuse mistreat, severely scold, injure, damage, ill-use appreciate

academy school, college, educational institution

accelerate hasten, speed up, quicken, hurry (*Slang* — step on it, hop to it) slow down, delay
ACCELERATION, ACCELERATOR

accent emphasis, stress on syllables of a word, tone, pronunciation, inflection

accept adopt, believe, approve, take what is offered, consent to (*Slang* — buy, swallow) deny, dissent
ACCEPTABLE, ACCEPTANCE

access way of approach ACCESSIBLE

accessory addition, extra, contributory, assistant, accomplice, supplement

accident mishap, injury, casualty, chance, event (*Slang* — fluke) ACCIDENTAL, ACCIDENTALLY

acclaim applaud, shout welcome, approve (*Slang* — root for) disapprove, reject

accommodate oblige, have room for, supply, conform
ACCOMMODATION

accomplice partner in crime (*Slang* — sidekick)

accomplish   do, carry out, finish, complete, fulfill, perform, achieve, realize (*Slang* — knock off, polish off, do the trick)   neglect   ACCOMPLISHMENT

accord   agreement, conformity, harmony   disagreement   ACCORDANCE, ACCORDINGLY

account   1. story, reason, information, description, tale, statement, 2. list, sum, record

accumulate   collect, store up, increase, assemble, gather, compile, amass   ACCUMULATION

accurate   correct, exactly right, perfect, O.K., all right   wrong   ACCURACY

accuse   blame, charge, impeach, indict, denounce, tattle, (*Slang* — put the finger on, rat on, frame)   absolve   ACCUSATION

accustom   get used to, familiarize, addict, condition

ache   continuous pain, hurt, throb

achieve   accomplish, carry out, do, finish, complete, fulfill, perform, realize (*Slang* — knock off, polish off, do the trick)   fail   ACHIEVEMENT

acknowledge   admit, recognize, make known, answer, accept, grant, concede   dissent   ACKNOWLEDGMENT

acme   top, highest point, summit, peak, crown, zenith   bottom, lowest point

acquaint   make familiar, inform, notify, teach, tell, enlighten, (*Slang* — wise-up)   ACQUAINTANCE

acquiesce   agree, submit, assent, concur, consent, comply, succumb (*Slang* — buy)   dissent

acquire   gain, obtain, get as one's own, secure, earn (*Slang* — get hold of)   lose   ACQUISITION

acquit   declare not guilty, absolve, forgive, cleanse, discharge, pardon, excuse   blame

acrid sharp, bitter, stinging, nasty, biting, harsh
sweet, pleasant

acrobat gymnast, athlete, tumbler

act 1. do, perform, behave, 2. pretend, 3. law

action 1. behavior, thing done, performance, way of working, 2. battle

active lively, working, energetic, vivacious, dynamic,
animated, spirited (*Slang* — peppy) idle, lazy

activity movement, use of power, energy, thing to do, action

actor stage player, performer, entertainer, trouper

actual real, factual, true, genuine, concrete, authentic
nonexistent ACTUALLY

acute sharp and severe, shrewd, discerning, quick, astute,
keen, smart (*Slang* — quick on the trigger, smart as a
whip, sharp as a tack, nobody's fool) dull

adamant firm, unyielding, obstinate yielding

adapt make fit, make suitable, modify, change, alter, vary,
adjust ADAPTABLE, ADAPTATION

add put together, increase, sum up, total, join, unite
subtract ADDITION, ADDITIONAL

address 1. apply oneself, 2. speech, greeting, 3. abode, home

adept skillful, expert, apt, proficient unskillful

adequate sufficient, enough, satisfactory, ample, plenty
inadequate, insufficient

adhere cling, stick fast ADHESIVE

adjacent near, adjoining, next to, touching, bordering,
neighboring

adjoin be next to, be close to, be side by side, connect,
come in contact with

adjourn   postpone, end, put off until a later time, discontinue, suspend, recess, dissolve

adjust   arrange, set just right, adapt, make fit, make suitable, modify, change, alter, vary   ADJUSTMENT

administer   1. manage, execute, preside, 2. apply, give to, contribute

admirable   praiseworthy, excellent, very good, commendable, deserving   unfavorable, objectionable   ADMIRATION, ADMIRE

admit   1. consent, confess, acknowledge (*Slang* — talk, own up, sing, come clean)   deny,   2. allow to enter, induct, receive

admonition   warning, advice, reminder, caution, word to the wise, tip

ado   action, stir, fuss, trouble, commotion, excitement, hubbub, to-do   peace, calm

adopt   choose, assume, take to oneself, give a home to, accept as one's own   reject   ADOPTION

adore   love and respect, worship, idolize, cherish, admire, revere   hate   ADORATION, ADORABLE

adorn   beautify, decorate, ornament, garnish, glamorize

adroit   smart, clever, adept, skillful, expert, apt, proficient   unskillful

adult   full-grown, grown-up, mature, developed, of age   immature

advance   move forward, promote, progress, proceed   revert   ADVANCEMENT

advantage   benefit, upper hand, leverage, gain (*Slang* — edge)   disadvantage   ADVANTAGEOUS

adventure   unusual experience, undertaking, enterprise, event, happening, occurrence, exploit, project, incident   ADVENTURER, ADVENTUROUS

adverse unfriendly, hostile, unfavorable, contrary, opposite, harmful ADVERSARY

adversity distress, misfortune, hardship, affliction, grief, disaster, trouble prosperity

advertise announce, notify public, call attention to (*Slang* — plug, boost) conceal, hush ADVERTISEMENT

advice counsel, plan, suggestion, recommendation, instruction, direction, tip ADVISE, ADVISABLE

advocate recommend publicly, speak in favor of, defend, support oppose

affable courteous, pleasant, friendly, sociable, gracious, approachable, amiable, communicative
unsociable, unfriendly

affair occasion, occurrence, event, happening, matter, concern, business, party, festivity

affect influence, sway, move, persuade

affection friendly feeling, admiration, love and respect dislike AFFECTIONATE

affirm assert, confirm, ratify, state, pronounce, declare, endorse, certify veto, deny AFFIRMATIVE

afflict cause pain, trouble, bother, distress greatly, disturb, perturb, agitate soothe AFFLICTION

affluent wealthy, abundant, plentiful, ample, rich, bountiful, well-off, well-to-do, well-fixed (*Slang* — well-heeled, filthy rich) poor

afford 1. have the means, 2. yield, supply, furnish

affront an open insult, offense, provocation (*Slang* — slap in the face)

afraid frightened, fearful, scared, cowardly (*Slang* — chicken) courageous

after 1. later than, following, next, subsequently before,

2. behind, 3. in search of, in pursuit, 4. because of, 5. in spite of, despite AFTERWARD

again another time, once more, anew, afresh, repeatedly

against in opposition to, versus with

age 1. time of life, period in history, 2. grow old, mature, ripen AGED

agency operation, office, management, work

agent doer, performer, actor, worker, operator

aggravate annoy, irritate, provoke, make worse, exasperate, infuriate, irk, vex (*Slang* — miff, peeve, rile) pacify

aggregate total, amount to, add up, accumulate, compile

aggression attack, assault, offense, invasion defense AGGRESSOR

aggressive belligerent, offensive, hostile, militant, combative peaceful

aghast astonished, surprised, amazed, astounded, bewildered, thunderstruck, awed, flabbergasted

agile nimble, fast, alert, quick, spry, athletic dull, slow AGILITY

agitate disturb, incite, instigate, excite, stir up, inflame, provoke calm AGITATION

agony suffering, pain, grief, distress, anguish, torture, torment, heartache, woe peace AGONIZING

agree consent, assent, accept, approve of, comply disagree AGREEABLE

agreement pact, contract, understanding, concord, bargain, treaty, alliance, deal disagreement

agriculture farming, cultivation, husbandry AGRICULTURAL

ahead   in front, before, forward, in advance, leading, winning   behind

aid   help, remedy, relief, assistant, helper, service, benefit   hindrance

ail   1. trouble, bother, disturb, perturb, 2. be ill, suffer, feel awful, feel sick   AILMENT

aim   1. direct, point, intend, try, 2. purpose, intention, objective, goal, end, target

airy   light, breezy, fanciful, lighthearted, gay, graceful, merry   grave, gloomy

aisle   passageway, corridor, alley, lane, channel, artery, opening

ajar   open, gaping   closed

akin   related, alike, similar, connected, associated, affiliated, allied

alarm   1. startle, arouse, frighten, shock, jar, jolt, agitate, disturb, unnerve   calm,   2. signal, call, warning, summons

alcoholic   drunkard, inebriate, sot, tippler (*Slang* — boozer, wino, lush, drunk, souse)   ALCOHOL

alert   watchful, wide awake, clear-witted, attentive, ready, prompt, lively, nimble, on the job, on one's toes   dull   ALERTNESS

alibi   excuse, story

alien   foreign, different, strange

allay   lessen, check, quiet, relieve, calm, ease, pacify, moderate, restrain, alleviate   excite

allege   declare, state

allegiance   loyalty, faithfulness, devotion, fidelity

alley   narrow back-street, path, aisle, passageway, corridor, lane, opening

alliance   agreement, pact, contract, understanding, bargain, treaty   ALLIED

allot   distribute, share, divide, assign, apportion, allocate, budget (*Slang* — give out, deal out, dole out, mete out, hand out, dish out, shell out, fork out)

allow   1. let, permit, consent, grant, admit, 2. acknowledge, concede, recognize   deny

allowance   allotment, portion, fee, grant, ration, budget

allude   refer indirectly, imply, mention slightly, suggest, hint, infer, intimate

allure   fascinate, attract, charm, tempt, captivate, infatuate

almighty   powerful, great, divine, omnipotent

almost   nearly, close to, just about

alms   charity, dole, contribution, donation (*Slang* — handout)

aloft   high up, overhead

alone   isolated, solitary, solo, lonely, unaccompanied accompanied

aloof   away, apart, distant, remote, unsociable, reserved, standoffish, cool   friendly

also   too, in addition, as well, besides

alter   make different, change, vary, deviate, modify, diversify   maintain   ALTERATION

alternate   take turns, switch, interchange, spell

alternative   choice, substitute, replacement

altogether   completely, wholly, entirely, thoroughly, totally partly

always   forever, all the time (*Slang* — for good, for keeps) never

amass accumulate, collect, heap up, store up, increase, assemble, gather, compile

amateur non-professional, beginner professional

amaze surprise, astonish, astound, aghast, bewilder, thunderstruck, flabbergast AMAZEMENT

ambitious aspiring, set on, intent upon indifferent AMBITION

amble stroll, saunter, slow pace rush

ambush 1. surprise attack, lying in wait, 2. hiding place, trap

amend change, correct, improve, mend AMENDMENT, AMENDS

ammunition powder, shot, bullets, bombs, shells (*Slang* — ammo)

among amid, between, surrounded by, in with

amount sum, quantity, value, measure, price

ample large, abundant, enough, full, sufficient, plenty insufficient AMPLY

amuse entertain, divert, delight, tickle, titillate (*Slang* — slay) AMUSEMENT

anchor 1. fasten, secure, fix, attach, 2. ship hook ANCHORAGE

ancient old, aged, antique, archaic, elderly young, new

anecdote story, tale, yarn, account, narrative, joke

angelic heavenly, pure, good, lovely, innocent, virtuous, saintly, godly devilish ANGEL

anger wrath, ire, rage, fury, annoyance, irritation ANGRILY, ANGRY

anguish agony, suffering, pain, grief, distress, torture, torment, heartache, woe peace

animal creature, beast

animated lively, gay, vigorous, spry, active, vivacious, snappy, chipper inactive ANIMATION

animosity hatred, dislike, ill will, bitterness
love, good will

annex 1. add, attach, join, unite with, 2. something joined, addition, wing, extension ANNEXATION

annihilate demolish, destroy, abolish, end, wreck
ANNIHILATION

announce make known, proclaim, report, broadcast, declare, state, notify, tell
ANNOUNCEMENT, ANNOUNCER

annoy tease, vex, disturb, irritate, make angry
please, calm ANNOYANCE

anoint oil, grease

answer reply, respond

antagonize oppose, cross, go against, counter, provoke, embitter soothe
ANTAGONISM, ANTAGONIST, ANTAGONISTIC

anticipate expect, await, hope for, foresee
ANTICIPATION

antics capers, pranks, funny gestures, practical jokes, tricks
(*Slang* — shenanigans)

antipathy hatred, strong dislike love

antique ancient, old, aged, archaic new
ANTIQUATED, ANTIQUITY

anxious 1. uneasy, concerned, fearful, troubled, bothered, perturbed, agitated, worried relaxed, 2. eager, desirous, keen ANXIETY, ANXIOUSLY

apartment   flat, suite, dormitory

apathy   indifference, unconcern, lethargy   feeling, interest

aperture   opening, hole, gap

apex   tip, acme, highest point, summit, top, peak, crown, zenith   lowest point

apologize   beg pardon, ask forgiveness, express regret, offer an excuse   APOLOGETIC, APOLOGY

appall   horrify, shock, dismay, terrify, stun (*Slang* — scare stiff)

apparatus   equipment, gear, rig, tackle, furnishings

apparel   clothing, dress, garments, garb, attire

apparent   plain, seeming, obvious, evident, clear   hidden, mysterious   APPARENTLY

apparition   ghost, illusion, vision, phantom, dream, fantasy

appeal   ask earnestly, beg, plead, implore, entreat

appear   seem, look   APPEARANCE

appease   calm, satisfy, quiet, allay, lessen, check, relieve, ease, pacify, moderate, restrain, alleviate   irritate

appendage   something attached, addition, supplement, tail

appetite   hunger, desire, craving

applaud   approve, praise, cheer, hail, acclaim, clap (*Slang* — root for)   disapprove, reject   APPLAUSE

appliance   tool, machine, device, instrument, implement, utensil

apply   1. request, ask, petition, 2. put on, administer   APPLICANT, APPLICATION

appoint   elect, choose, name, vote for, assign, nominate   APPOINTMENT

appreciate value, enjoy, think highly of, respect, admire, be grateful repel
APPRECIABLE, APPRECIATION, APPRECIATIVE

apprehend 1. fear, dread, 2. seize, arrest, capture, take prisoner (*Slang* — pinch, run in, nab) release
APPREHENSION

apprehensive afraid, worried, anxious, uneasy, concerned, fearful, troubled, bothered, agitated, perturbed relaxed

apprentice beginner, learner, novice, amateur experienced APPRENTICESHIP

approach 1. come near, advance retreat, 2. entrance, inlet, passageway, access

appropriate 1. suitable, proper, fitting, becoming inappropriate, 2. allot, distribute, share, divide, assign, apportion, allocate, budget (*Slang* — give out, deal out, dole out, mete out, hand out, dish out, shell out, fork out)
APPROPRIATION

approve like, think well of, accept, ratify, endorse, O.K. disapprove, frown on APPROVAL

approximate approach, near, close, roughly correct
APPROXIMATELY

apt 1. likely, suitable, appropriate, proper, fitting unlikely, 2. quick to learn, bright, clever, acute, sharp, shrewd, discerning, astute, keen, smart (*Slang* — quick on the trigger, smart as a whip, sharp as a tack, nobody's fool)

aqueduct waterway, gully, canal, channel, pipe

arbitrary unreasonable, willful fair, reasonable

arbitrate settle, referee, umpire, negotiate, mediate
ARBITRATION

architecture building, structure, construction
ARCHITECT

ardent   enthusiastic, eager, zealous, earnest, sincere, fervent, passionate, warm   apathetic, cool

arduous   difficult, strenuous, hard, laborious (*Slang* — tough, rough)   easy

area   1. extent, space, region, expanse, zone, territory, district, section, neighborhood, 2. size

argue   reason, object, persuade, bicker (*Slang* — hassle) ARGUMENT

arid   1. dry, waterless   wet, fertile,   2. dull, stuffy, flat, unimaginative   colorful

aristocrat   gentleman, nobleman (*Slang* — swell, blueblood) ARISTOCRACY, ARISTOCRATIC

arm   1. part of a body, 2. weapon. 3. equip, defend, fortify, empower

armistice   peace, truce, treaty, agreement, pact, contract, understanding, concord, alliance, deal

army   legion, forces, troops, military, militia

aroma   fragrance, odor, perfume, scent   AROMATIC

arouse   stir, excite, awaken, move, provoke, pique, kindle, inflame, foment, stimulate, agitate, disturb, shake

arrange   settle, put in order, adapt, fit, classify, catalog, organize, systematize   confuse, muddle
ARRANGEMENT

array   1. order, 2. display, 3. dress, adorn

arrest   stop, check, seize, catch, apprehend, capture, take prisoner (*Slang* — pinch, run in, nab)   release

arrive   come, reach, get to (*Slang* — show up)   leave
ARRIVAL

arrogant   too proud, haughty, insolent, cavalier (*Slang* — stuck-up, uppish)   humble, modest   ARROGANCE

art 1. drawing, painting, sculpture, design, work, composition, masterpiece, 2. skill, knack, craft, technique

artery 1. blood vessel, 2. main road, aqueduct, channel, pipe

artful 1. crafty, sly, deceitful, 2. skillful, clever, cunning, shrewd, knowing (*Slang* — shifty, cagey, slick) artless

article 1. composition, story, essay, report, treatise, 2. object, thing

artifice clever device, trick, ruse, foul play, scheme

artificial false, pretended, substitute, ungenuine, unreal, fake, synthetic, imitation, counterfeit real, authentic

artisan craftsman, worker, mechanic

artless 1. natural, simple, without trickery, 2. without art, unskilled, ignorant artful

ascend go up, rise, climb, mount descend

ascertain find out, learn, solve, answer, clear up

ascribe assign, attribute

ashamed embarrassed, humiliated, abashed, mortified proud

ask question, find out, inquire, request, invite answer

askance 1. with suspicion, with disapproval, 2. sideways

askew crooked, disorderly, twisted, awry straight

aspect view, look, appearance

aspire seek, desire, be ambitious, aim, strive ASPIRANT, ASPIRATION

ass 1. donkey, mule, burro, 2. dunce, stupid, stubborn, silly, fool (*Slang* — dope, dumbbell, dumb-bunny)

assail attack, assault (*Slang* — go for, sail into)

assassinate kill, murder, purge
ASSASSIN, ASSASSINATION

assault attack, offense, onslaught, charge (*Slang* — drive, push)

assemble meet, gather together, congregate, collect, crowd, throng, cluster, group   scatter, disperse   ASSEMBLY

assent agree, consent, accept, approve of, comply   dissent

assert declare, state, insist on, affirm, pronounce
ASSERTION

asset valuable things, property, funds, wealth, accounts, resources, goods, capital

assign appoint, elect, allot, choose, name, distribute, apportion, allocate (*Slang* — give out, deal out, dole out, mete out, hand out, dish out, shell out, fork out)
ASSIGNMENT

assimilate absorb, digest, soak up, blot up

assist help, aid, support, lend a hand
ASSISTANCE, ASSISTANT

associate 1. join, connect, combine, unite   disconnect, 2. companion, partner, ally   ASSOCIATION

assorted various, different, classified, grouped, several
ASSORTMENT

assuage quiet, calm, allay, lessen, check, ease, relieve, pacify, moderate, restrain, alleviate   excite

assume 1. suppose, take for granted, presume, suspect, understand, believe, think, 2. put on, adopt
ASSUMPTION

assure convince, make certain, promise, guarantee, pledge
ASSURANCE, ASSUREDLY

astonish surprise, astound, amaze   ASTONISHMENT

astound amaze, surprise, astonish

asunder apart, separate, divided together

asylum refuge, shelter, institution, home, madhouse (*Slang* — booby hatch)

athletic active, strong, muscular, brawny, able-bodied, well-built, sporting, gymnastic ATHLETE

atone make up, make amends, repay ATONEMENT

atrocious wicked, cruel, savage, brutal, ruthless, terrible, horrible, dreadful, awful, vile, wretched, contemptible kind, good

attach fasten, join, connect, affix, add, put together, increase, unite detach ATTACHMENT

attack raid, siege, bombardment, assault, offense, onslaught, charge, drive, push

attain 1. reach, arrive, come, get to, 2. gain, accomplish, finish, complete, fulfill, achieve, realize ATTAINMENT

attempt try, endeavor, make an effort (*Slang* — take a fling at, have a go at)

attend 1. be present, visit, go to be absent, 2. serve, help, work for, administer to, care for ATTENDANCE, ATTENDANT

attention care, courtesy, consideration, concern, thoughtfulness, politeness ATTENTIVE

attest give proof, testify, certify, give evidence, swear, vouch

attire dress, array, adorn

attitude viewpoint, standpoint, position, opinion

attract pull, interest, draw, fascinate, allure, charm, tempt, captivate, infatuate ATTRACTION

attractive pleasing, winning, charming, desirable, beautiful unattractive

attribute   1. assign, ascribe, give, place, apply, 2. characteristic, quality, trait, nature, feature

audacious   bold, daring, foolhardy, arrogant, haughty, insolent, cavalier   shy, humble   AUDACITY

audible   hearable, distinct, clear, plain   inaudible

augment   increase, enlarge, expand, raise, extend, broaden, magnify   decrease

auspicious   favorable, fortunate, lucky, promising, timely   unfortunate, untimely

austere   harsh, stern, strict, severe (*Slang* — tough, hardboiled)   soft, lenient

authentic   real, reliable, genuine, legitimate, actual, factual, true (*Slang* — straight, sure enough, honest to goodness)   false, artificial

authoritative   commanding, powerful, influential, official   AUTHORITY

authorize   give power to, legalize, enable, assign

autocrat   ruler, monarch, dictator, tyrant

autograph   sign, endorse, approve

automatic   self-acting, spontaneous, self-working   manual   AUTOMATICALLY, AUTOMATION

auxiliary   helping, assisting, aiding

avail   use, help, benefit, profit, advantage, value, worth, serve

available   handy, convenient, ready, at hand, obtainable   unavailable, unobtainable

avarice   greed, lust, desire for money   AVARICIOUS

average   1. usual, ordinary, passable, fair   unusual, extraordinary, 2. middle, medium   extreme

averse   opposed, unwilling, against, forced, involuntary   willing

aversion   strong dislike, hatred, loathing   love

avert   prevent, avoid, turn away, prohibit   invite

avid   eager, greedy

avocation   hobby, minor occupation, sideline

avoid   keep away from, shun, evade, snub   seek
AVOIDANCE

award   prize, grant, gift, trophy, reward, medal

aware   knowing, realizing, conscious, cognizant
ignorant, unaware

awe   fear and wonder, astonishment, surprise, dread, respect,
alarm

awful   unpleasant, atrocious, wicked, cruel, savage, brutal,
ruthless, terrible, horrible, dreadful, vile, wretched
pleasant   AWFULLY

awkward   clumsy, ungraceful, cumbersome, ungainly
graceful   AWKWARDLY, AWKWARDNESS

awry   wrong, askew, crooked, disorderly, twisted
right, straight

B

babble   baby talk, foolish talk, chatter, prattle, gabble

background   experience, knowledge, training, practice,

bad   evil, wrong, unfavorable   good   BADLY

badger   1. question, tease, annoy, torment, bother, pester,
harass, bait (*Slang* — pick on, ride), 2. small hairy animal

baffle   puzzle, perplex, confound, mystify, bewilder (*Slang*
— stump, stick, flaw, get, beat)

bait   1. badger, question, tease, annoy, torment, bother, pester, harass (*Slang* — pick on, ride), 2. trap, lure, tempt

balance 1. equalize, weigh, measure, stabilize, steady, 2. scale

bald hairless, bare, simple, open, nude, uncovered hairy, covered

baleful harmful, damaging, injurious harmless

balk be unwilling, be stubborn, be obstinate be willing

ballad song, poem, ditty

ballot vote, choice, poll

balmy mild, soft, gentle, fragrant

ban prohibit, forbid, outlaw, bar, block, obstruct, exclude, shut out allow

bandit highwayman, robber, thief, gangster, brigand

bang strike, hit, slam

banish exile, expel, force away, drive away, deport, outlaw BANISHMENT

bank 1. shore, barrier, slope, 2. treasury, storage, 3. series, row, string

banquet feast, formal dinner, affair

banter tease, joke, jest (*Slang* — rib, kid)

bar 1. block, obstruct, exclude, shut out, forbid, ban, prohibit allow, 2. pole, rod, stick, 3. lawyers as a group, 4. saloon, tavern, counter, 5. music staff

barbarian uncivilized, cruel, coarse, savage, uncouth, brutal, uncultured, primitive civilized BARBARIC, BARBAROUS

bare naked, nude, bald, open, uncovered covered

barely scarcely, hardly, just

bargain   1. agree, contract, 2. sale (*Slang* — a buy, a steal)

barren   unproductive, childless, unfertile, sterile, blank
fertile, productive

barricade   obstruction, barrier, fortification

barrier   barricade, obstruction, fortification

barter   trade, deal, exchange, swap

base   1. found, establish, set, settle, fix, 2. low, mean, selfish,
cowardly, inferior, 3. bottom, foundation, groundwork,
4. station, headquarters

bashful   awkward, uneasy, shy, timid, coy   aggressive

basic   essential, fundamental, underlying

bat   hit, knock, strike, crack, clout (*Slang* — clobber, belt,
slug)

bathe   1. swim, 2. launder, rinse, 3. pour over, drench, cover,
soak, saturate, medicate

batter   1. beat, pound, smash, thrash, 2. mixture, 3. baseball
player

battery   set, series

battle   struggle, fight, combat, war, contest, conflict   peace

bauble   toy, plaything, trinket

bawl   shout, cry, wail, weep, sob, howl

beach   shore, coast, waterfront, seaside

beacon   watchtower, signal, alarm, flare

beam   1. shine, smile, glow, 2. timber, bar, shaft

bear   1. carry, endure, withstand, hold, support, produce,
yield, 2. animal

bearing   1. manner, air, 2. reference, relation, connection,
3. direction, way, course

beast animal, creature BEASTLY

beat 1. strike, blow, bat, hit, knock, crack, clout (*Slang* — clobber, belt, slug), 2. mix, stir, 3. accent in music, 4. outdo, surpass, win, defeat, triumph (*Slang* — lick) BEATEN

beautiful pretty, handsome, attractive, lovely ugly BEAUTEOUS, BEAUTIFY, BEAUTY

beckon gesture, motion, invite, signal

bedlam uproar, confusion, racket, tumult, rumpus peace, calm

bedraggled sloppy, shabby, wet and limp

beefy strong, solid, heavy, stocky, muscular weak

before earlier, prior, previously, formerly, in advance after

beg ask, beseech, appeal, plead, implore, entreat

begin start, commence, take off (*Slang* — dig in, get the show on the road) end, finish BEGINNER

beguile 1. deceive, cheat, trick, dupe, bamboozle, 2. amuse, entertain, charm

behalf interest, good, benefit, welfare

behavior conduct, action, acts, manner BEHAVE

behest command, order, bidding

behind 1. after, later than, 2. retarded, backward ahead

behold see, look, notice, view, perceive, observe, sight

belated delayed, late, tardy, overdue early

belie 1. misrepresent, distort, twist, 2. disappoint

believe trust, suppose, think, surmise (*Slang* — swallow) doubt BELIEF

belittle minimize, underrate, underestimate overrate

belligerent warlike, aggressive, offensive, hostile, militant, combative peaceful

bellow   roar, yell, shout

belly   abdomen, stomach, paunch (*Slang* — breadbasket, pot, corporation)

belongings   possessions, property   BELONG

below   under, lower, less   above

bend   1. curve, turn, 2. bow, stoop, kneel, 3. yield, submit

beneath   below, under   above

benediction   blessing, thanks, prayer

beneficial   favorable, helpful, profitable, useful, advantageous   harmful   BENEFIT

benevolence   kindness, generosity, good will, charity   ill will   BENEVOLENT

bent   determined, inclined

berate   scold, yell at

beseech   beg, ask, appeal, plead, implore, entreat

beset   attack, surround

besides   moreover, also, too, in addition, as well

besiege   attack, assault, raid, siege, bombard, charge

bespeak   1. reserve, engage, 2. show, indicate, express, signify

best   prime, choice, select   worst

bestial   beastly, brutal, cruel, savage

bestow   give, put, place, present, award

bet   wager, gamble

betray   mislead, deceive, trick (*Slang* — double-cross)

betrothal   engagement, marriage contract   BETROTH

better   superior, preferable, improved   worse
    BETTERMENT

between betwixt, among

beware be careful, guard against, take care, look out, watch out, look sharp (*Slang* — keep one's eyes peeled, watch one's step)

bewilder confuse, baffle, puzzle, perplex, confound, mystify (*Slang* — stump, stick, get, beat) clarify
BEWILDERMENT

bewitch 1. put under a spell, hex, 2. charm, delight, enchant

beyond farther, past, exceeding

bias 1. slanting, oblique, diagonal, 2. prejudice, prejudgment, sway

bid command, order, direct, instruct, ask, invite, enjoin

big large, important, great, grand, considerable, grown-up, adult, mature little, small

bind 1. tie, fasten, restrain, wrap, weld, 2. oblige, require

birth beginning, origin, inception, infancy end, death

bit 1. small amount, piece, 2. harness, restraint

bite cut with teeth, nip, pierce BITTEN

biting sharp, cutting, sneering, sarcastic, acid

bitter distasteful, unpleasant pleasant BITTERLY

blade sword, knife

blame accuse, charge, impeach, indict, denounce, tattle (*Slang* — hang on, put the finger on, rat on, frame) absolve

blameless innocent, faultless (*Slang* — clean) guilty

bland 1. smooth, mild, soft, gentle harsh, 2. agreeable, polite disagreeable

blank empty, void, vacant

blast explosion, blowout, burst, discharge

blaze   1. fire, flame, flare, 2. notch, marking

bleak   bare, chilly, cold, dreary, dismal   cheerful

bleed   1. to lose blood, 2. grieve, pity, sorrow

blemish   stain, scar, injury, defect

blend   mix, combine, beat, join, stir   separate

bless   praise, thank, glorify   curse   BLESSED

blight   1. spoil, ruin, destroy, decay, wither, 2. decaying, disease

blind   1. sightless, visionless, 2. without thought, without judgment   BLINDLY, BLINDNESS

bliss   happiness, joy, delight, glee, elation   sadness
BLISSFUL

blithe   airy, light, breezy, fanciful, lighthearted, gay, graceful, merry   gloomy   BLITHESOME

bloat   swell, puff up, inflate   deflate

blob   bulge, bubble, globule

block   1. clog, obstruct, hinder   clear,   2. lump, solid, mass

blockade   obstruction, barrier, barricade, fortification

bloodthirsty   cruel, murderous

bloom   flourish, thrive, flower, glow, blossom

blossom   develop, flower, bloom

blot   erase, wipe out, obliterate

blow   1. puff, breeze, 2. knock, stroke, whack, rap

blowout   burst, explosion, blast

bluff   1. deceive, trick, delude, 2. steep cliff, bank

blunder   stumble, mistake, flounder (*Slang* — goof, put one's foot in one's mouth)

blunt   1. dull, unsharp   sharp,   2. outspoken, candid, frank, straightforward, direct

blur   dim, smear, cloud

board   1. mount, embark, get on, 2. committee, cabinet, 3. wood, lumber, 4. food, meals (*Slang* — grub)

boast   brag, pat oneself on the back   BOASTFUL

body   1. substance, firmness, 2. the main part, mass, bulk, 3. group, collection, throng, crowd

boil   1. fume, seethe, rage, 2. cook, bubble, 3. swelling, pimple

boisterous   violent, rough, noisy, rowdy, tumultuous serene

bold   1. defiant, impudent, brazen, arrogant, haughty, insolent, cavalier   modest,   2. vigorous, free, clear BOLDNESS

bolt   1. flee, break away, take flight (*Slang* — make a break for it, clear out), 2. lock, fastener

bombard   attack, fire upon, shell, torpedo, open fire BOMBARDMENT

bonus   extra, more, premium

boom   1. progress, increase, advance, gain, grow, swell, thrive, flourish, 2. thunder, roar, rumble, 3. pole, beam

boon   1. blessing, godsend, gift, windfall, 2. pleasant, jolly, merry, jovial

boost   lift, push, shove, help, thrust, hoist

boot   1. kick, 2. shoe

bootless   useless, purposeless   useful

booty   plunder, prize, loot, stolen goods

bore   1. drill, pierce, puncture, 2. make weary, irk (*Slang* — put to sleep)

born   brought forth, hatched, produced

borrow   take (*Slang* — touch)   lend

boss 1. supervise, oversee, look after, direct, 2. foreman, manager

bother worry, fuss, trouble, concern, annoy

bottom base, foundation, lowest part   top

bound 1. enclosed, surround, 2. spring back, leap, jump, 3. going, on the way, 4. boundary, limit

boundary bound, limit, border, division, barrier

boundless unlimited, endless, infinite   limited

bounteous generous, plentiful, abundant, liberal   scarce

bountiful fertile, bounteous, generous, plentiful, abundant scarce

bout 1. test, contest, trial, struggle, battle, 2. spell, length of time, turn, round

bow bend, stoop, kneel

box 1. fight, hit, 2. container, crate

boy lad, youth, fellow, male, buddy

boycott strike, revolt, picket, blackball, ban

brace 1. support, strengthen, tighten, tie, 2. a support, prop

bracket 1. couple, join, relate, enclose, 2. support, brace

brag boast, pat oneself on the back

brake stop, slow down, decelerate, curb   accelerate

branch 1. spread, divide, expand, 2. part of a tree

brand 1. mark, burn, label, tag, 2. kind, sort, type, stamp

brave courageous, bold, valiant, gallant, heroic   cowardly BRAVERY

brawl quarrel, riot, racket, fracas

brawn muscle, strength   weakness   BRAWNY

brazen   shameless, immodest, bold, forward   modest

breach   break, gap, falling-out, quarrel

break   1. fracture, rupture, crack, burst   heal, mend,   2. violation, 3. interruption, interval, pause, rest, letup

breed   raise, produce, train, race, develop, bring up, cultivate

breezy   brisk, lively, jolly, carefree, spry, energetic, active, spirited (*Slang* — peppy)   gloomy

brevity   shortness, conciseness, briefness   length

brew   1. plan, plot, scheme (*Slang* — cook up), 2. cook, prepare, ferment

bribe   buy off (*Slang* — grease the palm)   BRIBERY

bridle   1. restrain, control, check, hold back, 2. harness

brief   short, concise, terse, curt   long

brigand   robber, bandit, thief

bright   1. shining, clear, vivid, 2. smart, alert, intelligent, 3. pleasant, cheerful, lively   dull   BRIGHTNESS

brilliant   1. sparkling, bright, shining, clear, vivid, 2. smart, alert, intelligent   BRILLIANCE

brisk   1. breezy, 2. spirited, lively, jolly, spry, energetic, active, quick   dull

brittle   fragile, crisp, breakable, frail   strong, sturdy

broad   wide, large, expansive, roomy   narrow   BROADEN

broadcast   publish, distribute, scatter, announce, circulate

broken   burst, ruptured, shattered   repaired   BROKE

brood   1. ponder, contemplate, study, reflect, consider, meditate, 2. family group

brotherhood   bond, kinship, relationship, fraternity, fellowship

browse   1. read, scan, 2. feed, graze

bruise   injure, hurt, wound   heal

brush   1. clean, rub, remove, wipe, 2. shrubs, bushes

brusque   abrupt, blunt, gruff, curt, harsh, surly   courteous

brutal   coarse, barbarian, cruel, savage   kind
  BRUTALITY

buccaneer   pirate, sea robber, privateer

buck   1. jump, leap, spring, vault, 2. male animal

buckle   1. fasten, clasp, hook, clip, 2. bend, distort, wrinkle,
  3. belt, strap, catch, clip

bud   1. sprout, flourish, develop, 2. baby plant

buddy   friend, pal, companion, partner, comrade, chum
  (*Slang* — sidekick, crony)

budge   move, stir

budget   ration, allowance, schedule

buff   polish, rub, shine, wax, burnish

buffet   blow, beat, bat, hit, knock, strike, crack, clout
  (*Slang* — clobber, belt, slug)

build   construct, make, create   BUILDER, BUILDING

bulk   lump, mass, majority

bulletin   message, circular, news, statement, flash, news-
  letter

bully   tease, pester, annoy, badger, torment, bother, harass

bump   push, collide, shake, hit

bunch   group, set, batch, cluster

bundle   parcel, package, bale, packet

bungle   botch, tumble, blunder (*Slang* — goof)

buoyant   1. light, floating, elastic, springy   heavy,   2.

cheerful, lighthearted, carefree   gloomy, sad
BUOYANCY

burden   load, charge, task, hard work   BURDENSOME

burglar   robber, thief, housebreaker   BURGLARY

burly   strong, sturdy, brawny   weak

burn   blaze, fire, flame, flare

burnish   buff, polish, rub, shine, wax

burrow   1. dig, tunnel, excavate, 2. search, hunt, seek

burst   broken, ruptured, exploded

bury   cover, conceal, hide, immerse, cache   uncover
BURIAL

business   work, occupation, profession, trade, affair, job

bustle   fuss, noise, activity, flurry, ado, action, stir, trouble, commotion, excitement, hubbub, to-do   calm

busy   working, active, occupied, engaged, on the job
idle, inactive

busybody   meddler, gossip, tattletale, kibitzer

button   fasten, clasp, hook, close   unbutton, open

buxom   1. plump, 2. cheerful, healthy, merry, jolly

buy   purchase, shop, market   sell   BUYER

by   near, beside, at

byway   path, passage, detour, back street

C

cab   taxi, carriage, coach, car

cabin   house, cottage, bungalow, hut

cable 1. telegraph, wire, 2. rope, cord, wire

cache store, bury, cover, conceal, hide

cackle shrill laugh, babble, chatter, prattle

cafeteria restaurant, cafe, snack bar, diner

calamity 1. misfortune, mishap, accident, 2. disaster, catastrophe, tragedy

calculate 1. count, compute, figure, estimate, reckon, 2. plan, reason, think, suppose
CALCULATION, CALCULATOR

call 1. cry, shout, yell, 2. speak, ask, command, invite, telephone CALLER

calling profession, occupation, trade, vocation

callous hard, unfeeling, insensitive, heartless, cold
sensitive

calm quiet, still, peaceful, serene, tranquil excited

camouflage disguise, masquerade

campaign crusade, drive, cause, movement

can container, tin, receptacle

canal waterway, aqueduct, gully, duct, tube

cancel wipe out, erase, obliterate, repeal

candid sincere, blunt, outspoken, frank, straightforward, direct

candidate applicant, seeker, nominee

candor frankness, sincerity, fairness

canine dog, pooch, puppy

canny 1. shrewd, artful, crafty, skillful, clever, cunning
(*Slang* — slick) artless, 2. cautious, prudent, careful

canopy cover, awning, shelter, screen

cantankerous quarrelsome, cranky, cross, irritable, mean

cap 1. cover, top, crown, lid, 2. excel, beat

capability ability, power, fitness, capacity, skill, talent, competency, efficiency (*Slang* — know-how, what it takes) inability

capacity 1. size, volume, content, 2. intelligence, mentality, power, fitness, 3. position, function, duty, role

caper 1. leap, jump, hop, skip, romp, cavort (*Slang* — cut up, horse around), 2. frolic, prank, trick, play, antic (*Slang* — monkeyshine, shenanigan)

capital 1. important, leading, top, chief, 2. money, funds, stock, 3. city, government seat, 4. large letter

caprice whim, fancy, fad, unreasonable desire
CAPRICIOUS

capsize upset, overturn, overthrow, tip over

caption title, heading, headline

captivate charm, fascinate, delight, bewitch

capture arrest, seize, imprison, apprehend (*Slang* — pinch) free CAPTIVE, CAPTIVITY

car automobile, vehicle (*Slang* — buggy, jalopy, wreck, heap, crate, wheels)

caravan 1. group, procession, parade, 2. wagon, van

carcass animal corpse, body

care 1. thought, worry, attention, concern, 2. protection, charge, supervision, keeping, custody neglect

career profession, occupation, vocation, calling, trade

carefree happy, gay, lighthearted, breezy, lively, jolly, spry, energetic, spirited, active unhappy

careful cautious, watchful, prudent careless
CAREFULLY

careless   reckless, slovenly, sloppy   careful

caress   stroke, touch, fondle, pet

cargo   load, freight, shipment

carnival   fair, festival, fete, jamboree

carol   song, hymn, ballad

carp   1. complain, find fault, pick, tear to pieces   praise, 2. fresh-water fish

carpet   rug, mat, floor covering

carriage   1. vehicle, conveyance, 2. posture, position, bearing

carry   hold, transport, take

carve   cut, slice

case   1. condition, state, circumstance, 2. covering, box, receptacle, 3. lawsuit, legal action

cash   money, currency (*Slang* — dough, jack, cabbage, wampum) CASHIER

casket   box, coffin, crate

cast   1. throw, fling, pitch, toss, 2. mold, form, shape, 3. company, troupe, actors, 4. sort, kind, type, variety, 5. color, tint, shade

castle   palace, mansion, chateau

casual   accidental, chance, informal, unexpected, natural planned

casualty   misfortune, accident, mishap, injury, fluke

catalog   1. list, classify, record, group, sort, 2. file

catastrophe   calamity, misfortune, tragedy, disaster, accident

catch   1. take, arrest, seize, apprehend, capture, 2. surprise, discover CATCHER

catchy   1. attractive, 2. tricky, deceptive, misleading

cater 1. pamper, coddle, spoil, oblige, indulge, 2. serve, provide

cause motive, reason, interest, basis, grounds

caution warn, advise, alert, admonish, remind, tip CAUTIOUS

cavalcade procession, column, parade

cavalier 1. haughty, contemptuous, arrogant, insolent, 2. gentleman, horseman, knight, escort

cave cavern, shelter, den, lair

cavity hole, pit, crater

cavort prance about, caper, frolic, leap, jump, hop, skip, romp (*Slang* — horse around, cut up)

cease stop, end, halt, quit, discontinue (*Slang* — drop it) continue

cede give up, surrender, yield, relinquish   acquire

celebrate 1. proclaim, observe, commemorate, 2. make merry, revel (*Slang* — make whoopee)   CELEBRATION

celebrity notable, well-known person, somebody   unknown

celestial heavenly, divine, godly, angelic

cement fasten, solidify, secure, weld

cemetery graveyard, burial ground

censure blame, reproach, denounce, criticize, condemn (*Slang* — pan, knock)   approve

center middle, heart, core, nucleus

central main, chief, principal, leading

ceremonious 1. formal, ritualistic, stately, pompous informal, 2. courteous, polite, gracious   CEREMONY

certain 1. sure, positive, definite uncertain, 2. some, particular, special   CERTAINLY, CERTAINTY

certify   guarantee, testify, vouch, affirm, confirm
CERTIFICATE

cessation   end, discontinuation, close   continuation

chafe   1. rub, heat, warm, 2. anger, annoy, vex, disturb, irritate

chagrin   embarrassment, mortification, humiliation, disappointment

chain   bind, restrain, fasten, shackle

chair   seat, bench

chairman   speaker, presiding officer

challenge   confront, question, defy, dare, dispute, doubt
CHALLENGER

chamber   room, compartment

champion   1. winner, victor, best, choice, select, conqueror loser, 2. defender, upholder, protector, advocate
CHAMPIONSHIP

chance   1. opportunity, occasion, opening, 2. possibility, probability, likelihood, prospect, 3. fate, luck, lot (*Slang* — the breaks)

change   1. alter, vary, deviate, substitute, replace, 2. cash, money, coins

channel   1. waterway, strait, passageway, corridor, artery, 2. TV station

chant   song, psalm, prayer, ballad

chaos   confusion, disorder, muddle, mix-up (*Slang* — snafu, hassle, foul-up)   order   CHAOTIC

chap   1. crack, break, split, become rough, 2. fellow, man, boy

chapter   section, part, division

char   burn, scorch, sear, singe

character 1. nature, makeup, constitution, temperament, disposition, 2. actor, performer, player, 3. letter, sign, symbol, 4. eccentric (*Slang* — crackpot, oddball, nut, screwball)

characterize describe, distinguish, represent, portray, picture, depict CHARACTERISTIC

charge 1. load, fill, stuff, 2. order, command, direct, bid, 3. blame, accuse, complain, denounce, impeach, indict (*Slang* — put the finger on, rat on, frame), 4. rate, ask as a price, 5. attack, rush at

charitable generous, kindly, giving, big-hearted selfish CHARITY

charming pleasing, delightful, fascinating, appealing, enchanting, alluring obnoxious CHARM

charter 1. hire, lease, rent, 2. treaty, alliance

chase 1. follow, pursue, run after, 2. drive away, repulse, reject

chaste pure, clean, virtuous, modest, decent impure

chasten punish, chastise, discipline, restrain

chastise chasten, punish, discipline, restrain

chat talk, converse, gossip

chatter 1. babble, foolish talk, prattle, gabble, 2. shiver, rattle, chill, quiver

cheap 1. inexpensive, low-priced dear, 2. common, plentiful, abundant scarce CHEAPEN

cheat defraud, swindle, beguile, deceive, trick, dupe, bamboozle

check 1. stop, control, restrain, curb, 2. prove, mark, verify, 3. bill, certificate, money

checkup examination, physical

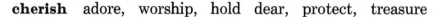

cheer 1. comfort, praise, gladden, 2. hope, good spirits, gladness, happiness sadness CHEERFUL

cherish adore, worship, hold dear, protect, treasure

chest 1. box, locker, safe, dresser, 2. breast, thorax

chew bite, grind, nibble, munch

chicken-hearted cowardly, timid, lily-livered (*Slang* — yellow) brave

chide reproach, blame, scold, reprimand, lecture (*Slang* — bawl out, chew out, give what-for)

chief leader, head, authority (*Slang* — big cheese, big wheel)

chiefly mainly, mostly, above all, especially

child youngster, baby, tot, juvenile, youth, young boy or girl, offspring (*Slang* — kid)

chilly cold, cool, brisk, nippy, wintery, snappy warm

chime 1. ring, jingle, peal, 2. agree, harmonize

chip 1. break, crack, 2. piece, bit, crumb

chisel 1. make, sculpture, carve, 2. engrave, inscribe, 3. tool, point

chivalrous courteous, gallant, knightly, polite, noble CHIVALRY

choice 1. selection, pick, decision, option, alternative, preference, 2. best, cream

choke smother, suffocate, strangle, muffle

chop cut, cleave, sever (*Slang* — hack, whack)

chore task, job, work, assignment, duty, function

chorus 1. choir, group, unison, 2. verse, stanza, refrain

chronic constant, established, fixed, set, lasting, continuing

chronicle history, story, account, journal, narrative

chubby plump, round, stout, fat, fleshy, corpulent, pudgy, stocky, tubby, chunky skinny

chuck 1. pat, tap, flick, 2. throw, toss, pitch, fling

chuckle laugh, giggle, titter

chum friend, mate, buddy, pal, companion, partner, comrade (*Slang* — sidekick, crony)

chunk lump, wad, bulk, mass (*Slang* — hunk)

cinch grip, bind, hold, wrap, tie, fasten

circulate go around, publish, broadcast, distribute, scatter, announce CIRCULATION, CIRCULATORY

circumstance condition, situation, state

citadel fortress, stronghold

citation 1. honorable mention, decoration, medal, 2. summons, subpoena, 3. quotation

cite quote, name, refer, mention, illustrate

citizen inhabitant, occupant, resident CITIZENRY, CITIZENSHIP

city metropolis, municipality

civil 1. public, common, social, 2. ceremonious, courteous, polite uncivil

civilization culture CIVILIZE

clad clothed, dressed, attired (*Slang* — dolled up, fixed up, spruced up)

claim 1. demand, require, 2. right, due, interest, title

clammy cold and damp, sweaty

clamor cry out, demand, complain

clamp fasten, clasp, brace

clan group, crowd, clique, tribe, folk, family

clap strike, bang, applaud

clarify explain, refine, make clear, simplify confuse

clash 1. contradict, oppose, disagree, differ, conflict agree, 2. collide, bump, bang, hit

clasp grasp, buckle, fasten, hook, clip

class 1. rank, grade, quality, 2. group, category, division

classify organize, group, categorize, sort

clatter noise, rattle, racket, din

clean cleanse, purify, wash, tidy dirty CLEANLINESS

clear 1. remove, eliminate, get rid of retain, 2. free, acquit apprehend, 3. clean, cleanse, purify, wash, tidy CLARITY, CLEARLY

cleavage split, division, break

cleft space, opening, crack, crevice, notch, indentation

clemency mercy, pity, sympathy, compassion, lenience, mildness harshness, severity

clench grasp, grip, clutch, hold release

clever skillful, cunning, bright, smart, alert, intelligent dull

client customer, prospect, patron

climate weather, elements, atmospheric conditions

climax 1. result, end, conclusion (*Slang* — payoff), 2. turning point

climb mount, ascend, rise

clinch 1. seize, grip, cinch, bind, hold, wrap, tie, fasten, 2. establish, insure, make certain

cling hold, grasp, adhere, stick

clip 1. cut, shear, crop, 2. fasten, attach, 3. pace

clique set, clan, group, crowd, folk, family

cloak 1. hide, conceal, cover, protect, 2. robe, wrap, coat

clod 1. lump, hunk, chunk, 2. stupid person, oaf, lout

clog stuff, block, obstruct, choke

close 1. shut, fasten, lock open, 2. end, finish, stop, conclude, terminate start

close 1. near, approaching, imminent far, 2. stuffy, airless, stifling, suffocating CLOSELY

clothe dress, cover, wrap, attire

cloudy dark, unclear, overcast, gloomy, dismal

clout rap, bat, hit, knock, strike (*Slang* — crack, clobber, belt, slug)

clown 1. fool, play (*Slang* — horse around), 2. comic performer, prankster

club 1. hit, beat, strike, blow, bat, knock (*Slang* — crack, clout, clobber, belt, slug), 2. bat, stick, 3. group, society, clique

clue hint, evidence, proof, sign, key, lead

clump cluster, lump

clumsy awkward, ungraceful, ungainly, cumbersome

cluster bunch, group, set, batch

clutch cling, hold, grasp, adhere, stick

clutter 1. rubbish, trash, debris, 2. confusion, disorder, jumble

coach 1. train, teach, tutor, 2. carriage, car

coagulate thicken, clot, set

coarse 1. rough, choppy, bumpy fine, smooth, 2. common, poor, inferior, 3. crude, vulgar refined

coast 1. slide, glide, ride, 2. seashore, seaside, waterfront, beach COASTAL, COASTLINE

coat   wrap, cloak, robe

coax   persuade, influence, urge, pressure, push

cocky   conceited, impudent, swaggering, saucy

coddle   pamper, cater to, spoil, oblige, indulge

code   laws, rules, arrangement, system, signal

coerce   compel, force (*Slang* — strong-arm)

coin   1. invent, make up, devise, originate, 2. money, silver
COINAGE

collapse   break down, fail, crash, topple (*Slang* — fizzle out)

collar   1. seize, nab, capture, 2. neckband

colleague   associate, buddy, friend, companion, partner, comrade

collect   assemble, gather, accumulate, store up
COLLECTION, COLLECTOR

collide   conflict, bump, clash, bang

colony   settlement, community

COLONIAL, COLONIZATION

colorful   vivid, picturesque, bright, gay, rich   colorless

colorless   dull, uninteresting, flat, dreary   colorful

colossal   huge, gigantic, vast, enormous, immense, mammoth
insignificant

column   1. division, section, part, 2. tower, pillar, cylinder, monument

combat   battle, struggle, fight, contest, conflict, war

combine   join, unite, mix, connect, couple, blend, fuse
separate   COMBINATION

combustible   flammable, burnable, fiery
COMBUSTION

comedian comic, gagman, funnyman COMEDY

comely attractive, fair, good-looking, pleasing, personable

comfort console, ease, assure, relieve, cheer, gladden
COMFORTABLE

comical amusing, funny, humorous tragic COMIC

command 1. bid, order, direct, instruct, enjoin, 2. power,
control COMMANDER

commemorate honor, celebrate, observe, proclaim

commence begin, start, take off, fire away
COMMENCEMENT

commend 1. praise, compliment, approve (*Slang* — boost,
plug) criticize, disapprove, 2. commit, assign, trust
COMMENDATION

comment remark, note, observe, mention

commerce trade, business, dealings COMMERCIAL

commit 1. entrust, promise, pledge, 2. perform, do

committee council, group, delegation

commodious roomy, spacious, comfortable close

commodity product, ware, article

common 1. public, general private, 2. usual, familiar,
ordinary, everyday odd, 3. low, crude, coarse, vulgar,
poor, inferior refined COMMONLY

commotion disturbance, tumult, confusion, rumpus, ado,
action, stir, fuss, trouble, excitement, row, stir, hubbub,
to-do order

communicable contagious, catching, transferable, infectious

communicate inform, tell, enlighten, report, convey (*Slang*
— wise up) COMMUNICATION

community 1. society, people, colony, district, town, 2. ownership together

commute 1. exchange, substitute, replace, switch, 2. travel, move COMMUTER

compact 1. concise, short, brief lengthy, 2. agreement, contract, pact, understanding, concord, bargain, treaty, alliance, deal

companion partner, accompanist, buddy, friend, pal, comrade, chum (*Slang* — sidekick, crony) COMPANIONSHIP

company 1. group, association, 2. business, firm, enterprise, 3. guest, visitors, companions

compare match, liken, contrast, measure COMPARABLE, COMPARATIVE, COMPARISON

compassion clemency, mercy, pity, sympathy, leniency, mildness harshness, severity COMPASSIONATE

compatible agreeing, harmonious incompatible, differing

compel force, make, require

compensate pay, reward, atone for, balance, make up for COMPENSATION

compete rival, vie with COMPETITION, COMPETITIVE, COMPETITOR

competent able, effective, adequate, capable, qualified, fit incompetent

compile gather, collect, assemble, accumulate, store up

complacent self-satisfied, contented dissatisfied COMPLACENCY

complain grumble, squawk, find fault, fret (*Slang* — crab, bellyache, kick, grouch) COMPLAINT

complement supply, complete, supplement

complete 1. finish, conclude, terminate, end, clean up, wind up, close up (*Slang* — put the lid on it, button up, call it a day) start, begin, 2. whole, entire, thorough incomplete COMPLETELY, COMPLETION

complex 1. complicated, confused, involved, mixed simple 2. prejudice, bias, leaning, inclination COMPLEXITY

complexion appearance, look, color, pigment

complicate confuse, confound, involve, complex, mix up (*Slang* — foul up) simplify COMPLICATION

compliment commend, flatter, praise, congratulate COMPLIMENTARY

comply conform, agree, assent, submit, obey dissent

compose 1. make up, devise, put together, construct, build, create, make, 2. calm, pacify, soothe, quiet COMPOSER, COMPOSITE

composition 1. writing, work, paper, document, script, 2. composite, combination, mixture, blend

composure calmness, quiet, self-control, peace, rest, serenity tranquility excitement, agitation

comprehend 1. understand, realize, know (*Slang* — catch on, get the drift), 2. include, contain, cover exclude COMPREHENSION, COMPREHENSIVE

compress squeeze, press, reduce, condense, concentrate, crush expand, spread COMPRESSOR

comprise include, consist of, contain, involve exclude

compromise settle, yield, concede, adjust, meet halfway (*Slang* — go 50-50)

compulsory compelled, required, necessary

compute calculate, count, figure, estimate, reckon COMPUTATION

comrade buddy, friend, pal, companion, partner, chum (*Slang* — sidekick, crony)

conceal hide, cover, cloak, veil, camouflage disclose CONCEALMENT

concede admit, allow, grant, confess refuse, deny

conceited vain, boastful, proud, cocky, saucy CONCEIT

conceivable imaginable, thinkable, possible, likely, plausible inconceivable, doubtful CONCEIVE

concentrate 1. think about, focus wander (in thought), 2. strengthen, intensify, make stronger weaken CONCENTRATION

concept thought, notion, idea, opinion CONCEPTION

concern 1. interest, affect, trouble, involve, 2. business, company, firm, enterprise

concert 1. music, recital, 2. agreement, harmony, unison, teamwork

conciliate soothe, allay, quiet, calm, pacify, moderate, restrain, alleviate irritate CONCILIATORY

concise brief, short, terse, curt lengthy

conclude 1. close, end, finish, stop, terminate begin, 2. reason, suppose, assume, presume, infer, gather CONCLUSION

concoct make, invent, prepare, devise, create, manufacture (*Slang* — cook up)

concord peace, harmony, agreement

concrete 1. real, solid, substantial, tangible abstract, flimsy, 2. cement, pavement

concur agree, cooperate (*Slang* — play ball) disagree

concussion shock, head injury

condemn disapprove, doom, censure, blame, reproach,

.denounce, criticize (*Slang* — pan, knock)   approve
CONDEMNATION

condense   compress, squeeze, reduce, concentrate
enlarge, expand   CONDENSATION

condition   1. circumstance, situation, state, 2. provision,
specification   CONDITIONAL

conduct   1. manage, direct, guide, lead, 2. behavior, action,
manner   CONDUCTOR

confederation   league, alliance, association, union
CONFEDERATE

confer   consult, discuss, talk over (*Slang* — go into a huddle)
CONFERENCE

confess   admit, acknowledge, consent (*Slang* — talk, sing,
come clean)   deny   CONFESSION

confide   trust in, rely, depend, tell a secret, disclose

confident   certain, sure, convinced, believing   doubtful
CONFIDENCE

confidential   secret, unpublishable, off the record (*Slang*
— inside)

confine   enclose, surround, contain, keep in, coop up, imprison, restrain   free, release

confirm   establish, verify, substantiate, prove, O.K.
CONFIRMATION

confiscate   seize, take

conflagration   fire, blaze

conflict   1. clash, oppose, disagree, differ   agree,   2. fight,
struggle, opposition, contest, battle   peace

conform   comply, agree, assent, submit, obey   dissent

confound   confuse, perplex, baffle, puzzle, mystify, bewilder,
stump (*Slang* — stick, floor, get, beat)   clarify

confront   oppose, face, meet squarely, encounter

confuse   complicate, mix up, mistake, muddle, jumble (*Slang* — ball up, foul up)   clarify   CONFUSION

congeal   freeze, thicken, stiffen, clot, solidify   melt, soften

congenial   agreeable, pleasing, compatible, harmonious, like-minded   conflicting

congested   overcrowded, overloaded, stuffed, full (*Slang* — jam-packed)   empty

congratulate   bless, compliment, flatter, commend, praise CONGRATULATION

congregate   crowd, mass, gather, meet, assemble (*Slang* — gang around)   disperse, scatter

conjecture   guess, suppose

conjure   entreat, appeal, plead, implore

connect   join, unite, combine, link, attach disconnect, separate   CONNECTION

conquer   overtake, vanquish, defeat, crush, win, triumph CONQUEROR, CONQUEST

conscientious   exacting, particular, faithful, scrupulous neglectful

conscious   1. alive, awake   unconscious, 2. knowing, realizing, sensitive, sensible, aware, cognizant   unaware

consecutive   following, successive, continuous   interrupted

consent   permit, agree, assent, accept, approve of, comply refuse

consequently   therefore, as a result, accordingly, hence CONSEQUENCE

conservative   cautious, opposed to change, unextreme, protective   changing

conserve   preserve, save, keep, guard, protect, maintain CONSERVATION

consider 1. think, study, ponder, reflect, contemplate, deliberate (*Slang* — mull over), 2. think of, regard, look upon

considerable important, much, great, significant, powerful insignificant, unimportant

considerate thoughtful, mindful of others, kind, sympathetic inconsiderate, thoughtless CONSIDERATION

consign hand over, deliver, transfer, entrust, send, convey

consist comprise, make up, include

consistency 1. firmness, stiffness, 2. steadiness, uniformity, keeping changing CONSISTENT

console comfort, cheer, solace, sympathize CONSOLATION

consolidate unite, combine, condense, concentrate, merge, compress, squeeze, reduce

consort 1. husband or wife, spouse, mate, 2. associate, companion, buddy, friend, pal, partner, comrade

conspicuous noticeable, distinct, clear, obvious, prominent, outstanding inconspicuous

conspire plot, scheme (*Slang* — cook up) CONSPIRACY, CONSPIRATOR

constantly always, often, without stopping, continual seldom, scarcely

consternation dismay, alarm, terror, fright, scare, dread

constitute organize, form, set up, establish, compose CONSTITUTION, CONSTITUENT

constrain force, compel, urge, press

constrict contract, compress, squeeze, press, crush expand, spread

construct manufacture, form, build, make, create CONSTRUCTION

constructive   helpful, useful, worthwhile   destructive

construe   explain, interpret, infer   misconstrue, misunderstand

consult   confer, discuss, talk over (*Slang* — go into a huddle)

consume   1. use up, spend, eat up, drink up, 2. waste, destroy, exhaust   CONSUMER, CONSUMPTION

contact   touch, connect, reach, join, approach

contagious   catching, spreading, infectious, epidemic   CONTAGION

contain   1. hold, include, comprise, consist of, involve   exclude, 2. control, restrain, curb (*Slang* — keep under wraps)   CONTAINER

contaminate   pollute, corrupt, defile, infect   purify

contemplate   1. consider, think, study, ponder, reflect, deliberate, 2. plan, intend, expect   CONTEMPLATION

contemptible   mean, atrocious, wicked, cruel, brutal, ruthless, terrible, horrible, dreadful, awful, vile, wretched   good, angelic   CONTEMPTUOUS

contend   fight, struggle, argue, quarrel

contented   satisfied, pleased, delighted   dissatisfied   CONTENTMENT

contest   1. contend, fight, struggle, argue, quarrel, 2. game, sport, tournament   CONTESTANT

continue   last, endure, go on, keep on, persist   discontinue, stop   CONTINUITY, CONTINUOUS

contortion   twist, distortion, crookedness

contour   outline, profile, form

contraband   prohibited, forbidden, illegal, smuggled, outlawed   legal

1. contract   1. form, start, enter into,   2. agreement, pact, understanding, bargain, treaty, alliance, deal
CONTRACTOR

2. contract   shrink, reduce, compress   expand
CONTRACTION

contradict   deny, oppose, dispute   agree
CONTRADICTION, CONTRADICTORY

contrary   opposed, opposite, different, clashing, conflicting
agreeable

contrast   compare, match, liken, measure

contribute   give, donate, participate, provide
CONTRIBUTION

contrite   regretful, sorry, penitent

contrive   invent, scheme, plan, plot, devise, conspire
CONTRIVANCE

control   1. command, influence, master,   2. restrain, check, contain, curb (*Slang* — keep under wraps)

controversy   dispute, argument, quarrel (*Slang* — hassle)

convalesce   recover, rally, heal, recuperate, improve
relapse   CONVALESCENT

convene   gather, meet, assemble   disperse

convenient   handy, suitable, timely, nearby   inconvenient
CONVENIENCE

conventional   customary, usual, traditional, accepted, established, formal   unusual   CONVENTION

converse   talk, speak with, discuss, communicate with (*Slang* — chew the rag, shoot the breeze)   CONVERSATION

convert   change, transform
CONVERSION, CONVERTIBLE

convey   1. carry, transport, take,   2. communicate, inform, tell, enlighten, report, 3. transfer, consign, hand over, deliver, entrust, send CONVEYANCE

convict condemn, doom, sentence acquit
CONVICTION

convince persuade, assure, make certain, promise, guarantee, pledge

convoy accompany, escort, protect, conduct, guide, lead

convulsion fit, tantrum, seizure, spasm, attack
CONVULSE

cook prepare

cool 1. chilly, fresh warm, 2. calm, unexcited excited

cooperate work together, collaborate (*Slang* — play ball)
COOPERATION, COOPERATIVE

coordinate arrange, organize, harmonize

cope struggle, put up, face

copious plentiful, abundant, ample scarce

copy imitate, repeat, duplicate, reproduce

cordial sincere, hearty, warm, friendly, hospitable
unfriendly CORDIALITY

corporation industry, company, business, firm, enterprise

corpulent fat, stout, chubby, plump, round, fleshy, pudgy, stocky, tubby, chunky thin

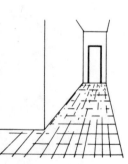

corral hem in, surround, capture, herd, round up, enclose, fence in release, free

correct 1. mark, change, remedy, adjust, 2. true, right, proper, accurate incorrect, wrong CORRECTION

correspond 1. write, communicate with, 2. agree, harmonize, resemble CORRESPONDENCE, CORRESPONDENT

corridor hallway, passageway, aisle

corroborate confirm, establish, verify, substantiate, prove, O.K.

corrode deteriorate, eat away, rot, rust

corrupt wicked, evil, rotten, dishonest, crooked, shady CORRUPTION

cost 1. price, charge, rate, amount (*Slang* — damage, score, tab), 2. loss, sacrifice, expense COSTLY

costume outfit, dress, equip, fit, suit

council conference, assembly, committee, group, delegation

counsel advise, recommend, instruct, suggest, confer COUNSELOR

count 1. add, total, number, 2. depend, rely (*Slang* — bank on), 3. consider, regard, judge

countenance appearance, expression, face, looks (*Slang* — mug, kisser, puss)

counteract 1. offset, balance, neutralize, 2. act against, oppose, contradict, cross agree

counterfeit copied, imitation, fake, artificial (*Slang* — phony) authentic, real

countersign password, secret signal, watchword

countless many, endless, unlimited, innumerable limited

country land, region, nation, territory

couple join, pair, team

courage bravery, boldness, valor, gallantry cowardice COURAGEOUS

courier messenger, runner

course direction, line, way, track, channel

court 1. please, pursue, chase, woo (*Slang* — run after, play up to), 2. yard, enclosure, 3. playground, field, 4. tribunal

courteous polite, civil, gracious, obliging, respectful rude COURTESY

courtly elegant, courteous, polite, civil, gracious, obliging, respectful ill-bred

covenant agreement, pact, contract, understanding, concord, bargain, treaty, alliance

cover 1. hide, protect, shelter, conceal uncover, 2. include, consist of, comprise, contain, involve exclude

covert 1. secret, hidden, disguised, covered, veiled, concealed open, 2. shelter, hiding place, hideaway, refuge

covet desire, crave, lust, want, envy

coward weakling (*Slang* — weak sister, chicken, scaredy-cat) hero, brave person COWARDICE, COWARDLY

cower crouch, squat, cringe

coy shy, modest, bashful, timid, demure bold

cozy comfortable, snug, relaxing, homey uncomfortable COZILY

crack 1. break, split, open, slit, 2. blow, shot, bang, noise

crack-up 1. crash, smash, collide, 2. collapse, breakdown

cradle 1. support, hold, carry, 2. rocker, bed

craft skill, trade, art, handicraft

crafty sly, scheming, calculating, plotting, cunning

cram stuff, fill, load, pack, gorge, saturate

cramp 1. confine, box in, limit, restrict, 2. pain, twinge

cranky cross, irritable, churlish good-humored

crash strike, shatter, break, smash

crate box, container

crave covet, desire, lust, want, envy

crazy insane, mad, lunatic, daft, unbalanced (*Slang —* cracked) sane CRAZE

crease fold, ridge, wrinkle, crinkle

create 1. make, form, invent, originate, manufacture, 2. cause, produce, bring about
CREATION, CREATIVE, CREATOR

credit belief, trust, faith, honor

credulous undoubting, believing, trusting, gullible doubting

crest 1. decoration, insignia, 2. tuft, feathers, plume, 3. peak, ridge, summit, top, crown base

crestfallen dejected, depressed, discouraged, downcast (*Slang —* down in the mouth) cheerful, merry

crevice cleft, rift, gap, break

crew staff, force, gang

crime wrongdoing, sin, vice, evil CRIMINAL

cringe crouch, cower, squat

crinkle wrinkle, ripple, crease

cripple damage, weaken, disable, injure

crisis emergency, critical point, crucial period, turning point

crisp 1. brittle, fragile, frail, breakable strong, 2. fresh, sharp, clear, bracing

critical 1. disapproving, faultfinding approving, 2. crucial, decisive, urgent, pressing unimportant CRITIC

crony friend, pal, buddy, companion, partner, comrade, chum

crook 1. hook, bend, curve, 2. criminal, gangster, lawbreaker, thief

croon hum, sing, vocalize

crop 1. cut, clip, shear, 2. produce, growth, yield, harvest

cross 1. pass, step over, 2. mate, interbreed, 3. oppose, go against, 4. cranky, irritable, churlish good-humored

crouch cower, squat, cringe

crowd group, mass, throng, mob

crown 1. honor, reward, glorify, decorate, 2. head (*Slang* — noodle), 3. crest, peak, ridge, summit, top base, 4. head ornament, tiara

crucial important, critical, urgent, decisive, pressing unimportant

crucify torture, torment, punish, execute
CRUCIFIXION

crude rough, unrefined, raw, vulgar refined

cruel mean, heartless, brutal, ruthless kind
CRUELTY

crumble break up, disintegrate

crumple crush, crinkle, wrinkle, crease, ripple

crusade cause, movement, drive, campaign
CRUSADER

crush 1. subdue, conquer, 2. compress, squeeze, press, reduce expand

crutch support, prop, brace

cry wail, sob, weep, bawl laugh

cuddle snuggle, nestle, fondle

cudgel beat, club, whip

cue hint, signal, clue, key, lead

cull select, pick out, separate

culminate top, crown, end, terminate

culpable guilty, faulty, blamable innocent

culprit offender, sinner, wrongdoer

cultivate condition, prepare, train, develop, improve
CULTIVATION

cultured refined, learned, polished, well-bred uncouth
CULTURE, CULTURAL

cumbersome bulky, clumsy, awkward, unmanageable, burdensome, troublesome manageable

cunning skillful, clever, crafty, sly, scheming, calculating, plotting

curb 1. check, stop, control, restrain, 2. pavement

cure restore, remedy, heal

curious 1. strange, odd, unusual, queer, peculiar, 2. inquisitive CURIOSITY

currency money, cash, legal tender

current 1. flow, stream, 2. prevalent, present, happening
past

curse 1. swear, 2. affliction, trouble, burden

curt abrupt, sudden, short, unexpected

curtail shorten, abbreviate, condense, abridge, contract, reduce, cut, compress lengthen

curve bend, turn, wind, twist, curl

cushion 1. soften, support, 2. pillow

custodian guardian, keeper, caretaker CUSTODY

custom tradition, use, habit, practice, way, manner
CUSTOMARY

cut 1. reduce, contract, abbreviate, shorten, curtail, condense, abridge, compress increase, 2. sever, split

cute 1. pretty, dainty unattractive, 2. clever, shrewd, smart, cunning dull

cycle   series, circle

D

dab   pat, smear, coat

dabble   splash, splatter, putter, toy, fiddle

daft   1. silly, foolish, 2. crazy, insane (*Slang* — loony, goofy, wacky, balmy, batty, nutty, screwy, bugs, cuckoo)   sane

daily   regularly, day by day

dainty   fresh, delicate, small, pretty, cute   gross DAINTILY

dally   loiter, dawdle, lag, linger, delay   rush

damage   harm, hurt, impair, spoil, ruin, upset (*Slang* — mess up, foul up, gum up the works)   remedy

dame   lady, woman

damn   condemn, doom, denounce, censure, curse

dampen   1. moisten, wet, sprinkle, 2. depressed, discouraged, 3. muffle, mute, dull, deaden, smother, suppress   encourage DAMP

dangerous   unsafe, hazardous, risky, perilous, chancy   safe DANGER

dangle   hang, droop, sag, swing, flap

dank   wet, moist, damp, humid, muggy   dry

dapper   neat, trim, smart, chic, well-dressed, natty, sporty, dressy, swanky (*Slang* — sharp, spiffy, classy, nifty, sprucy, swell)

daring   bold, fearless, audacious, foolhardy, adventurous cautious   DARE

dark   1. black, obscure   light, 2. gloomy, dismal, somber, solemn, grave, dreary   cheerful, 3. hidden, secret, concealed, obscured   open   DARKEN, DARKNESS

darling   beloved, dear, precious, adored, cherished

darn   mend, repair, fix, patch up

dart   1. dash, rush, scurry, scoot, hurry, 2. throw, fling, toss, cast

dash   1. hurry, rush, dart, scamper, hasten, 2. drop, trace, touch, pinch

data   facts, information, evidence, proof, grounds

date   1. time, day, 2. appointment, engagement, 3. fruit

daub   1. grease, lubricate, coat, cover, 2. soil, dirty, stain, spot, smear, 3. scribble, scrawl, paint badly

daunt   frighten, discourage, deter, dishearten   encourage

dauntless   brave, fearless, unafraid   fearful

dawdle   idle, loiter, linger, delay, tarry, dillydally (*Slang* — stick around)   rush

dawn   1. daybreak, sunrise, 2. beginning, start, commencement, outset   ending

daze   confuse, bewilder, muddle, upset, ruffle

dazzle   shine, glow, flash, glaze, glare, blind

dead   1. lifeless, deceased, gone, 2. dull, inactive, flat, dreary   alive   DEADEN, DEADLY, DEATH

deal   1. allot, grant, give, 2. trade, buy, sell, 3. act, behave, 4. bargain, compact, agreement, understanding, transaction   DEALER

dear   1. precious, darling, beloved, adored, admired, idolized, 2. expensive, costly, high-priced (*Slang* — stiff, steep)   inexpensive

dearth   lack, scarcity, shortage   abundance

debase   lower, discredit, degrade, demote, run down   lift

debate   discuss, argue, reason, dispute

debris ruins, rubbish, trash, scrap, litter, residue, junk

debt obligation, amount due DEBTOR

decay rot, spoil, crumble, disintegrate flourish, bloom

decease die, perish, depart, expire (*Slang* — croak, kick the bucket, pop off)

deceive beguile, trick, hoax, dupe, betray, mislead, lie
DECEIT, DECEITFUL, DECEPTION

decent 1. respectable, proper, correct, right improper,
2. adequate, good enough, suitable, fit inadequate
DECENCY

decide settle, determine, resolve, judge
DECIDEDLY, DECISION

decipher solve, explain, figure out

declare state, assert, announce, affirm, say, pronounce
DECLARATION

decline 1. refuse, reject (*Slang* — turn down, not buy)
accept, 2. sink, fail, run down, fall, weaken strengthen,
3. slope, descent, slant, hill DECLIVITY

decompose decay, rot, crumble, disintegrate

decorate adorn, trim, beautify, ornament, fix up (*Slang* —
doll up) DECORATIVE, DECORATION

decorum decency, etiquette, manners, social graces, formality

decoy bait, lure (*Slang* — come-on)

decrease lessen, diminish, reduce, curtail, cut, shorten,
compress increase

decree pronounce, order, rule, pass judgment, command,
dictate

dedicate inscribe, devote, address, assign
DEDICATION

deduct subtract, remove, withdraw, take away, discount add DEDUCTION

deed 1. act, action, performance, doing, fete, 2. contract, policy

deem think, believe, consider, judge, regard, suppose, assume

deface mar, blemish, disfigure, deform improve

defeat overcome, win, triumph (*Slang* — lick, do in)

defect fault, flaw, weakness, failing, shortcoming, blemish, imperfection, deficiency perfection DEFECTIVE

defend protect, safeguard, shield, support attack DEFENSE, DEFENSIVE

defenseless helpless, unprotected protected

defer 1. put off, delay, postpone, 2. yield, submit, bow to, respect, accept, acknowledge DEFERENCE

deficient lacking, incomplete, wanting, needing, missing (*Slang* — shy on) complete DEFICIENCY

defile 1. dirty, pollute, contaminate purify, 2. march, parade, file

define 1. explain, describe, clarify, 2. fix, set, establish, outline DEFINITION

definite clear, precise, distinct, plain, obvious, evident, clear-cut, exact indefinite, unclear DEFINITELY

deform disfigure, blemish, mar, spoil, make ugly improve, beautify DEFORMITY

defraud cheat, swindle, gyp (*Slang* — beat, cook, stick, shortchange, chisel)

deft skillful, nimble, clever, adept, expert, proficient, apt, handy, ingenious (*Slang* — crackerjack) unskillful

defy resist, confront, challenge, disobey, ignore, disregard obey DEFIANT, DEFIANCE

degrade demote, reduce, lower, downgrade (*Slang* — take down a peg, run down, knock, bump, bust)

degree 1. step, grade, notch, amount, extent, measure, period, 2. rank, title, honor

deign stoop, lower oneself, yield, concede, give in

deity divinity, god

dejected sad, depressed, discouraged, downcast, disheartened, despondent, blue (*Slang* — down in the mouth) cheerful

delay detain, put off, postpone, hold up

delegate 1. assign, authorize, entrust, appoint, charge, 2. representative, envoy, agent, deputy DELEGATION

deliberate 1. ponder, consider, think over, study, meditate, reflect, mull over, 2. slow, leisurely, easy, unhurried hasty DELIBERATELY, DELIBERATION

delicate mild, soft, fine, dainty, frail, light, fragile, sensitive, tender gross DELICACY

delicious tasty, savory, luscious (*Slang* — scrumptious, yummy)

delightful pleasant, lovely, charming, appealing, pleasing (*Slang* — out of this world) unpleasant DELIGHT

delirious giddy, raving, frantic, mad, violent, hysterical (*Slang* — out of one's head) DELIRIUM

deliver 1. transfer, pass, hand over, consign, give, 2. say, voice, express, communicate, recite, relate, 3. free, rescue, release, liberate DELIVERANCE, DELIVERY

delude mislead, deceive, beguile, hoax, dupe, fool, betray (*Slang* — slip one over on, double-cross) DELUSION

deluge 1. flood, overflow, run over, overwhelm, 2. rain, flood, torrent, storm

delve search, dig, scoop, hunt, look, explore

demand   1. ask, inquire, want to know, 2. require, need, call for, want

demeanor   behavior, manner, conduct, way, actions

demolish   destroy, wreck, tear apart, dismantle, shatter restore

demon   devil, fiend, evil spirit, monster, ogre

demonstrate   display, show, illustrate, clarify
DEMONSTRATION

demote   degrade, reduce, lower (*Slang* — bump, bust) promote

demure   coy, timid, bashful, prim, overmodest bold

denomination   group, sect, class, kind, brand, sort, name

denote   indicate, mean, say, signify, imply, show, mark, express

denounce   blame, censure, reproach, condemn, accuse, charge, indict, damn (*Slang* — knock, pan, slam) commend

dense   1. crowded, packed, compact, thick, heavy, close, solid, compressed empty, 2. stupid, dull (*Slang* — dumb, thick) bright, smart DENSITY

dent   pit, notch, nick, impress

deny   refute, contradict, dispute, renounce, reject admit DENIAL

depart   1. leave, go away, exit, 2. die, decease, perish, pass on arrive DEPARTURE

depend   rely, trust, confide
DEPENDENCE, DEPENDENT

depict   represent, portray, describe, picture, illustrate, characterize

deplore   regret, be sorry for, lament

deportment behavior, conduct, manners, action

deposit 1. put down, lay, place, leave, store withdraw, 2. pledge, stake DEPOSITOR

depot 1. station, stand, post, 2. storehouse, depository, warehouse

depress 1. sadden, deject, discourage, dishearten cheer, 2. lower, sink raise, 3. weaken, reduce, lessen increase DEPRESSION

deprive take away, take from give

deputy agent, representative, delegate

deride ridicule, laugh at, make fun of (*Slang* — ride, pan, razz) DERISION, DERISIVE

derive get, obtain, acquire, gain, secure, receive

derogatory belittling, unfavorable, slanderous flattering

descend decline, fall, drop, plunge ascend DESCENT

descendant child, offspring

describe define, characterize, portray, picture, depict, represent, paint, tell DESCRIPTION, DESCRIPTIVE

desert leave, forsake, abandon (*Slang* — walk out on, pull out, sell out) DESERTER

deserve merit, earn, be worthy of (*Slang* — rate)

design 1. sketch, draw, paint, picture, portray, depict, 2. intend, plan, propose DESIGNING

designate 1. show, indicate, point out, specify, 2. name, nominate, appoint

desire wish, want, fancy, lust DESIRABILITY, DESIRABLE, DESIROUS

desist stop, cease, end, halt, discontinue, abandon continue

desolate 1. empty, vacant, void, barren dense, 2. gloomy, dismal, dreary cheerful DESOLATION

despair   lose hope, give up

desperate   frantic, wild, reckless, mad   DESPERATION

despise   hate, scorn, loathe, disdain   love

despoil   rob, plunder, loot

despondent   depressed, dejected, downhearted, downcast, discouraged (*Slang* — down in the mouth)   cheerful

despot   ruler, tyrant, dictator, oppressor, slave driver

destination   1. end, goal, objective, 2. lot, fortune, fate   DESTINE, DESTINY

destitute   poor, penniless, bankrupt, down-and-out (*Slang* — broke, flat, strapped)   wealthy

destroy   1. spoil, ruin, wreck, devastate   restore, 2. kill, slay, exterminate, finish   DESTROYER, DESTRUCTION, DESTRUCTIVE

detach   1. separate, unfasten, disconnect   join, attach, 2. assign, delegate, draft   DETACHMENT

detail   1. itemize, elaborate, dwell on, tell fully, 2. commission, assign, delegate, 3. part, portion, fraction, division, segment, fragment

detain   delay, retard, hold up, slow up   hurry

detect   discover, spot, spy, recognize, perceive, catch   DETECTIVE

deter   discourage, hinder, prevent, prohibit   encourage

determined   firm, sure, convinced, resolute, resolved, serious   doubtful   DETERMINE, DETERMINATION

detest   hate, dislike, loathe, abhor, despise, scorn   love   DETESTABLE

dethrone   remove, dismiss, overthrow

detour   shift, go around, bypass

devastate   destroy, ruin, wreck

develop 1. grow, flourish, mature, 2. progress, advance
DEVELOPMENT

device 1. machine, apparatus, tool, instrument, implement,
2. plan, scheme, trick

devil demon, fiend, ogre, monster

devise plan, invent, contrive, arrange, create, make up

devoid empty, vacant, bare, blank   full

devote dedicate, assign, apply, attend to

devotion 1. affection, love, fondness, liking   hatred, 2.
loyalty, dedication   infidelity

devour 1. eat, consume, swallow, 2. waste, destroy, ruin

devout 1. religious, pious, 2. earnest, sincere, hearty, devoted, serious, zealous   indifferent

dexterity skill, cleverness, competence

diagnose interpret, gather, deduce, analyze   DIAGNOSIS

diagram draw, sketch, portray, design, depict

dial tune in, call, ring

dialogue conversation, talk, speech, words

diary record book, memo, journal, account, chronicle

dice 1. cube, cut, 2. cubes (*Slang* — ivories)

dictate 1. order, demand, direct, instruct, rule, charge,
2. advise, recommend, suggest
DICTATION, DICTATORSHIP

die decease, perish, expire, pass away (*Slang* — croak, kick
the bucket, pop off)   live   DYING, DEAD

different unlike, distinct, opposite, contrary, reverse, dissimilar, varied, assorted   same, alike
DIFFER, DIFFERENCE

difficult hard, rough, rugged, arduous (*Slang* — tough, wicked, mean) easy DIFFICULTY

dig scoop, excavate, gouge, tunnel DUG

digest 1. absorb, 2. understand, comprehend, grasp, catch on (*Slang* — get the drift), 3. brief, summary DIGESTION, DIGESTIVE

digit 1. number, numeral, figure, 2. finger or toe

dignified noble, worthy, stately, majestic, grand undignified DIGNIFY, DIGNITY, DIGNITARY

dilapidated decayed, ruined, battered, broken-down, run-down (*Slang* — beat-up)

dilate expand, enlarge, widen, broaden, magnify, increase contract, reduce

diligent hard-working, industrious, energetic lazy DILIGENCE

dillydally loiter, delay, tarry, linger, dawdle (*Slang* — hang around, take one's sweet time, stick around) hurry, speed

dilute weaken, reduce, thin, cut, water down strengthen

dim faint, weak, pale, indistinct, vague, darkish bright

dimension measurement, size, expanse, proportions

diminish decrease, reduce, lessen, curtail, cut increase, enlarge

din noise, racket, clamor, uproar, tumult quiet

dine 1. eat, sup, 2. feed, nourish DINER, DINNER

dingy dirty, dull, grimy, dark, gray bright

dip sink, ladle, immerse, dunk

diplomat politician, envoy, ambassador, emissary, a tactful person DIPLOMATIC

dire   bad, terrible, dreadful, horrible, awful, wretched, disastrous, tragic, black

direct   1. manage, control, conduct, handle, head, govern, rule, regulate, 2. order, command, dictate, instruct, charge, 3. show, point, aim, 4. address, inscribe
DIRECTION, DIRECTLY, DIRECTOR, DIRECTORY

dirty   grimy, soiled, muddy, untidy, dingy, messy, sloppy   clean   DIRT, DIRTINESS

disable   cripple, make useless, put out of order, weaken   enable   DISABILITY

disadvantage   drawback, handicap, liability, inconvenience   advantage

disagree   differ, quarrel, conflict, dispute (*Slang* — row, scrap, hassle)   agree
DISAGREEABLE, DISAGREEMENT

disappear   vanish, go away, fade out   appear
DISAPPEARANCE

disappoint   dissatisfy, let down, displease   satisfy
DISAPPOINTMENT

disapprove   disfavor, frown upon, object to, oppose (*Slang* — turn one's thumbs down on, take a dim view of)   approve

disarm   demilitarize, paralyze, make powerless   strengthen

disaster   casualty, calamity, misfortune, mishap, catastrophe, tragedy, accident   fortune   DISASTROUS

disband   separate, scatter, disperse, split, break up, dismiss, dissolve   assemble

discard   reject, throw away, get rid of, dispose of, scrap, cast off (*Slang* — junk)   keep

discern   see, behold, observe, view, perceive, recognize, know, realize, understand, detect, spot, spy

discharge   unload, release, dismiss, expel, dump, fire, let go

disciple   believer, follower, convert

discipline   1. train, drill, exercise, practice, prepare, condition, groom (*Slang* — lick into shape), 2. punish, chastise, correct, penalize (*Slang* — give what-for)

disclaim   deny, refuse, withhold, reject   accept

disclose   uncover, open, reveal, show, expose, unmask hide, conceal

discolor   fade, dull, tarnish, bleach

discomfort   distress, trouble, bother, disturb, perturb, upset comfort, please

discord   1. disagreement, difference, dispute, conflict, friction   agreement, 2. noise, racket, din, clamor   quiet

discount   1. deduct, subtract, remove   add, 2. allow for, consider, take into account

discourage   deter, prevent, hinder, disapprove, keep from, deject, daunt   encourage   DISCOURAGEMENT

discourse   talk, converse, lecture, preach, expound, address

discover   reveal, learn, observe, see, notice, perceive, find, disclose, expose   DISCOVERY

discredit   1. doubt, disbelieve   believe, 2. disgrace, dishonor, shame, humiliate (*Slang* — knock)

discreet   careful, prudent, considerate, thoughtful, cautious indiscreet   DISCRETION

discriminate   separate, segregate, distinguish, set apart DISCRIMINATION

discuss   debate, talk over, reason, consider, confer (*Slang* — kick around, chew the rag)   DISCUSSION

disdain   scorn, despise, reject, spurn   respect DISDAINFUL

disease   sickness, illness, ailment, malady, infirmity   health DISEASED

disfigure deform, deface, blemish, mar, injure, scar, spoil

disgrace shame, dishonor, discredit, humiliate, embarrass
DISGRACEFUL

disguise conceal, hide, cover, camouflage, misrepresent

disgust sicken, offend, repel, revolt, nauseate

dish 1. give, serve, 2. receptacle, container

dishearten discourage, depress, sadden, deject cheer

disheveled rumpled, mussed, untidy, sloppy neat

disintegrate break up, separate, decompose, crumble, decay, rot

dismal dark, gloomy, dreary, miserable, bleak, depressing
bright, cheerful

dismantle disassemble, take apart, demolish, wreck

dismay bewilder, disturb, embarrass, bother, confuse, alarm, frighten

dismiss discharge, expel, send away (*Slang* — fire, can, sack, bump, give the gate, show the door) enlist
DISMISSAL

dispatch 1. send, transmit, forward, discharge, 2. hurry, hasten, speed, rush

dispel scatter, disperse, drive away assemble

dispense distribute, give out, deal out, issue, allot, grant, dole out, mete out (*Slang* — hand out, dish out, fork out, shell out)

disperse scatter, distribute, spread

display demonstrate, illustrate, exhibit, present, parade, flaunt conceal

disposal 1. removal, elimination, release, 2. arrangement, settlement, adjustment, administration

disposition 1. nature, temperament, character, inclination, 2. arrangement, settlement, order, adjustment, administration

dispute argue, debate, quarrel, oppose, resist, fight, bicker, contest agree

dissect cut, examine, analyze

dissent disagree, differ, take exception agree
DISSENSION

dissipate 1. scatter, spread, dispel, disperse, 2. squander, waste, spend foolishly save

dissolve 1. melt, liquefy, 2. cease, end, fade, pass away, disappear

dissuade discourage, talk out of

distance 1. space, length, extent, reach, 2. far away
nearness DISTANT

distend expand, swell, stretch, widen, enlarge, magnify, increase, blow out, bulge contract, decrease

distinct 1. different, dissimilar, diverse, separate similar, 2. clear, plain, obvious, precise, exact, clear-cut, definite, unmistakable indefinite
DISTINCTION, DISTINCTIVE

distinguish 1. tell apart, define, see, detect, 2. honor, dignify, make famous

distinguished important, great, outstanding, famous, well-known, noted, popular, celebrated, honored

distort twist, contort, misrepresent, falsify

distract divert, confuse, disturb

distress pain, hurt, afflict, torment, torture, agonize, trouble, bother, disturb, upset please

distribute   scatter, disperse, spread, dispense, allot, dole out, mete out (*Slang* — hand out, dish out, fork out, shell out) collect   DISTRIBUTION

district   region, area, zone, territory, place, section, neighborhood

disturb   1. annoy, irk, vex, bother, irritate, 2. trouble, perturb, concern, agitate, upset, excite, alarm DISTURBANCE

dive   plunge, drop, fall   DIVER

diverse   1. different, unlike, distinct, 2. various, several same   DIVERSITY

divert   1. distract, detract, confuse, 2. amuse, entertain, delight, tickle   DIVERSION

divide   separate, portion, partition, split, share, sort   unite DIVISIBLE, DIVISION, DIVISOR

divine   1. heavenly, sacred, holy, 2. superb, delightful, excellent, great, beautiful, 3. foretell, predict, guess, forecast, prophesy, anticipate   DIVINITY

divorce   separate, disjoin, divide, disconnect

divulge   reveal, tell, make known, publish, broadcast, circulate, let out, come out with

dizzy   giddy, staggering, spinning, unsteady, confused steady   DIZZINESS

do   perform, act, behave, produce   DOINGS

docile   obedient, willing, receptive, responsive, yielding, gentle, tame, mild   stubborn

dock   1. anchor, moor, tie, 2. clip, cut off

doctor   1. treat, remedy, heal, cure, 2. physician, medic

doctrine   belief, teachings, creed

document   writing, paper, certificate, statements

dodge   avoid, duck, recoil

doff   remove, take off, undo   don, put on

dogged   stubborn, willful, headstrong, obstinate   yielding

doldrums   blues, low spirits, gloom (*Slang* — dumps) cheerfulness

dole   give, donate, allot, dispense, grant, deal out, mete out (*Slang* — hand out, fork out, shell out)

doleful   sad, mournful, dreary, dismal

dolt   dunce, blockhead, numskull (*Slang* — dope)

domain   sphere, realm, province, field, property

domestic   1. household, family, internal, 2. tame, 3. servant, maid   DOMESTICATE

dominate   control, rule, command, lead DOMINANT, DOMINATION

domineering   arrogant, overbearing, high-handed, bossy

dominion   1. rule, control, command, power, hold, grasp, 2. lands, sphere, country, domain

don   put on, slip on, dress in, wear

donate   give, contribute, present, bestow, award, allot, grant   DONATION, DONOR

done   finished, complete, ended, concluded, terminated, over, wound up, through with (*Slang* — fini, washed up)

donkey   1. dolt, stubborn person, 2. ass, mule, burro

doom   condemn, damn, censure, convict, sentence

dormant   sleeping, inactive   active, awake

dose   amount, quantity, portion (*Slang* — slug)

double   1. duplicate, copy, 2. fold, turn over, 3. twice as much   DOUBLY

doubt   mistrust, suspect, question, challenge, dispute
believe   DOUBTFUL

douse   1. dip, immerse, dunk, 2. extinguish, quench

dowdy   shabby, untidy, messy, mussy, sloppy, seedy   tidy

downcast   dejected, sad, discouraged, disheartened,
depressed, gloomy, melancholy, glum (*Slang* — down in
the mouth)   cheerful

downfall   1. ruin, failure, defeat, upset, overthrow   success,
2. rainstorm, cloudburst, flood, downpour

downhearted   discouraged, dejected, depressed, downcast,
sad, glum, melancholy (*Slang* — down in the mouth)

downpour   rainstorm, cloudburst, flood, downfall

downright   thorough, complete, plain, positive, utter, absolute, entire, total

dowry   1. settlement, endowment, 2. talent, gift, ability,
genius

drab   dull, unattractive, flat, lifeless   bright

draft   1. wind, air, 2. sketch, drawing, rough copy, outline,
3. enlistment, enrollment, induction, call-up, recruitment,
4. note, bill, check

drag   1. pull, heave, haul, draw, tug, tow, 2. crawl, creep,
linger on, tarry, lag, dillydally, delay   speed

drain   1. dry, empty, draw off, 2. deprive, filter, use, spend,
exhaust   replenish   DRAINAGE

dramatize   stage, produce, present, feature, put on
DRAMA, DRAMATIC, DRAMATICALLY,
DRAMATIZATION

drape   cover, hang, flow   DRAPERY

drastic   extreme, severe, intense, rough, violent, fierce, tough
mild

draw 1. pull, drag, haul, 2. attract, lure, magnetize, interest repel, 3. sketch, portray, picture, design, 4. tie, equal, match

drawback disadvantage, handicap, fault, obstacle, objection, failing, shortcoming, flaw, catch (*Slang* — bug) advantage

dread fear, be afraid

dreadful bad, terrible, awful, unpleasant, horrible, vile, wretched, detestable, ghastly splendid

dream imagine, vision, muse DREAMER, DREAMY

dreary gloomy, dull, dismal, somber, depressing, discouraging, disheartening pleasant

dredge dig, excavate, scoop, pick up

drench soak, wet, saturate, flood

dress clothe, adorn, decorate, attire, outfit DRESSER

dressing 1. medicine, bandage, 2. sauce, seasoning

dribble drip, trickle, leak

drift wander, roam, stray, meander, ramble, float, cruise, glide

drill 1. practice, instruct, teach, train, exercise, prepare, condition, discipline (*Slang* — lick into shape), 2. tool

drink swallow, sip, guzzle

drive 1. steer, ride, handle, operate, work, run, conduct, manage, 2. move, thrust, compel, force, make, impel DRIVER, DRIVEN, DROVE

drizzle rain, shower, sprinkle

droll amusing, humorous, laughable, funny, witty dull

drone 1. hum, buzz, 2. male bee, 3. loafer, nonworker, unemployed, idler

drool salivate, dribble, trickle

droop 1. hang, dangle, drag, 2. weaken, sink, fade, fail, decline, 3. despond, despair, lose heart, give up

drop 1. fall, dive, plunge, descend rise, 2. end, cease, stop start, 3. dismiss, let go, give up, abandon, 4. hardly anything, small amount much

drown submerge, sink, immerse, inundate

drowsy sleepy, dreamy, heavy-eyed awake, alert
DROWSE

drudge work away, plod (*Slang* — grind, plug away)
DRUDGERY

drug 1. numb, deaden, put to sleep, knock out (*Slang* — dope), 2. medicine, potion, narcotic (*Slang* — dope)
DRUGGIST

drum 1. beat, tap, strike, pound, 2. repeat, drill, 3. musical instrument DRUMMER

drunk intoxicated, tipsy, dizzy (*Slang* — soused, pickled, crocked, tight, high, lit up, stiff)
DRUNKARD, DRUNKEN

dry waterless, arid, parched, thirsty wet DRYER

dual twofold, double, duplicate

dub name, call, title, label, tag, christen

dubious doubtful, uncertain, questionable certain

duck 1. plunge, dip, submerge, sink, immerse, dunk, 2. sidestep, 3. web-footed bird

due 1. proper, rightful, fitting, just, fair, square, equitable unfair, 2. owed paid DULY

duel fight, contest, contend, struggle

dull 1. blunt, unsharp sharp, 2. gray, dingy, dreary bright, 3. stupid, slow clever, 4. boring, uninteresting, dry, flat interesting, 5. slow, inactive, sluggish busy

dumb 1. silent, mute, speechless, 2. stupid, dull, dense (*Slang* — numskulled) smart

dummy 1. imitation, copy, model, figure, doll, fake, 2. dolt, dunce (*Slang* — dope)

dump empty, unload, discharge, discard, throw away, scrap

dunce dolt, dummy, fool (*Slang* — dope)

dupe deceive, trick, beguile, betray, hoax, bamboozle

duplicate copy, repeat, reproduce, double

durable longlasting, enduring, permanent, endless, sturdy, solid, strong perishable

duration time, period, term (*Slang* — hitch)

dusk 1. sundown, sunset, twilight, evening, nightfall dawn, 2. shade, dark, gloom DUSKY

dust 1. clean, wipe off, 2. sprinkle, powder, 3. fine powder DUSTY

duty 1. task, work, job, chore, assignment, charge, function, obligation, responsibility, 2. tax, toll, tariff DUTIFUL

dwarf midget, runt, shrimp

dwell live, reside, inhabit, occupy (*Slang* — hang out) DWELLER, DWELLING

dwindle shrink, decrease, diminish, lessen, decline, subside, waste away increase

dye color, stain, tint

dynamic active, energetic, forceful, strong, lively, intense, animated, spirited (*Slang* — peppy) weak

E

eager wanting, wishing, desirous, anxious, keen, ready, willing unconcerned

early 1. beforetime, in advance late, 2. long ago, in the past, back EARLIER, EARLIEST

earn get, gain, obtain, require, secure, make, deserve, merit, be in line for (*Slang* — rate) EARNINGS

earnest determined, sincere, serious, decided, resolute, devoted insincere

earth 1. world, globe, 2. ground, dirt, soil, land, sod
EARTHEN, EARTHLY

ease 1. relieve, reduce, soothe, allay, comfort, lighten, relax, loosen aggravate, 2. help, aid, facilitate

easy 1. simple, effortless, plain, not hard hard, 2. comfortable, restful, relaxing, cozy, snug uncomfortable, 3. kindly, mild, gentle, lenient strict, 4. pleasant, smooth, natural, informal formal EASIER, EASIEST, EASILY

eat 1. dine, consume, chew, swallow, 2. corrode, erode, waste away EATABLE, EATEN, EDIBLE

ebb decrease, diminish, lessen, decline, subside, recede, retreat, withdraw increase

eccentric unusual, peculiar, odd, abnormal, irregular, queer (*Slang* — screwy, wacky, nutty) normal

echo repeat, duplicate, imitate

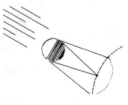

eclipse hide, conceal, cover, screen, veil, obscure, darken, shadow, overcast

economy thrift, frugality, saving
ECONOMIC, ECONOMICS, ECONOMIZE

ecstasy joy, rapture, happiness, delight, glee, elation sadness

edge border, bound, fringe EDGEWAYS, EDGEWISE

edict decree, order, law, ruling, proclamation

edifice building, structure, construction, establishment

edit correct, check, rewrite, revise, amend
EDITION, EDITOR, EDITORIAL

educate teach, instruct, school, train, tutor, enlighten, direct, guide, show EDUCATION, EDUCATIONAL

eerie strange, weird, spooky, deathlike, ghastly, ghostly
EERIER, EERIEST

efface erase, destroy, rub out, obliterate

effect cause, influence, produce, bring about, evoke, determine, achieve, make, accomplish, execute, complete
EFFECTIVE

efficacy ability, capacity, competence, proficiency
inability EFFICIENCY, EFFICIENT

effort attempt, try, endeavor, undertaking, fling (*Slang* — crack, whack, stab, whirl)

egg 1. ovum, embryo, 2. urge, stir, agitate, incite, provoke, arouse (*Slang* — put up to)

eject remove, eliminate, drive out, expel, oust (*Slang* — bounce, kick out, give the bum's rush, give the old heave-ho, give the 1-2-3, throw out on one's ear) receive, include

elaborate dwell on, develop, work out, detail

elapse pass, expire, run out, slip away

elastic 1. flexible, pliable, yielding, adaptable inflexible, 2. rubber band ELASTICITY

elated overjoyed, enchanted, delighted, jubilant, rejoicing
unhappy ELATION

elder older, senior younger ELDERLY, ELDEST

elect choose, pick, select, vote for, appoint ELECTION

electrify 1. charge, generate, shock, 2. excite, thrill, jolt, agitate, stir, ruffle, shake, upset
ELECTRIC, ELECTRICAL, ELECTRICIAN, ELECTRICITY, ELECTROMAGNET, ELECTRON

elegant refined, superior, tasteful, polished, cultured, fine vulgar ELEGANCE

elementary fundamental, basic, primary, essential, simple, beginning, introductory, initial, underlying advanced
ELEMENTARY SCHOOL

elevate lift, raise, boost ELEVATION, ELEVATOR

elf mischief-maker, devil, imp, fairy ELVES

elicit draw forth, summon, secure, get from

eligible qualified, fit, desirable, suitable ineligible

eliminate remove, discard, reject, throw out, get rid of, exclude, dispose of include ELIMINATION

elongate lengthen, extend, stretch, prolong shorten

elope flee, run, escape

eloquent fluent, well-spoken, expressive, meaningful
ELOQUENCE

else other, different, instead, another

elude avoid, escape, evade, miss, dodge (*Slang* — duck)
ELUSIVE

emaciated thin, undernourished, wasted, starved, haggard

emancipate free, release, liberate, deliver, rescue, save enslave, restrain EMANCIPATION

embalm preserve, keep

embankment bank, buttress, shore, barrier, dam, fortification

embark depart, start, board disembark

embarrass fluster, confuse, bewilder, humiliate, shame, mortify EMBARRASSMENT

embed enclose, fix, root, plant, lodge, wedge, inset, inlay EMBEDDED

embezzle steal, thieve, take, rob

embitter anger, provoke, incense, arouse, inflame, antagonize, alienate, set against

emblem symbol, sign, token, badge, mark

embody include, comprise, contain, cover, take in, embrace, incorporate exclude

embrace 1. grasp, hug, clasp, enfold, press, hold, clutch, 2. include, contain, comprise, cover, involve, 3. accept, adopt, take up

embroider 1. stitch, decorate, ornament, adorn, trim, embellish, 2. exaggerate, overstate, overdo, stretch, magnify EMBROIDERY

emerge appear, come out, come into view

emergency crisis, crucial period, pinch (*Slang* — squeeze, clutch)

emigrate leave, migrate EMIGRANT, EMIGRATION

eminent high, great, prominent, noble, distinguished, superior, important, outstanding, famous unknown EMINENCE

emissary delegate, messenger, envoy, agent, diplomat, minister, ambassador, spy

emit give off, discharge, ooze, send out receive

emotion feeling, sentiment, sensitivity, excitement EMOTIONAL

emphasis stress, importance, accent, insistence EMPHASIZE, EMPHATIC, EMPHATICALLY

employ hire, engage, contract, sign, retain, occupy, busy, use EMPLOYEE, EMPLOYER, EMPLOYMENT

empower permit, enable, authorize, sanction, license, warrant, commission, delegate, assign, entrust

empty 1. discharge, let out, eliminate, evacuate, 2. flow out, drain, run out, 3. vacant, void, barren, blank full EMPTINESS

emulate imitate, follow, copy, rival, vie with, compete with EMULATION

enable empower, qualify, authorize, sanction, license forbid

enact 1. pass, legislate, 2. portray, represent, act out, perform, stage

enchant delight, charm, thrill, enthrall, titillate, fascinate, captivate (*Slang* — tickle to death, tickle pink, knock dead, slay) ENCHANTMENT

encircle include, take in, comprise, enclose, surround, encompass, bound

enclose surround, fence, contain, include, encircle, envelop, shut in ENCLOSURE

encompass encircle, include, surround, enclose

encore 1. again, 2. repetition, curtain call

encounter 1. meet, come across, 2. battle, confront, collide, oppose

encourage support, urge, invite, promote, sponsor, cheer, inspire discourage ENCOURAGEMENT

encroach intrude, interfere, infringe, trespass, break in upon (*Slang* — barge in, bust in, butt in)

encumber burden, load, weigh down, hamper, saddle with relieve ENCUMBRANCE

end finish, stop, terminate, close, conclude, cease, quit, discontinue, halt, result, complete, wind up, clean up (*Slang* — put the lid on it, call it a day) ENDING

endanger risk, imperil, jeopardize, hazard

endear charm, captivate, allure   embitter

endeavor try, effort, strive, attempt, labor, struggle (*Slang* — take a fling at, have a go at, give it a whirl, make a stab at, take a crack at)

endless continuous, constant, ceaseless, incessant, uninterrupted, nonstop, eternal, infinite, perpetual, everlasting

endorse sign, approve, support, accept, ratify, certify, confirm, O.K., validate, pass

endow give, invest, bequeath, provide, supply, furnish, contribute   ENDOWMENT

endure 1. last, continue, persist, remain, stay   vanish, 2. stand, undergo, bear, experience, feel, suffer, tolerate   ENDURANCE

enemy opponent, foe, opposition   friend, ally

energy force, strength, vigor, potency, vim, drive, might, power, vitality, stamina (*Slang* — pep, guts) weakness   ENERGETIC, ENERGETICALLY

enfold embrace, clasp, wrap, hug, surround, envelop

enforce compel, force, make, oblige, drive, execute   ENFORCEMENT

engage 1. involve, entangle, absorb, engross, occupy, hold, grip, 2. employ, busy, hire, contract for, 3. promise, agree, commit   ENGAGEMENT

engaging interesting, absorbing, fascinating, engrossing, enthralling, spellbinding, charming, enchanting, captivating, appealing, tempting, enticing, delightful, lovely, exquisite   dull, boring

engender cause, produce, develop, generate, breed

engineer guide, manage, direct, regulate, conduct, run, lead, maneuver ENGINE, ENGINEERING

engrave carve, cut, fix, print, inscribe, stamp, sketch, impress ENGRAVING

engross occupy, absorb, engage, fascinate, enthrall

engulf swallow, devour, flood, inundate

enhance improve, better, enrich, uplift (*Slang* — step up, soup up, jazz up) impair

enigma riddle, puzzle, mystery, problem, stumper (*Slang* — brain twister)

enjoy like, appreciate, savor, relish (*Slang* — get a kick out of) disgust ENJOYABLE, ENJOYMENT

enlarge increase, expand, broaden, magnify reduce, shrink ENLARGEMENT

enlighten clarify, inform, instruct, illuminate, explain, simplify, acquaint, teach, educate

enlist 1. join, enroll, sign up, 2. induce, prompt, move, influence, sway, persuade

enliven stimulate, inspire, cheer, brighten (*Slang* — pep up) calm

enmity hate, dislike, loathing, unfriendliness love

enormous large, great, vast, immense, huge, colossal, giant (*Slang* — whopping) tiny

enough sufficient, ample, plenty, satisfactory, adequate insufficient

enrage madden, infuriate, anger, inflame, provoke

enrich improve, enhance, better, uplift

enroll 1. list, register, write, record, join, 2. enlist, draft, induct, recruit ENROLLMENT

enshrine   entomb, inter, bury

ensign   1. flag, banner, pennant, standard, colors, 2. officer

enslave   subject, capture, hold down   free

ensue   follow, succeed, result

ensure   1. assure, make certain, guarantee (*Slang* — clinch), 2. protect, guard, defend, shelter, cover, shield, screen

entangle   involve, complicate, confuse, trap, snare
ENTANGLEMENT

enter   go into, set foot in, join   exit
ENTRANCE, ENTRY

enterprise   ambition, project, fete, undertaking, business, venture, deed, exploit, achievement, adventure
ENTERPRISING

entertain   1. amuse, delight, interest, excite, fascinate, give a party, 2. consider, contemplate, have in mind
ENTERTAINMENT

enthrall   fascinate, charm, captivate, intrigue, enchant, delight, titillate, thrill (*Slang* — send)

enthrone   crown, glorify, exalt, install, instate, inaugurate
impeach

enthusiastic   interested, attracted, eager, keen about (*Slang* — wild about, crazy about, mad about)
unconcerned, disinterested
ENTHUSIASM, ENTHUSIAST, ENTHUSIASTICALLY

entice   attract, tempt, lure, seduce (*Slang* — give the come-on, rope in)

entirely   wholly, fully, altogether, completely, thoroughly, totally, exclusively, solely   partly
ENTIRE, ENTIRETY

entitle   name, call, designate, tag, label, title, identify, authorize, empower, enable, license   forbid

entrance 1. fascinate, charm, intrigue, enthrall, enchant, delight, thrill, 2. hypnotize, spellbind

entreat beg, ask, implore, plead ENTREATY

entrust delegate, assign, charge, commission

enumerate list, count, tally, number

enunciate speak, pronounce, announce, state, express ENUNCIATION

envelop wrap, cover, embrace, surround, encompass, hide, conceal

environment surroundings, neighborhood, vicinity, setting

envoy messenger, delegate, agent, diplomat

envy covet, be jealous of ENVIABLE, ENVIOUS

epidemic widespread, prevalent, contagious, infectious, catching

episode occurrence, happening, experience, event, incident, affair

epoch era, period, age

equal match, rival, tie, parallel (*Slang* — break even) unequal EQUALITY, EQUALIZE, EQUALLY

equilibrium balance, stability, firmness, soundness, steadiness instability

equip provide, furnish, fit, prepare, rig, costume EQUIPMENT

equitable fair, just, square, even, rightful, due, fit, proper EQUITY

equivalent equal, match, like, rival, substitute, replacement (*Slang* — ringer)

era epoch, period, age

eradicate eliminate, get rid of, remove, exterminate

erase cancel, wipe out, obliterate, cross off ERASER

erect 1. build, construct, make rise, 2. upright, vertical, straight bent ERECTION

erode disintegrate, break up, corrode, wear away, rust EROSION

err misjudge, go wrong, slip, sin

errand task, job, chore, assignment, duty, exercise

errant wandering, roving, roaming, rambling, meandering, drifting, straying, vagrant

erratic uncertain, irregular, queer, abnormal, unusual, changeable, unstable constant

erroneous mistaken, incorrect, untrue, wrong, false true ERROR

erupt burst forth, vomit, discharge, pour out ERUPTION

escape evade, get away, flee (*Slang* — jump, skip, fly the coop, ditch, shake, skip, duck)

escort accompany, conduct, guide, lead, usher, attend, squire, chaperon

especially particularly, principally, chiefly, mainly, mostly, primarily

espionage spying

essay 1. try, attempt, test, experiment, undertake (*Slang* — take a fling at, have a go at, give it a whirl), 2. composition, article, study, paper, thesis

essence 1. meaning, significance, substance, 2. perfume, scent, smell, odor, fragrance

essential needed, necessary, important, vital, fundamental, required, basic ESSENTIALLY

establish 1. fix, set, settle, found, organize, 2. prove, demonstrate, show ESTABLISHMENT

estate property, land

esteem 1. think, consider, judge, regard, 2. prize, value, appreciate, treasure, rate highly

estimate judge, calculate, evaluate, rate, value, figure, compute, gauge ESTIMATION

etch engrave, imprint, stamp, impress ETCHING

eternal always, forever, endless, perpetual, everlasting, permanent, infinite, continual, constant, ceaseless temporary ETERNITY

ethereal light, airy, delicate dense

etiquette manners, social code, formalities

evacuate leave, withdraw, remove, depart, quit, empty, abandon, vacate arrive EVACUATION

evade avoid, escape, miss, bypass (*Slang* — ditch, shake, dodge, duck) EVASION

evaporate vanish, disappear, fade away EVAPORATION

even 1. level, flat, smooth uneven, 2. same, uniform, equal, identical, 3. still, yet

evening nightfall, sunset, sundown

event happening, occurrence, incident, episode, experience

eventually finally, ultimately, in time EVENTUAL

everlasting perpetual, permanent, eternal, infinite, endless, continual, constant, ceaseless temporary

evermore forever, always temporarily

every each, all

evict expel, oust, turn out EVICTION

evidence facts, proof, grounds, data, indication, sign, clue

evident clear, plain, apparent, obvious, clear-cut doubtful, vague

evil   bad, wrong, sinful, wicked   good

evoke   bring forth, summon, induce, prompt

evolve   unfold, develop, grow, progress, advance
EVOLUTION

exact   detailed, precise, correct, accurate   vague
EXACTING, EXACTLY

exaggerate   overstate, stretch, overdo, magnify, enlarge
(*Slang* — talk big, lay it on thick)   minimize
EXAGGERATION

exalt   honor, praise, laud, extol, glorify, compliment, elevate
condemn, disapprove

examine   1. inspect, observe, study, consider, review, analyze, 2. test, quiz, question   EXAMINATION

example   1. sample, model, pattern, representative, symbol,
2. arithmetic problem

exasperate   irritate, aggravate, annoy, anger, infuriate, madden (*Slang* — give one a pain, get one's goat, burn one up,
get under one's skin, get in one's hair)   EXASPERATION

excavate   dig, scoop, pull up, unearth, burrow
EXCAVATION

exceed   surpass, better, excel, top, cap, beat
EXCEEDINGLY

excel   surpass, better, top, cap, beat, exceed
EXCELLENCE, EXCELLENT

except   1. excluding, omitting, leaving out, barring, besides,
save, outside of, aside from   including, 2. reject, exclude,
deny   accept, include   EXCEPTING, EXCEPTION

exceptional   unusual, extraordinary, remarkable, notable,
outstanding   ordinary

excess   left over, addition, extra, surplus, remaining   lack
EXCESSIVE

exchange change, substitute, switch, trade, swap

excite arouse, stir, stimulate, provoke, incite, move, affect compose, calm
EXCITABLE, EXCITED, EXCITEMENT

exclaim cry out, clamor, shout
EXCLAMATION, EXCLAMATORY

exclude bar, shut out, outlaw, keep out, reject, forbid, prohibit include
EXCLUSION, EXCLUSIVE, EXCLUSIVELY

excursion trip, journey, outing, tour

excuse 1. pardon, forgive, absolve, 2. reason, alibi

execute 1. do, perform, complete, carry out, put into effect, accomplish, 2. put to death, kill
EXECUTION, EXECUTIONER

executive directing, managing, administrative

exemplify illustrate, demonstrate, show

exempt free, release, excuse, except, let off liable

exercise practice, use, train, drill, prepare, condition, perform (*Slang* — lick into shape)

exert use, employ, put forth, utilize EXERTION

exhale breathe out, give off, expel, blow inhale

exhaust 1. empty, drain, use up, consume, finish, spend save, 2. tire, fatigue, wear out, knock out (*Slang* — poop, bush)

exhibit show, demonstrate, display, present, flaunt (*Slang* — flash, sport) EXHIBITION

exhilarate cheer, gladden, enliven, encourage, inspire, stimulate, refresh, excite (*Slang* — give a lift, pep up) sadden, deject EXHILARATION

exhort urge, advise, press, coax, prompt (*Slang* — twist one's arm)

exile   banish, expel, cast out, deport, ban, exclude   admit

exist   1. be, live, 2. occur, prevail, stand   EXISTENCE

exit   depart, go out, leave   enter

exodus   departure, leaving, going, parting, exit   entrance

exorbitant   excessive, unreasonable, outrageous, overpriced
  cheap

exotic   1. foreign, strange   native, 2. colorful, bright, rich,
  vivid, gay   dull

expand   spread, swell, unfold, grow, enlarge, extend, broaden,
  increase, magnify   contract, reduce
  EXPANSE, EXPANSION

expect   anticipate, look for, await, think, suppose, hope
  EXPECTANT, EXPECTATION

expedient   useful, helpful, fitting, desirable, appropriate,
  wise, sensible   unwise, absurd

expedition   1. journey, trip, trek, pilgrimage, 2. speed,
  promptness, swiftness, haste, hurry   delay

expel   remove, get rid of, eliminate, eject, dispose of, dismiss,
  discharge, oust, banish, outlaw (*Slang* — bounce, give the
  hook, kick out, give the bum's rush, give the old heave-ho,
  give the 1-2-3)   admit

expend   spend, use up, consume, exhaust, waste   store
  EXPENDITURE

expensive   costly, high-priced, dear (*Slang* — stiff, steep)
  cheap   EXPENSE

experience   1. happening, occurrence, incident, episode,
  adventure, 2. sensation, feeling, emotion, 3. practice,
  knowledge, know-how   inexperience   EXPERIENCED

experiment   try, test, prove, verify (*Slang* — play around
  with, fool around with, try it for size)
  EXPERIMENTAL, EXPERIMENTATION

expert skillful, adept, apt, handy, clever, proficient, masterful, ingenious (*Slang* — crack, crackerjack) incompetent

expire end, cease, perish, die, pass away, vanish, disappear continue, commence EXPIRATION

explain solve, answer, clarify, simplify, illustrate, show, demonstrate EXPLANATION, EXPLANATORY

explicit clear, distinct, definite, direct, candid, express, positive, unmistakable indefinite, unclear

explode blow up, burst, erupt
EXPLOSION, EXPLOSIVE

exploit 1. use unfairly, take advantage of (*Slang* — play for a sucker), 2. deed, feat, adventure, bold act

explore search, hunt, look, research, examine, investigate, delve into, probe EXPLORATION, EXPLORER

export send abroad, ship import

expose open, uncover, show, display, reveal, disclose, unmask hide, conceal EXPOSITION, EXPOSURE

expound explain, clarify, illuminate, demonstrate, teach, lecture, present

express 1. say, voice, present, tell, describe, 2. show, indicate, imply, 3. send, dispatch, ship, 4. fast, quick, speedy, rapid, swift slow EXPRESSION, EXPRESSIVE

expressly plainly, definitely

expulsion removal, ejection, elimination, discharge admittance

exquisite 1. lovely, delicate, beautiful, superb, magnificent, marvelous, wonderful, delightful, charming, appealing, enchanting, heavenly, attractive ugly, 2. sharp, intense, acute dull

extend 1. stretch, reach out, lengthen, increase, enlarge,

expand, broaden, magnify   decrease, shorten,   2. give, grant, donate, present, allot, contribute, supply, provide, furnish   take
EXTENSION, EXTENSIVE, EXTENT

exterior   outside, outer, external, surface   interior

exterminate   destroy, get rid of, eliminate, kill, dispose of, wipe out

external   outside, outer, exterior, surface   internal

extinct   dead, gone, past, obsolete   EXTINCTION

extinguish   put out, smother, quench, suppress, crush (*Slang* — crack down on, shut down, squelch, sit on, put the lid on)

extol   praise, glorify, laud, compliment, exalt

extra   additional, supplementary, surplus, more, spare

extraordinary   special, unusual, remarkable, exceptional, wonderful, marvelous, noteworthy, memorable   ordinary
EXTRAORDINARILY

extravagant   extreme, excessive, overdone, exaggerated, unreasonable, luxurious, grand   meager
EXTRAVAGANCE

extreme   1. extravagant, excessive, exaggerated, overdone, drastic, radical   moderate,   2. final, last, conclusive, terminal, endmost   first, beginning
EXTREMELY, EXTREMITY

extricate   release, free, liberate, rescue, clear   capture

exult   rejoice, delight, be glad   lament, grieve
EXULTANT, EXULTATION

eye   look, glance, watch, observe, regard, view, inspect, stare (*Slang* — size up, give the once-over)

F

fable   story, legend, myth, fairy tale, fiction   truth

fabric   cloth, textile, goods, material

fabulous   unbelievable, amazing, remarkable, striking, notable, marvelous

facade   front, face

face   1. confront, oppose, meet, encounter, brave avoid, 2. features, looks, countenance (*Slang* — mug, kisser, puss), 3. look, expression   FACIAL

facet   side, aspect, view, phase

facilitate   ease, help, assist, speed, smooth the way   FACILITY

fact   detail, item, point, truth, certainty, evidence, data, clue lie   FACTUAL

factor   cause, element, part, ingredient, basis

factory   plant, works

faculty   1. talent, gift, power, ability, capacity, qualification, aptitude, 2. teachers, staff

fad   fashion, craze, rage

fade   1. dim, lose color, pale, dull, bleach, 2. weaken, sink, fail, droop, decline (*Slang* — cave in, fizzle out, peter out, hit the skids, conk out, give out, poop out)

fag   tire, fatigue, weary, exhaust

fagot   sticks, twigs, firewood

fail   1. flunk, be unsuccessful, lose out (*Slang* — flop, lay an egg) succeed, 2. neglect, fall short, 3. weaken, fade, decline (*Slang* — cave in, fizzle out, peter out, hit the skids, conk out, give out, poop out)   FAILING, FAILURE

faint   1. swoon, black out, weaken, keel over (*Slang* — pass out), 2. weak, dim, pale, indistinct, vague, hazy, blurred clear, strong

fair   1. light, pale, whitish dark, 2. clear, sunny, bright, pleasant cloudy, 3. average, mediocre outstanding, 4.

honest, just, square, right, impartial unfair, unjust, 5. festival, fete, affair, bazaar, exposition, market FAIRLY

fairy sprite, elf, goblin, pixie, sylph

faith 1. trust, belief, confidence, hope, 2. religion, teaching FAITHFUL, FAITHLESS

fake 1. pretend, deceive, falsify, disguise, distort, feign (*Slang* — go through the motions, put on an act, put up a false front), 2. false, mock, make-believe, imitation, counterfeit, artificial, fraudulent (*Slang* — phony) real, genuine

fall 1. drop, plunge, descend, tumble ascend, 2. lapse, slip, 3. ruin, destruction, defeat, overthrow, 4. autumn, 5. wig, hairpiece

fallow unprepared, uncultivated, idle, unproductive cultivated

false 1. untrue, incorrect, lying, wrong true, 2. deceitful, disloyal, two-faced loyal, 3. artificial, fake, counterfeit, mock, imitation real, genuine FALSEHOOD

falter hesitate, stumble, stagger, waver, flounder

fame reputation, name, renown, glory, popularity, notoriety FAMED, FAMOUS

familiar 1. well-known, popular unknown, 2. friendly, close, personal, intimate distant, 3. well acquainted, informed in, versed in, knowledgeable unfamiliar FAMILIARITY

family group, household, kin, relatives, folks

famine starvation, lack, need, want, shortage, deficiency, absence sufficiency, plenty

famish hunger, starve

fan 1. stir, arouse, whip, stimulate, spread, flare soothe, calm, 2. blower, 3. admirer, follower, devotee, fancier (*Slang* — hound, rooter)

fanatic enthusiast, zealot (*Slang* — bug, nut)

fancy 1. imagine, visualize, picture, dream, suppose, think, 2. like, care for, love (*Slang* — go for, have eyes for) dislike, 3. elaborate, ornate, flowery, fussy, frilly (*Slang* — classy) simple FANCIFUL

fang tooth, tusk

fantastic odd, unreal, strange, wild, unusual, incredible, outrageous ordinary, usual

fantasy 1. imagination, vision, illusion, fancy, 2. fiction, myth, fable, legend, story, fairy tale

far 1. distant, remote, removed near, 2. much, a great deal FAR OFF, FARTHER

fare 1. eat, be fed, 2. prosper, get on, progress, thrive, 3. charge, toll, fee, 4. passenger

farewell 1. good-by, good luck, good day, so long, cheerio, see you later hello, 2. departing, leaving, parting, taking leave arriving

farm 1. cultivate, grow, raise, ranch, harvest, 2. hire, let, rent, lease, charter, 3. plantation, ranch, homestead FARMER

far-reaching broad, wide, extensive, sweeping, widespread limited

fascinate interest, excite, attract, enthrall, captivate, charm, intrigue, enchant, thrill, delight bore FASCINATION

fashion 1. make, shape, form, create, mold, 2. style, mode, vogue, custom FASHIONABLE

fast 1. go hungry, starve eat, 2. speedy, swift, rapid, quick, hasty slow, 3. firm, stable, sure, dependable, solid, steady changing

fasten tie, lock, attach, secure, close, bind, connect untie, separate, open

fastidious particular, selective, critical, choosy

fat 1. stout, fleshy, plump, chubby, tubby, chunky thin, 2. oil, lubrication, grease FATTEN

fatal 1. deadly, destructive, killing, mortal, disastrous, 2. important, fateful, serious, significant unimportant

fate fortune, destiny, lot, end FATED, FATEFUL

father 1. originate, cause, produce, bring about, breed, 2. priest, 3. male parent, daddy, sire FATHERLY

fathom 1. understand, follow, grasp, comprehend (*Slang* — dig, get the picture, get the drift, get), 2. measure, gauge

fatigue tire, exhaust, wear out

fault mistake, error, defect, flaw, shortcoming, wrongdoing, misdeed, catch (*Slang* — bug) FAULTY

favor 1. prefer, rather, like better, 2. resemble, look like, 3. kindness, service, good deed, benefit, courtesy FAVORABLE

favorite choice, cherished, prized, beloved, precious, pet, adored, treasured

fealty loyalty, faithfulness, allegiance, devotion, faith, attachment disloyalty

fear dread, be afraid FEARFUL, FEARLESS

feasible possible, practical, workable, attainable impossible

feast 1. enjoy, like, love, delight in, rejoice in, appreciate (*Slang* — get a kick out of), 2. banquet, treat, feed, spread

feat deed, act, action, exploit, achievement, accomplishment, stunt

feature 1. show, headline, star, 2. part, characteristic, trait, mark

fee charge, dues, toll, fare

feeble weak, powerless, frail strong

feed 1. nourish, supply, nurture, 2. eat, dine FED

feel 1. touch, finger, handle, 2. be, seem, look, appear, 3. experience, know, encounter, meet, undergo, endure, suffer, sense FEELER, FEELING

feign pretend, fake, act, bluff, assume, affect, play FEINT

felicity 1. happiness, bliss, gladness, delight, joy, cheer, glee, enchantment, 2. blessing, good fortune, luck

fellow 1. lad, boy, man, chap, guy, 2. companion, counterpart, mate, partner, comrade, associate FELLOWSHIP

female ladylike, womanly, feminine male FEMININE

fen marsh, swamp

fence 1. enclose, wall, fortify, blockade, 2. fight, joust, duel, 3. sell illegally, black-market, bootleg FENCER, FENCING

ferment 1. change chemically, sour, 2. excite, agitate, disturb, stir, trouble, ruffle calm, pacify

ferocious fierce, savage, vicious, brutal, wild, cruel, ruthless, bloodthirsty gentle, tame FEROCITY

ferret 1. hunt, search, 2. weasel

ferry 1. carry, transport, haul, cart, 2. boat

fertile productive, fruitful, enriched, abundant, creative unproductive, barren FERTILITY, FERTILIZATION, FERTILIZE FERTILIZER

fervent sincere, devoted, ardent, zealous, passionate, intense, enthusiastic FERVOR

festive merry, gay, jolly, jovial, joyous, gala FESTAL, FESTIVAL, FESTIVITY

fetch bring, go get

fetching enchanting, appealing, interesting, enticing, inviting, alluring, fascinating, captivating, delightful, exquisite, lovely displeasing

fete festival, party, gala affair

fetter bind, tie, chain, shackle, restrain

feud quarrel, dispute, controversy, fight, squabble, animosity, bitterness peace

fever heat, flush, sickness, high body temperature FEVERISH

few not many, small number, very little many

fib lie, falsehood, untruth, tale, story, yarn truth

fickle changing, unstable, not constant, flighty, uncertain, unreliable, unfaithful constant

fiction fantasy, untruth, invention, legend, myth, fable, fairy tale truth

fidelity 1. loyalty, faithfulness, allegiance, devotion, faith, attachment, fealty disloyalty, 2. accuracy, exactness, correctness, precision

fidget fuss, twitch, jerk, wriggle, squirm, twist, wiggle

field 1. land, space, region, tract, plot, ground, pasture, 2. sphere, range, realm, area

fiend 1. devil, monster, demon, ogre, 2. addict FIENDISH

fierce savage, raging, wild, violent, vicious, brutal, ferocious, cruel calm, kind

fiery 1. hot, burning, flaming, 2. aroused, excited, violent, heated, ardent, feverish, fervent unemotional

fiesta festival, holiday, festivity, fete

fight quarrel, struggle, combat, contest, battle, contend, oppose, attack, row (*Slang* — scrap)

figure   **100**

figure   1. symbol, number, numeral, digit, 2. price, cost, charge, amount, 3. shape, form, physique, build, structure, 4. person, individual, 5. picture, drawing, diagram, illustration, design, pattern, outline, chart, sketch

filch   steal, take, pilfer, thieve (*Slang* — lift, swipe, cop, pinch)

file   1. sort, classify, group, categorize, catalog, store, 2. march, parade, 3. smooth, grind, sand, sharpen, edge

fill   1. load, pack, stuff, cram   empty, 2. supply, provide, furnish   FILLING

filly   mare, female colt

film   1. photograph, take a picture (*Slang* — shoot), 2. coat, coating, layer, covering   FILMY

filter   strain, percolate, screen, sift, refine, purify, cleanse, drain, separate

filth   dirt, muck, foul matter, rot   FILTHY

final   last, deciding, closing, terminal, conclusive   beginning   FINALLY

finale   end, finish, conclusion, termination   beginning, opening

finance   sponsor, back, support, aid, assist, subsidize, stake (*Slang* — bankroll)   FINANCIAL, FINANCIER

find   1. discover, disclose, come upon   lose, 2. learn, get, gain knowledge, gather, 3. decide, declare, determine

fine   1. penalize, tax, charge, 2. delicate, minute   coarse, 3. refined, tasteful, polished, 4. excellent, good, nice, splendid (*Slang* — great, grand, dandy, swell, keen, nifty)

finery   clothes, frillery, ornaments (*Slang* — glad rags)

finger   1. touch, handle, feel, manipulate, 2. digit

finish   1. end, complete, close, terminate, conclude, stop, cease (*Slang* — wind up, clean up, button up, put the lid on it, call it a day)   begin, 2. perfect, polish, refine

fire   1. ignite, heat, kindle, 2. dismiss, discharge, expel, lay off, release (*Slang* — sack, can, bounce, boot, give the ax, give the gate)   hire, 3. arouse, excite, inflame, stir, provoke, agitate   calm, soothe, 4. shoot, discharge, blast

firearms   guns, artillery, ammunition

firebrand   1. lighter, 2. troublemaker, agitator, provoker, instigator, rabble-rouser

firm   1. solid, fixed, secure, unyielding, inflexible, stationary, immovable, rigid   flexible, 2. company, business, enterprise

first   1. principal, main, chief, leading, primary, dominant, 2. beginning, foremost, before, ahead, in front   last, 3. rather, sooner, preferably

fissure   split, crack, opening, break, crevice, gap

fit   1. suit, adapt, adjust, 2. proper, right, suitable, qualified improper, 3. strong, healthy, well   unfit, 4. attack, seizure, spell, spasm, convulsion, frenzy, rage   FITTING

fitful   irregular, sporadic, choppy, disconnected, broken regular, constant

fix   1. mend, repair, adjust, regulate, doctor   break, impair, 2. settle, establish, stabilize, solidify, 3. dilemma, quandary

fixture   appliance, attachment, accessory

flag   1. signal, wave, 2. weaken, droop, wilt, fade, 3. pennant, banner, standard, colors

flair   talent, perception, insight

flamboyant   flaming, brilliant, striking, ornate, vivid, dazzling, fancy   simple

flame   blaze, burn   FLAMMABLE

flank   1. side, border, 2. attack, strike

flare 1. flame, blaze, glow, burn, 2. spread, expand, open up, unfold

flash 1. flame, flare, blaze, 2. telegraph, wire, cable, radio FLASHY

flat 1. level, even, horizontal, smooth uneven, 2. dull, lifeless exciting, 3. off-key, unmusical, 4. apartment, suite FLATTEN

flatter praise, compliment (*Slang* — soft-soap, butter up) FLATTERY

flaunt display, exhibit, parade (*Slang* — flash, sport) hide, conceal

flavor season, spice, give taste FLAVORING

flaw damage, defect, crack, fault, weakness, blemish perfection FLAWLESS

flay 1. peel, skin, strip, 2. criticize, attack, assail (*Slang* — roast, pitch into, sail into)

fleck spot, mark, speckle, dot

flee run away, disappear (*Slang* — beat it, blow, scram, clear out, make off, skip) FLED

fleece 1. rob, cheat, swindle (*Slang* — rook, beat, con), 2. wool

fleet 1. rapid, swift, fast, quick, nimble slow, 2. ships, 3. group, band, company

flesh 1. meat, body, 2. skin, 3. family FLESHY

flex bend, arch, curve stiffen, straighten FLEXIBLE

flick strike, snap, crack, jerk, flip

flicker 1. flutter, waver, 2. woodpecker

flimsy slight, frail, weak, delicate, dainty, fragile strong, sturdy

flinch shrink, cringe, recoil, draw back

fling 1. throw, sling, pitch, toss, cast, hurl (*Slang* — peg, fire), 2. celebration, spree, escapade, lark

flip 1. toss, throw, fling, sling, pitch, cast, hurl (*Slang* — peg, fire), 2. jerk, snap, flick

flippant rude, disrespectful, saucy, pert, impudent, cocky, flip, cheeky, smart, smart-alecky (*Slang* — fresh, nervy) polite

flit fly, glide, flutter

float 1. buoy up, sustain, hold up   sink, 2. raft, 3. parade car

flock group, crowd, throng, mob, bunch, pack, multitude

flog beat, whip, lash, spank, thrash

flood overfill, drench, overflow, inundate, oversupply, deluge

floor 1. defeat, overcome, upset, overthrow, 2. ground, pavement, 3. level, story

flop 1. drop, fall, sink, go down, droop, slump, sag   rise, 2. fail, lose (*Slang* — lay an egg, fold up, strike out) succeed

flounder 1. struggle, have trouble, stumble, 2. fish

flourish 1. thrive, prosper, grow, develop, sprout, bloom fade, 2. wave, flaunt, display, parade, exhibit, show

flout sneer, insult, mock, ridicule, jeer, taunt

flow glide, stream, pour, run, gush

flower blossom, bloom, develop, flourish, thrive
FLOWERING, FLOWERY

fluffy soft, downy, feathery, woolly, furry

fluid liquid, flowing, watery solid

flurry 1. fluster, excite, agitate, confuse, ruffle, 2. commotion, confusion, disturbance, 3. light snowstorm

flush 1. blush, redden, color, 2. rush, chase, 3. level, flat, even, 4. full, stuffed, packed

fluster   excite, confuse

flutter   wave, flap, flourish, tremble, move

fly   1. glide, coast, sail, wing, 2. flee, run away (*Slang* — take to one's heels, make off, clear out), 3. insect   FLIGHT

foam   bubble, lather, froth

focus   adjust, concentrate

foe   enemy, adversary, opponent   friend

fog   cloud, blur, dim, confuse   clarify   FOGGY

foil   1. outwit, frustrate, thwart, spoil, ruin, 2. metal, 3. sword

fold   1. bend, double over   unfold, 2. pen, enclosure, 3. church   FOLDER

folk   1. people, persons, society, public, 2. tribe, nation, race, clan, breed

follow   1. come next, succeed, ensue, trail   lead, precede, 2. pursue, trace, 3. use, obey, act according to   ignore   FOLLOWER, FOLLOWING

folly   foolishness, silliness, stupidity (*Slang* — dumb thing to do)   cleverness

fond   loving, liking, affectionate, adoring, romantic, sentimental, tender   disliking

fondle   pet, caress, cuddle

font   1. fountain, spring, 2. basin

food   edibles, provisions, nutriment, nourishment (*Slang* — grub, eats, chow)

fool   1. play, joke, 2. deceive, trick, mislead (*Slang* — kid, spoof), 3. ninny, ignoramus, know-nothing, dunce, blockhead, scatterbrain, simpleton (*Slang* — chump, numskull, silly, jerk, dope, dumbbell, simp)   FOOLISH

foolhardy   bold, rash, daring, audacious, reckless cautious

foolproof   safe, tight, resistant

foot   1. walk, hoof it, march, hike, 2. part of body, sole (*Slang* — dog, kicker, tootsy), 3. base, lowest part, foundation top

footing   1. support, toehold, standing, 2. relationship, position

forage   1. hunt, search, look, explore, 2. animal food, fodder, feed, grain

foray   plunder, pillage, raid, invade

forbear   refrain, hold back, abstain, avoid, control oneself indulge FORBEARANCE

forbid   prohibit, disallow, bar, ban, taboo, prevent, deter encourage FORBIDDEN

force   1. compel, make, drive, oblige, pressure, motivate, 2. thrust, push, shove, ram, break through, 3. power, strength, might, vigor, energy weakness, 4. group, body, staff, personnel, crew, gang FORCEFUL, FORCIBLE

fore   front, forward, foremost, first, chief, head, primary

foreboding   warning, prediction, foretelling, forecast, promise, omen, prophecy, premonition

forecast   prophecy, prediction, foretelling, promise, omen

forefather   ancestor, predecessor, forebear

foreign   alien, external FOREIGNER

foreman   supervisor, superintendent, overseer, boss

foremost   first, chief, leading, head, main, principal, dominant, primary

foresee   anticipate, predict, forecast, foretell, prophesy FORESEEN, FORESIGHT

forest   wood, timberland FORESTRY

foretell   predict, prophesy, forecast, promise

forever   always, evermore, eternity

forfeit lose, sacrifice, let slip retain

forge 1. make, shape, form, create, mold, 2. counterfeit, falsify, make up, 3. progress, push onward, 4. blacksmith's shop, smelter

forget not remember, escape one, lose sight of remember
FORGETFUL, FORGOT

forgive pardon, excuse, absolve, quit blame
FORGIVEN, FORGIVENESS

forgo give up, sacrifice, surrender, yield, relinquish, do without, waive retain, keep

fork 1. silverware, 2. branch, offshoot

forlorn hopeless, miserable, desperate, despondent, forsaken, abandoned, deserted, defenseless, helpless

form 1. develop, compose, make, create, fashion, construct, shape, mold, 2. kind, sort, class, grade, type, variety, species, make, 3. manner, method, fashion, style, way, procedure
FORMATION

formal orderly, regular, systematic, businesslike, stiff, arranged, structural, correct, proper, customary informal
FORMALITY

former earlier, past, previous, preceding, prior, first latter
· FORMERLY

formidable difficult, hard, rough, rugged, tough (*Slang* — wicked, mean) easy, simple

formulate define, describe, express, voice, put

forsake leave, give up, abandon, quit
FORSAKEN, FORSOOK

forth forward, onward, on, ahead back

forthcoming approaching, imminent, coming, near, close (*Slang* — in the cards)

forthwith immediately, promptly, without delay, instantly, at once, quickly, swiftly (*Slang* — pronto)

fortify strengthen, brace, invigorate, reinforce weaken
FORTIFICATION

fortitude courage, strength, vigor, vitality, stamina, spunk
(*Slang* — guts) weakness

fortunate lucky, auspicious unlucky

fortune 1. riches, wealth, prosperity, treasure poverty, 2.
luck, chance, fate, lot, destiny

forum 1. square, plaza, 2. discussion, debate, deliberation,
consideration, study, 3. tribunal, law court

forward 1. send, dispatch, deliver, pass, 2. onward, ahead,
frontward, advanced backward, 3. pert, bold, aggressive,
insolent, presumptuous, brazen, immodest (*Slang* — crusty,
nervy, cocky, cheeky, smart-alecky) shy

fossil remains, trace, vestige, relic

foster nourish, nurture, feed, cultivate, nurse, care for,
support, mind, tend, rear

foul 1. dirty, nasty, smelly, stinking, offensive, disgusting,
vile savory, 2. wicked, vicious, evil, bad, wrong, sinful,
base, low good, 3. unfair fair

foundation 1. base, ground, 2. establishment, institution,
organization

founder 1. fall, stumble, tumble, topple, 2. break down,
collapse, sink, fail, 3. producer, creator, maker, author,
originator, inventor, builder

foundling orphan, waif

foundry forge, smelter, blacksmith's shop

fountain 1. spring, spout, spray, 2. source

fowl bird, poultry

foxy crafty, shrewd, artful, cunning, knowing, sly, clever,
canny artless

fraction part, portion, division, segment, section whole

fracture break, crack, burst, rupture, chip

fragile delicate, frail, slight, dainty, breakable, flimsy, brittle sturdy, strong

fragment part, portion, segment, section, fraction, division whole

fragrant sweet-smelling, perfumed, odorous, aromatic foul FRAGRANCE

frail weak, slight, delicate, dainty, fragile strong FRAILTY

frame 1. make, plan, put together, build, construct, form, design, devise, arrange, 2. border, edge, bound, trim, 3. body, figure, form, 4. support, skeleton FRAMEWORK

frank open, candid, sincere, straightforward, forthright, outspoken, blunt deceitful

frantic excited, frenzied, wild, violent, delirious, hysterical calm, unexcited FRANTICALLY

fraternal brotherly, kind, sympathetic, friendly, congenial, sociable unfriendly, antisocial FRATERNITY

fraud cheating, trickery, dishonesty, swindle (*Slang* — gyp)

fraught loaded, filled lacking

fray 1. wear away, rub, tatter, 2. fight, quarrel, battle, conflict, clash, brush, tussle, skirmish, scuffle, struggle, melee (*Slang* — scrap, run-in)

freak unusual, queer, incredible, grotesque, bizarre

free 1. clear, acquit, dismiss, release, discharge, relieve, reprieve, deliver, liberate, emancipate enslave, 2. loose, unfastened, untied restrained, 3. independent, open, unrestrained, at liberty restricted, 4. complimentary, gratis, untaxed, without charge taxed FREEDOM

freeze 1. chill, refrigerate defrost, 2. stiffen, remain motionless FREEZER, FROZE, FROZEN

freight load, cargo, burden, shipment, goods FREIGHTER

frenzy fury, madness, excitement, passion, rage, agitation, fit, delirium serenity, calmness FRENZIED

frequent 1. visit often, haunt (*Slang* — hang out at), 2. many, recurrent, common, prevalent, regular, habitual infrequent FREQUENCY, FREQUENTLY

fresh 1. new, unused, firsthand, original old, stale, 2. unsalty, 3. bright, alert, unfaded, brisk, vigorous, energetic, refreshed dull FRESHEN

fret worry, fuss (*Slang* — stew) FRETFUL

friction resistance, clash, conflict, grinding, scraping harmony

friend acquaintance, intimate, companion, comrade, mate, associate, colleague, partner, crony, playmate, chum, buddy (*Slang* — sidekick, pal) enemy FRIENDLINESS, FRIENDLY, FRIENDSHIP

fright 1. fear, terror, alarm, dismay, dread, awe, horror, phobia, panic fearlessness, 2. eyesore, mess beauty FRIGHTEN, FRIGHTFUL

frigid 1. cold, stiff, chilling, icy, reserved, unfeeling, restrained, aloof, distant warm, friendly, 2. freezing, wintry, crisp, brisk, nippy, raw, sharp, frosty warm

frill ornament, ruffle, flounce, embellishment, luxury

fringe border, trimming, edge, brim, rim

frisk frolic, play, romp, caper FRISKY

frivolous silly, shallow, unimportant, light, trivial, foolish, inane serious, important

frock gown, dress, garment, robe

frolic   play, frisk, romp, caper   FROLICSOME

front   fore, first part, face, head   back

frontier   back country, border, outskirt

frost   freezing, cold   FROSTY

frosting   icing, topping

froth   1. foam, lather, 2. trivia, rubbish, unimportant   important

frown   scowl, pout, look sullen, look displeased   smile

frugal   economical, thrifty, saving, prudent   wasteful   FRUGALITY

fruit   1. plant product, 2. yield, result   FRUITFUL, FRUITLESS

frustrate   foil, thwart, defeat, spoil, ruin   aid, help   FRUSTRATION

fry   cook, sauté

fuel   kindling, combustible

fugitive   1. runaway, escaping (*Slang* — hot), 2. temporary, passing, transient   lasting, permanent

fulfill   perform, do, carry out, execute, finish, complete, transact, discharge, satisfy   FULFILLMENT

full   1. complete, entire, stuffed, packed, crammed   empty, 2. plump, round, fat   thin, 3. broad, wide, expansive, roomy   skimpy   FULLNESS, FULLY

fumble   bungle, blunder, muff, grope awkwardly

fume   1. be angry, burn, seethe, rage, storm, rave, 2. smoke, vapor, gas

fumigate   disinfect, sterilize, sanitize

fun   amusement, playfulness, joking, sport, good time, pleasure, entertainment, enjoyment (*Slang* — picnic)   FUNNY

function 1. work, be used, act, operate, perform, serve, 2. ceremony, gathering, service, rite, ritual, exercise

fund stock, supply, resources, assets

fundamental essential, basic, underlying, primary, elementary

funeral burial, last rites

funnel channel, siphon, pipe

fur pelt, hide, skin FURRY

furious raging, violent, angry, mad, rabid, overwrought, upset, enraged, infuriated (*Slang* — hopping mad, fit to be tied) calm, placid FURY

furl roll up, fold unfold

furlough vacation, leave of absence, sabbatical

furnace stove, heater, oven, kiln, forge

furnish supply, provide, give, equip, outfit FURNITURE

furrow wrinkle, crease, groove

further 1. help, aid, advance, promote hinder, 2. farther, beyond, past, over FURTHEST

furthermore in addition, then, again, also, too, besides, similarly, likewise, by the same token

furtive secret, sly, stealthy, sneaky, underhanded open, honest

fuse 1. join, blend, melt, unite, combine, stick together, weld, solder, glue separate, 2. exploder, blaster FUSION

fuss worry, bother, fret (*Slang* — stew) FUSSY

futile useless, vain, unsuccessful, ineffective useful

future coming, hereafter, tomorrow past

fuzz fluff, fur, down FUZZY

G

gadget device, tool, instrument, implement, utensil, apparatus, appliance, contraption (*Slang* — gimmick)

gag 1. silence, muzzle, muffle, stop one's mouth, restrain, 2. joke, jest

gain 1. get, obtain, secure, acquire, earn, receive lose, 2. benefit, 3. advance, make progress, improve, look up, pick up, come along deteriorate

gait pace, walk, step, stride

gala festive, merry, gay, jolly, joyous, joyful

gale 1. wind, windstorm, tempest, squall, 2. noisy outburst, shout

gall 1. bitterness, impudence, nerve, 2. bile

gallant 1. brave, courageous, valiant, bold, heroic cowardly, 2. noble, chivalrous, courteous, knightly, manly, fine, grand, stately ungentlemanly, ill-mannered GALLANTRY

gallery 1. passage, corridor, hallway, arcade, 2. balcony, grandstand (*Slang* — peanut gallery)

gallop run, ride, sprint, bound, trot

gallows hanging, execution, rope, noose

galosh rubber, overshoe, boot

gamble speculate, risk, bet, wager, try one's luck GAMBLER

gambol frolic, run, play, sport, romp, caper, cavort, carry on (*Slang* — cut up, horse around)

game 1. brave, plucky, spirited, daring (*Slang* — spunky) unwilling, 2. contest, match, play, fun, 3. scheme, plan, plot, 4. hunted animals, wildlife, quarry, prey

gang   group, crew, ring, band, party, company, pack, troop, bunch, crowd (*Slang* — mob)

gangway   passageway, bridge

gap   1. break, opening, pass, cleft, crevice, rift, gulf, hole, 2. blank, unfilled space

gape   1. yawn, open mouth wide, 2. gap, gulf, hole, opening

garage   carport, auto repair shop

garb   clothing, apparel, dress, attire, garments (*Slang* — duds)

garbage   waste, scraps, refuse, rubbish, trash, debris, litter, junk

garden   grow, raise, cultivate, plant   GARDENER

gargle   mouthwash, antiseptic

gargoyle   waterspout

garland   wreath, spray, bouquet, lei

garment   robe, frock, article of clothing, togs (*Slang* — duds)

garner   store, collect, save up, accumulate, amass, stockpile, hoard

garnish   decorate, trim, adorn, beautify, embellish, dress up, spruce up, fix up (*Slang* — doll up)

garret   attic, loft

garrison   1. fort, stronghold, 2. military unit, regiment, battalion, company, troop

gas   1. vapor, fume, 2. gasoline, petroleum   GASEOUS

gash   cut, wound, laceration

gasoline   petroleum

gasp   pant, puff, choke

gate   fence, barrier

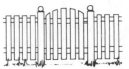

gateway   door, portal, entry, opening

gather   1. collect, bring together, assemble, accumulate, amass, bunch, group, cluster, compile   scatter, 2. fold, tuck, pleat   GATHERING

gaudy   showy, tasteless, garish, vulgar (*Slang* — loud) tasteful

gauge   measure, estimate, judge, rate, appraise, assess, size up

gaunt   1. thin, lean, skinny, scrawny, lanky, bony, 2. desolate, blank, bleak, empty

gavel   mallet

gay   1. happy, merry, spirited, lively, animated, vivacious, playful, joyful, joyous, jolly, jovial, cheerful, pleasant unhappy, solemn, 2. colorful, bright, vivid, rich   dull GAIETY, GAILY

gaze   stare, gape, gawk

gear   1. equip, furnish, outfit, rig, 2. wheel   mechanism

gem   1. jewel, precious stone, 2. treasure, good thing, joy, first-rater

general   1. common, widespread, indefinite, vague, broad, 2. officer, commander   GENERALLY

generate   produce, cause, bring about, create, originate GENERATOR

generous   1. unselfish, giving, kind, liberal, openhanded, bighearted   selfish, 2. large, plentiful, ample   small GENEROSITY

genial   pleasant, cheerful, friendly, kindly, warm, comforting, cordial, agreeable, amiable, good-natured disagreeable, unpleasant

genius   1. intelligence, inspiration, talent, creative thought, gift, 2. prodigy, master, wizard

genocide   slaughter, massacre, killing, butchery, carnage

gentle 1. mild, soft, moderate, tender rough, 2. kindly, friendly, good-natured, cordial, genial, amiable, sympathetic, humane harsh, mean, 3. refined, well-bred, cultured, polished, genteel, noble ill-bred
GENTILITY, GENTLY

genuine real, true, authentic, pure, legitimate, bona fide, sincere fake

germ 1. seed, origin, beginning, 2. microorganism

germinate grow, develop, sprout, flourish, thrive

gesture signal, sign, motion, movement

get 1. obtain, receive, gain, fetch, bring, retrieve, acquire, secure give, 2. become, turn, grow, 3. persuade, influence, induce, 4. incur, bring about

geyser spring, steam, volcanic water, jet, gush, fountain

ghastly 1. horrible, terrible, dreadful, deplorable, outrageous, vile, wretched, detestable, contemptible, frightful, shocking, appalling, repulsive (*Slang* — awful, atrocious) lovely, beautiful, 2. pale, sallow, deathlike ruddy

ghost spirit, specter, phantom, spook GHOSTLY

giant huge, immense, vast, enormous, tremendous, colossal, monumental, mammoth, gigantic tiny, minute

gibe jeer, sneer, scoff, mock, taunt, boo, hiss, hoot approve

giddy 1. dizzy, reeling, 2. silly, flighty, scatterbrained serious

gift 1. present, offering, 2. ability, talent, endowment, power, aptitude GIFTED

gigantic huge, immense, vast, enormous, tremendous, colossal, monumental, mammoth tiny, minute

giggle laugh, chuckle, titter, snicker

gild 1. coat, paint, cover, 2. sweeten, embellish GILT

gird 1. bind, belt, tie, wrap untie, 2. surround, encircle, 3. prepare, ready, get set GIRT

girl lass, female, maiden, damsel, miss GIRLISH

girth size, dimensions, measure, proportions, width, expanse

give 1. present, offer, hand over, bestow, donate, contribute, grant, award, furnish, provide, supply, allot, deliver, deal out, dole out, mete out (*Slang* — hand out, dish out, fork out, shell out, fork over, come across with, kick in) take, 2. yield, bend

given 1. presented, handed over, 2. stated, supposed, assumed, 3. inclined, disposed, addicted, bent

glacier iceberg GLACIAL

glad happy, pleased, bright, gay, delighted, charmed, thrilled, tickled, gratified, satisfied, joyful, joyous, cheerful sad GLADDEN

glade clearing, open space

gladiator fighter, battler, combatant, contestant, contender, competitor

glamorous fascinating, charming, entrancing, enchanting, bewitching, spellbinding, alluring, captivating, enthralling, attractive, interesting, appealing, enticing unattractive GLAMOUR

glance look, glimpse, skim

glare 1. stare, scowl, glower, 2. shine, glow, burn, glaze, flash, flare, dazzle, blind

glass 1. goblet, cup, tumbler, 2. crystal, pane GLASSY

glaze gloss, polish, luster, buff, wax, coat, cover

gleam shine, glow, beam, glare, radiate, burn, glimmer, glisten, twinkle, sparkle

glean gather, harvest, reap, pick, separate, select

glee   joy, delight, mirth, happiness, gladness, cheer, enchantment, elation, bliss, merriment   sadness   GLEEFUL

glen   valley, ravine

glide   cruise, coast, skim, slide, sweep, flow, sail, fly, move easily   GLIDER

glimmer   1. shimmer, blink, flicker, 2. hint, indication, suggestion, inkling, clue

glimpse   glance, see, notice, catch sight of

glint   gleam, flash, glimpse, glance, peek

glisten   sparkle, glitter, shine, glimmer, twinkle

glitter   sparkle, glimmer, twinkle, shine, glisten

gloat   exult, triumph, glory (*Slang* — crow over)

globe   1. sphere, ball, 2. earth, world, universe, 3. map   GLOBAL

gloomy   1. dark, dim, dismal, dreary, somber, bleak, depressing, discouraging, 2. sad, melancholy, glum   cheerful   GLOOM, GLOOMILY

glorify   worship, praise, laud, exalt, extol, honor, ennoble   belittle   GLORY

glorious   magnificent, splendid, grand, superb, fine, impressive, proud, stately, majestic, elegant, luxurious, extravagant (*Slang* — wonderful, divine, terrific, sensational, colossal, tremendous, swell, plush, super)   terrible

gloss   shine, luster, sheen, glow, gleam   GLOSSY

glossary   dictionary, wordbook, thesaurus

glow   1. burn, blaze, flame, flare, flicker, shine, radiate, glare, dazzle, 2. redden, blush, flush, 3. tingle, tremble, shiver, quiver, quake, thrill

glower   stare, scowl, glare, frown

glue   fasten, stick together, bind, paste, cement

glum sad, gloomy, dismal, sullen, moody cheerful

glutton greedy eater (*Slang* — hog, pig)

gnarled knotted, twisted, rugged GNARL

gnash crunch, gnaw, grind

gnaw grind, gnash, chew

go 1. move, leave, travel, pass, proceed, advance come, 2. act, work, 3. become, get to be, turn, grow into, 4. operate, function, 5. be given, aim, point, head for, 6. belong, have place GONE

goad urge, drive, pride, push, shove, poke, jab, spur

goal 1. end, finish, destination, objective, aim, object, target, 2. score, point

gobble 1. eat fast, devour, gulp, gorge, stuff, 2. turkey talk

goblet glass, cup

goblin spirit, elf, troll, dwarf

God Lord, the Maker, the Creator, the Supreme Being, the Almighty

godly religious, pious, obeying, loving, holy, righteous, spiritual, pure, saintly, divine

golden 1. metallic, 2. shining, bright dull, 3. very good, superior, excellent, fine, nice, splendid, valuable inferior GOLD

gong bell, chimes

good 1. excellent, fine, nice, splendid (*Slang* — dandy, swell, keen, nifty, hunky-dory), 2. well-behaved, proper bad, 3. desirable, right, appropriate, fitting, suitable, becoming, satisfying, seemly, nice, decent undesirable, 4. kind, friendly, gracious, nice, warmhearted, sympathetic, brotherly, fraternal unkind, unfriendly, 5. real, genuine, authentic, legitimate, bona fide fake, 6. benefit, profit, advantage GOODNESS

good-by farewell, so long, adieu hello

goods 1. belongings, property, holdings, possessions, 2. wares, merchandise

good will willingness, agreeability, readiness, friendly relations, harmony

gorge 1. stuff, devour, gulp, gobble (*Slang* — eat like a horse), 2. valley, ravine, gully

gorgeous splendid, beautiful, ravishing, stunning, glorious, divine, brilliant, dazzling hideous

gory bloody

gossamer 1. fine, delicate, dainty coarse, 2. filmy, sheer, transparent

gossip chat, talk, tattle, prattle

gouge dig, scoop, excavate, burrow, chisel, carve

govern rule, control, manage, regulate, influence, determine, head, lead, command, preside over, direct, supervise, minister, guide, conduct, handle, run, boss (*Slang* — mastermind) GOVERNMENT, GOVERNOR

gown dress, robe, garment, frock

grab snatch, seize, grasp, grip, clutch (*Slang* — collar, nab)

grace 1. honor, dignify, distinguish dishonor, 2. beauty, loveliness, attractiveness, 3. charm, elegance, taste, refinement, polish, culture tactlessness, vulgarity, 4. sympathy, clemency, mercy, pardon, excuse, reprieve, 5. favor, 6. thanks, prayer, thanksgiving, blessing GRACEFUL

gracious pleasant, kindly, courteous, good, nice, warmhearted, sympathetic, polite, respectful, cordial, friendly, hospitable, generous rude, unkind

grade 1. arrange, sort, classify, group, rank, rate, mark, place, 2. slope, incline, hill

gradual slow, little by little, easy sudden

graduate finish, pass, succeed, advance   fail
GRADUATION

graft 1. transplant, join, 2. bribery, corruption (*Slang —*
boodle)

grain 1. particle, speck, bit, 2. plant, seed, 3. texture, finish,
markings, fiber, 4. character, temper, nature, disposition,
tendency GRANARY

grand 1. large, great, considerable, sizable, big   small, 2.
important, main, outstanding, prominent, distinguished,
magnificent, glorious, impressive, majestic, dignified, stately unimportant, insignificant   GRANDEUR

grandstand gallery, bleachers

granite rock, stone

grant 1. give, donate, present, bestow, award, allot, give out,
deal out, mete out, dole out (*Slang —* hand out, fork out,
shell out), 2. allow, permit, let, consent, admit   deny

graph diagram, chart, plot, outline, draw up

graphic lifelike, vivid, meaningful, significant, representative, descriptive, pictorial

grapple 1. seize, grip, grab, grasp, clutch, clasp, hold
release, 2. struggle, fight

grasp 1. seize, hold, grapple, clutch, clasp, grip, 2. control,
possession, hold, command, domination, 3. understanding,
comprehension

grate 1. grind, file, scrape, pulverize, 2. scrape, scratch, rasp,
3. annoy, irritate, get on one's nerves, rub the wrong way, 4.
iron bars, grillwork GRATING

grateful thankful, appreciative, obliged   ungrateful

gratify satisfy, please GRATIFICATION

gratitude thankfulness, gratefulness, appreciation
ungratefulness

grave 1. serious, solemn, grim, earnest, thoughtful, sober, somber   cheerful, gay, 2. dignified, slow-moving, stately, imposing, majestic, 3. important, vital, essential   unimportant, 4. burial place, plot

gravel pebbles, stones, grain

gravitate move toward, incline, lean, tend
GRAVITATION, GRAVITY

graze 1. feed, 2. touch lightly, scrape, rub, contact, brush, skim

grease oil, lubrication, fat   GREASY

great 1. large, grand, sizable, considerable   small, 2. outstanding, prominent, famous, main, distinguished, remarkable, glorious, magnificent, impressive, majestic, stately   insignificant, unimportant   GREATNESS

greed avarice, piggishness, hoggishness, lust, desire
GREEDY

green 1. undeveloped, unripe, immature   ripe, 2. untrained, new, inexperienced, ignorant   experienced

greenhouse hothouse, plant nursery

greet 1. address, hail, talk to, 2. meet, approach
GREETING

grieve hurt, mourn, brood over, lament, sorrow   GRIEF

grievance wrong, evil, protest, objection, injury, injustice, complaint (*Slang* — beef, howl, kick, gripe, squawk, bellyaching, grumbling)

grievous 1. severe, outrageous, terrible, deplorable, awful, wretched, contemptible, 2. sorrowful

grill 1. broil, cook, barbecue, 2. question, cross-examine, interrogate, 3. gridiron, grating

grim 1. stern, strict, harsh, fierce, merciless, rough, unyielding, rigid, inflexible, adamant (*Slang* — tough, hard-boiled) relaxed, lenient, 2. horrible, frightful, ghastly, dreadful, terrible pleasant

grimace wry face

grime dirt, soot, smut, mud, slime, filth GRIMY

grin smile, smirk, beam

grind 1. crush, pulverize, grate, crumble, mash, squash, 2. sharpen, smooth, rub, edge, whet, file, 3. study, work, drudge, plod

grip 1. seize, hold, grasp, clutch, clasp, clench release, 2. suitcase, handbag, valise, 3. control, command, domination, possession, 4. understanding, comprehension

grit 1. grind, rub, grate, 2. gravel, sand, grain, 3. courage, pluck, stamina (*Slang* — spunk, backbone, guts)

groan moan, harsh sound, wail, howl

groom 1. tidy, clean up, tend, preen, 2. newlywed

groove 1. channel, furrow, track, rut, 2. routine

grope feel around, fumble, poke around

gross 1. whole, entire, total, 2. bad, terrible, stupid (*Slang* — dumb), 3. coarse, vulgar, unrefined, crude refined, 4. big, fat, obese, bulky, massive, clumsy petite, delicate, 5. thick, heavy, dense slight

grotesque 1. fantastic, incredible, bizarre, monstrous, ridiculous, absurd, 2. deformed, unnatural, queer, odd, disfigured, ill-shaped, ugly natural, normal

grotto cave, cavern, tunnel, hole

grouch complain, grumble, mutter, mope, sulk, fret (*Slang* — kick, howl, squawk, gripe, crab, bellyache, beef) GROUCHY

ground 1. fix, establish, root, set, 2. surface, soil, sod, dirt, land, base, floor

grounds 1. lawns, garden, real estate, 2. dregs, leftovers, sediment, 3. foundation, basis, reason, cause, premise, motive

group arrange, assemble, cluster, organize, grade, sort, classify, gather, collect, bunch disassemble

grovel crawl, creep, cower

grow 1. increase, mature, become, advance, gain, rise, develop, age, progress shrink, decrease, 2. raise, farm, cultivate GROWN, GROWTH

growl snarl, complain, grumble (*Slang* — kick, howl, grouch, squawk, bellyache)

grub 1. dig, gouge, excavate, scoop out, tunnel, burrow, 2. toil, drudge, plod (*Slang* — plug away), 3. larva, 4. food (*Slang* — eats, chow)

grudge ill will, dislike

grudgingly unwillingly, reluctantly, involuntarily, under protest, against one's will willingly

gruff 1. deep, husky, coarse, harsh, 2. rough, rude, unfriendly, brusque, curt, blunt polite

grumble complain, mutter (*Slang* — kick, grouch, squawk, gripe, crab, bellyache, beef)

grunt snort

guarantee promise, secure, pledge, swear, warrant, assure, certify, sponsor, back, endorse, underwrite, stand for

guard 1. watch, defend, shield, protect, secure, 2. check, restrain, control, curb GUARDIAN

guess think, believe, suppose, assume, imagine, consider, conjecture

guest visitor, caller, company (*Slang*—moocher, freeloader)

guide 1. lead, direct, show, steer, escort, conduct, squire, usher, 2. manage, control, regulate, advise, instruct, govern, rule GUIDANCE

guild   society, union

guile   deceit, cunning, craftiness, sneakiness

guilty   criminal, to blame, at fault, blameworthy, culpable GUILT

guise   1. garb, dress, cover, coat, attire, clothes, apparel, 2. appearance, look, show, form, manner

gulch   valley, gorge, ravine, gully, canyon

gulf   1. separation, break, cut, cleft, crack, crevice, hole, rift, opening, gap, chasm, pit, 2. bay

gullible   easily fooled, naive, deceivable

gully   gorge, valley, ditch, ravine, gulf, gulch

gulp   1. swallow, devour, 2. choke, repress, gasp

gun   1. shoot, fire, discharge, 2. weapon, firearm, pistol, rifle, revolver (*Slang* — shooting iron, gat, rod)

gurgle   bubbling sound

gush   1. rush out, pour, flow, spout, surge, flush, flood, spurt, 2. chatter, babble, prattle

gust   1. wind, blast, 2. outburst, outbreak, eruption, flare-up

gutter   channel, groove, trench, ditch

gymnasium   arena, athletic field, playground, court   GYM

gymnastics   exercises, drill, athletics, calisthenics, sports, acrobatics

gyp   cheat, swindle, defraud (*Slang* — rook, con)

gypsy   nomad

H

habit   1. custom, practice, nature, pattern, trait, 2. religious dress   HABITUAL

habitation   abode, dwelling place, residence, lodging, housing   HABITAT

hack　1. cut, sever, split, cleave, chop, 2. cough

hag　witch, crone (*Slang* — old girl, old battle-axe)

haggard　thin, poor, pale, deathlike, wild-eyed, tired-looking, seedy

hail　1. greet, cheer, welcome, call, shout, 2. sleet

hale　1. drag, haul, pull, tug, tow, 2. strong, mighty, powerful, healthy, sturdy, rugged, strapping, hardy, robust, vigorous, husky　weak

hall　1. passageway, corridor, arcade, vestibule, lobby, foyer, 2. large meeting room, assembly, auditorium, 3. building, community center, theater　HALLWAY

halo　1. circle, ring, 2. glory, glamour

halt　stop, come to a standstill, check, arrest, quit, cease, end (*Slang* — lay off, knock off)

halve　divide, dissect, split, share (*Slang* — fifty-fifty) HALF, HALVES

hamlet　village

hammer　1. hit, drive, pound, beat, knock, bang, 2. repeat, drill, 3. mallet

hamper　1. hinder, impede, cramp, obstruct, block, restrain, limit　help, 2. basket

hand　1. give, turn over, deliver, transfer, pass, 2. worker, person, laborer, 3. possession, central power, command, grasp, clutches, 4. handwriting, penmanship

handbag　pocketbook, purse

handicap　hindrance, burden, disadvantage, load　asset

handle　1. touch, feel, finger, manipulate, use, 2. manage, direct, regulate, carry on, govern, run (*Slang* — mastermind), 3. deal in, trade in

handsome　1. good-looking, attractive　ugly, 2. large, considerable, big, generous, liberal　meager

handwriting penmanship

handy 1. useful, convenient, nearby, available, ready (*Slang* — on deck) inconvenient, 2. skillful, adept, apt, proficient inept

hang 1. suspend, fasten up, 2. execute, string up, 3. droop, bend down, sag

haphazard chance, random, casual planned

happen 1. take place, occur, come off, pass, 2. chance, turn up HAPPENING

happy contented, glad, joyful, blissful, cheerful, bright, radiant unhappy, sad HAPPILY, HAPPINESS

harass 1. trouble, torment, molest, bother, badger, plague, persecute, haunt, bully, threaten, 2. disturb, worry, vex HARASSMENT

harbor 1. shelter, protect, shield, defend, guard, screen, cover, house, 2. keep in mind, consider, think, entertain the idea, 3. port, dock, wharf, pier

hard 1. firm, solid, stony, rigid soft, 2. stern, unyielding, strict, inflexible easygoing, 3. difficult, rough, rugged, tough (*Slang* — wicked, mean) easy, 4. with effort, with vigor, laboriously, strenuously, 5. unpleasant, harsh, ugly, severe, callous pleasant

hardly barely, just, not quite, scarcely, narrowly, nearly (*Slang* — by the skin of one's teeth)

hardship trouble, ups and downs

hardy 1. strong, healthy, robust, mighty, powerful, sturdy, rugged, hale weak, 2. bold, daring, courageous, valiant, gallant, heroic cowardly

hark listen, heed HARKEN

harm hurt, damage, wrong, injure, impair help, improve HARMFUL, HARMLESS

harmonious   1. agreeing, in accord, congenial, compatible
  conflicting, 2. musical, in tune, blending
  HARMONIZE, HARMONY

harness   1. control, use, 2. saddle, hitch up, yoke, hook up

harp   dwell on, elaborate

harrow   1. hurt, wound, pain, afflict, distress, irritate, torment, torture, agonize   soothe, 2. rake, plow

harry   1. raid, rob, storm, besiege, invade, 2. trouble, worry,
  torment, vex, harass

harsh   1. rough, coarse, husky, grating, raspy, gruff
  smooth, 2. cruel, unfeeling, severe, bitter, sharp, cutting,
  piercing, gruff, brusque, curt, strict, stern, tough   kind

harvest   1. reap, gather, pick, 2. crop, yield, product, proceeds, 3. result, consequences, effect, outcome
  HARVESTER

hash   1. mixture, assortment, mix (*Slang* — stew), 2. mess,
  muddle, jumble, scramble, fiasco

hasty   1. quick, hurried, fast, swift, speedy, rapid, fleet
  (*Slang* — snappy)   slow, 2. rash, reckless, unprepared,
  sudden, premature, impulsive, impetuous   planned, 3.
  quick-tempered, hotheaded
  HASTEN, HASTE, HASTILY

hat   cap, headdress, chapeau, millinery

hatch   1. arrange, plan, plot, scheme, intrigue, invent,
  concoct, make up (*Slang* — cook up), 2. produce, generate,
  incubate, breed, brood, be born, 3. opening, door, trap

hatchet   tomahawk, ax

hate   dislike, loathe, detest, abhor, abominate   love
  HATEFUL, HATRED

haughty   arrogant, proud, lofty, scornful (*Slang* — uppish,
  highfalutin)   modest

haul 1. pull, drag, draw, heave, tug, tow, 2. take, catch

haunch hip, side, flank

haunt 1. visit often, frequent, hang around, 2. obsess, torment HAUNTED

have 1. hold, possess, own, 2. must, be forced, should, ought, need, 3. cause, make, compel, require, 4. experience, feel, meet, undergo, endure, 5. permit, tolerate, suffer, put up with, stand for HAS

haven shelter, safety, harbor, refuge, sanctuary

havoc destruction, ruin, devastation, ravage, damage, harm, injury restoration

hawk 1. hunt, chase, 2. peddle, sell, vend buy

hay fodder, feed

hazard risk, chance, gamble, bet, wager HAZARDOUS

hazy 1. misty, smoky, dim, cloudy, overcast, foggy, 2. obscure, indistinct, unclear, indefinite, vague, faint, blurred, fuzzy, uncertain, confused, muddled clear HAZE

head 1. lead, come first, precede, initiate follow, 2. govern, command, lead, direct, manage, supervise, administer, control, rule, dominate, conduct, run (*Slang* — mastermind), 3. proceed, move toward, go, gravitate, 4. pate, crown, top (*Slang* — noodle, noggin, bean), 5. mind, intelligence, understanding, mentality, brain, 6. crisis, conclusion

headfirst hastily, rashly, impetuously, impulsively, recklessly, carelessly cautiously

heading topic, title, subject, issue, question, theme, headline

headquarters main office, base, central station

headstrong obstinate, stubborn, willful, bullheaded

headway progress, advance, improvement setback

heal   cure, remedy, correct, mend, repair   damage, impair

health   well-being, physical condition
HEALTHFUL, HEALTHY

heap   pile, gather, fill, stack, load

hear   listen, heed (*Slang* — get an earful) HEARD

hearsay   gossip, rumor, common talk

heart   1. body pump (*Slang* — ticker), 2. feelings, soul, spirit, temperament, 3. kindness, sympathy, warmth, love, affection, 4. courage, enthusiasm, stamina (*Slang* — spunk, guts)   cowardice, 5. middle, center, core, nucleus, hub, 6. substance, main part, meat, 7. valentine

hearten   cheer, encourage, inspire, gladden   dishearten

heartfelt   sincere, genuine, profound, deep   insincere

hearth   fireplace, fireside, home

heartily   sincerely, warmly, devotedly, completely, fervently, ardently   indifferently   HEARTY, HEARTINESS

heat   1. warm, make hot   cool, 2. cook, prepare, 3. excite, move, affect, stir, provoke, arouse, kindle, inflame   calm
HEATER

heave   1. lift, raise, hoist, pull, haul, lug, tug, tow, drag, 2. breathe hard, pant, 3. swell, rise, bulge, billow, surge   subside

heaven   1. sky, space, 2. paradise, bliss, ecstasy   hell
HEAVENLY

heavy   weighted, laden, bulky, fat, hefty   light, thin
HEAVILY, HEAVINESS

hectic   1. feverish, heated, hot, burning, 2. exciting, stirring, frantic, moving, busy   calm

hedge   1. dodge, sidestep, evade questions, duck (*Slang* — pussyfoot), 2. boundary, limit, border, borderline

heed   notice, observe, follow, care, mind, attend   ignore

height   1. altitude, elevation, tallness, stature, 2. top, summit, highest point, peak, crown, tip, apex, acme bottom   HEIGHTEN

hello   greetings, salutations, good day   (*Slang* — howdy)

helm   control, reins, driver's seat

help   1. aid, assist, lend a hand, avail   hinder, 2. benefit, relieve, 3. avoid, prevent, deter, keep from HELPFUL, HELPLESS

hem   border, edge, rim

hence   1. therefore, consequently, accordingly, because of this, thus, 2. away, elsewhere, 3. later, from now, in future time   HENCEFORTH

herald   1. announce, bring news, proclaim, cry out, shout, 2. messenger

herd   flock, assemble, join together, drive, shepherd, collect, gather   scatter

here   1. this place, this spot   there, 2. now, at present, at this time   later, 3. present, in attendance   absent HEREABOUT, HEREAFTER

hereditary   inherited, inborn HEREDITY

heresy   misbelief, dissent   HERETIC

heritage   heredity, birthright

hermit   recluse, shut-in

heroic   brave, gallant, valiant, stalwart, courageous, bold, chivalrous   cowardly   HERO, HEROINE, HEROISM

hesitate   1. pause, rest, let up, 2. feel doubtful, be undecided, flounder, falter, waver   HESITATION

hew   cut, chop, sever, split, cleave

hibernate   sleep, slumber, hole up

hide   1. conceal, cover up, screen, cloak, veil, mask   expose, 2. skin, pelt   HID, HIDDEN

hideous   ugly, frightful, horrible, horrid, dreadful, terrible, repulsive, ghastly (*Slang* — awful)   beautiful

high   1. tall, long, lofty, elevated, steep, towering, soaring, 2. great, chief, main, important, eminent, exalted, grand   unimportant, 3. shrill, sharp, piercing, screechy   low   HIGHLY

high-strung   sensitive, nervous, excitable, edgy, jumpy (*Slang* — jittery)   calm, steady

highway   road, thoroughfare, turnpike, expressway, thruway, freeway

hike   walk, march, tramp, parade

hilarious   merry, gay, joyful, gleeful   HILARITY

hill   elevation, mound, heap   HILLY

hind   back, rear   front

hinder   stop, obstruct, impede, check, curb, retard, restrain, hold back   help   HINDRANCE

hinge   1. fasten, clasp, lock   separate, 2. depend, rest on, revolve on

hint   suggest, imply, intimate, insinuate

hire   1. employ, engage   fire, 2. lease, let, rent, charter

hiss   boo, hoot   cheer

history   record, chronicle, annals   HISTORIAN, HISTORIC, HISTORICAL

hit   1. strike, blow, knock, punch, poke, smack, whack, slug, bat, crack, swat, sock, clout (*Slang* — clobber, belt, paste, wallop, clip), 2. meet, find, discover, come upon, reach, arrive at   miss, 3. affect, impress, strike, 4. success (*Slang* — smash, wow, sensation, killing)   failure

hitch   1. fasten, hook, clasp, bind, tie   separate, 2. jerk, yank, 3. obstacle, stopping, block, catch, snag, difficulty, drawback

hoard   save, store, collect, accumulate, amass, gather   use

hoarse   rough, gruff, harsh, husky   smooth

hoary   old, aged, elderly, white, gray   young

hobble   limp, totter, stagger

hobby   avocation, pastime

hobgoblin   goblin, imp, elf, ghost

hobo   tramp, vagabond, vagrant (*Slang* — bum)

hodgepodge   mixture, mess, jumble, scramble

hoe   plow, dig, loosen, till

hog   1. pig, swine, 2. glutton, greedy person   HOGGISH

hoist   raise, lift, elevate, boost   lower

hold   1. grasp, keep, grip, cling to, clutch, retain   release, 2. contain, support, bear, carry, 3. have, maintain, occupy, 4. apply, be true, stand up (*Slang* — hold water), 5. think, consider, suppose, assume, presume, regard, surmise

holding   land, property, possession, ownership, title, claim, stake

hole   opening, hollow, pit, gap, chasm, cavity

holiday   vacation, leave, furlough

hollow   1. empty, vacant, bare, void, blank, barren   occupied, 2. deep, sunken, concave   bulging, 3. false, unreal, insincere   sincere, 4. hungry, starved, famished, ravenous, empty   full

holy   sacred, spiritual, pure, religious, godly   HOLINESS

homage   respect, honor, reverence, regard, esteem, deference, acknowledgment   disrespect

home 1. abode, dwelling, residence, hearth, habitat, 2. institution, sanitarium, hospital, asylum HOMELIKE

homeland native land, mother country

homely 1. ugly, plain, unattractive attractive, 2. simple, ordinary, common, 3. homelike, comfortable, cozy, domestic

homestead farm, plantation, house and grounds

homework lesson, task, assignment, exercise, duty

honest fair, upright, truthful, frank, open, genuine, pure, sincere dishonest, insincere HONESTY

honk toot, blast, blare

honor glory, fame, renown, respect, regard, esteem, homage, deference, praise dishonor
HONORABLE, HONORARY

hood cover, lid, veil, cap

hoodlum rowdy, ruffian, thug, tough (*Slang* — bruiser, roughneck, gorilla, hooligan)

hoof foot, paw (*Slang* — kicker)

hook 1. fasten, clasp, bind, clip, snap, latch unhook, 2. catch, snare, trap release, 3. hanger, wire, crook

hoop circle, band, ring

hoot yell, call, cry

hop spring, jump, vault

hope wish for, desire, yearn for, expect
HOPEFUL, HOPELESS

horde crowd, swarm, multitude, throng, mob, force, pack

horizontal level, flat, even, plane

horrible frightful, shocking, terrible, dreadful, outrageous, horrid, ghastly, deplorable, scandalous (*Slang* — awful, atrocious) splendid HORRID, HORRIFY, HORROR

horse steed, colt, mare, stallion, stud (*Slang* — nag)

horseplay rowdiness, boisterous fun

hose 1. stockings, socks, 2. tube, pipe HOSIERY

hospitable friendly, receptive, welcoming, cordial, amiable, gracious, neighborly, generous unfriendly
HOSPITALITY

hospital clinic, sanitarium

host 1. receptionist, proprietor, 2. large number, quantity, multitude, score, flock, army, swarm HOSTESS

hostel inn, hotel, tavern, roadhouse

hostile unfriendly, unfavorable, bitter, antagonistic, aggressive, belligerent, militant friendly HOSTILITY

hot 1. torrid, burning, boiling, fiery cold, 2. spicy, sharp, peppery, nippy, tangy bland, 3. fresh, new stale

hotel inn, tavern, roadhouse, lodging, hostel, motel

hothouse greenhouse, nursery, conservatory

hound 1. hunt, chase, seek, search, follow, 2. urge, press, insist, 3. dog

house 1. shelter, building, dwelling, lodge, residence, home, 2. audience, congregation HOUSING

household family, brood, folks

housekeeper mistress, homemaker, housewife

hovel shack, pigsty (*Slang* — dump)

hover 1. float, sail, drift, 2. waver, hesitate, pause, falter

however 1. nevertheless, although, notwithstanding, yet, still, but, 2. whatever, whatsoever

howl cry, yell, shout, bawl, scream, screech, roar, bellow, bark, yelp, wail

hub   center, middle, nucleus, core

hubbub   noise, uproar, racket, din, clamor, tumult, commotion, fracas, ado, fuss, turmoil, bustle, row, rumpus   calm

huddle   assemble, crowd, gather, flock together, cluster, congregate   scatter

hue   color, tint, shade

huff   1. puff, blow, exhale, 2. fit of anger (*Slang* — stew)

hug   hold, clasp, embrace, press, enfold, squeeze

huge   great, very large, vast, immense, enormous, monumental, gigantic, tremendous (*Slang* — terrific, whopping, whacking)   tiny

hulk   1. ship, boat, 2. oaf, lout, clod (*Slang* — lummox, galoot)   HULKING

hum   1. drone, buzz, murmur, 2. active, busy   quiet, inactive

human   man, person, mortal, being   HUMANITY

humane   kind, good, gracious, warmhearted, brotherly, sympathetic   cruel

humble   modest, meek, plain, simple, homely, unpretentious   vain, showy   HUMBLY, HUMILITY

humbug   cheat, deceive, trick, hoax

humid   moist, damp, wet, muggy   dry   HUMIDITY

humiliate   embarrass, disgrace, shame, mortify, offend, insult, dishonor   honor, dignify   HUMILIATION

humor   1. cater to, give in to, pamper, spoil, coddle, oblige, please, satisfy, 2. wit, pleasantry, comedy, 3. mood, temper, frame of mind, disposition   HUMORIST, HUMOROUS

hump   bump, bulge, ridge, hunch

hunch   1. hump, bump, bulge, 2. feeling, suspicion, impression   HUNCHBACK

hunger   desire, eagerness, appetite, craving
HUNGRILY, HUNGRY

hunk   lump, piece, mass, bulk, wad, gob, chunk

hunt   search, seek, look, pursue, chase
HUNTER, HUNTSMAN

hurdle   1. leap, jump, vault, bound, 2. obstacle, block, difficulty, hitch, catch, snag, barrier

hurl   throw, fling, sling, pitch, toss, cast, heave, chuck, flip

hurrah   cheer, cry, shout, yell, applause   HURRAY

hurricane   storm, cyclone, blizzard, tornado, squall

hurry   hasten, speed, urge, rush, accelerate, hustle (*Slang* — step on it, make it snappy)

hurt   injure, bruise, harm, damage, wrong, impair, pain, wound, distress, grieve, offend   help, benefit, soothe
HURTFUL

hurtle   jostle, collide, clash, strike, bump, crash

husband   1. save, economize, preserve, keep, reserve, scrimp, skimp, 2. spouse, mate, married man

hush   silence, quiet, mute, muffle, calm

husky   1. strong, sturdy, mighty, powerful, rugged, strapping, well-built, muscular, athletic, hefty, beefy, 2. hoarse, harsh, rough, coarse, raspy   smooth, 3. Eskimo dog
HUSKINESS

hustle   1. hasten, speed, urge, rush, 2. push, shove, jostle, prod, bump, jolt, bounce

hut   cabin, shed, shanty, shack

hybrid   mongrel, crossbreed, half-breed

hydrophobia   rabies

hymn   song of praise, psalm, spiritual   HYMNAL

hypnotize   entrance, spellbind, mesmerize
HYPNOTISM, HYPNOTIST

hypocrite   pretender (*Slang* — fake, phony)
HYPOCRISY

hysterical   uncontrollable, frenzied, frantic, delirious, beside
oneself, overexcited, upset   calm, composed   HYSTERIA

I

ice   frozen water, sleet

icebox   refrigerator

ice cream   frozen dessert, sherbet

icing   frosting, topping

idea   thought, plan, notion, fancy, opinion

ideal   perfect, faultless, flawless, model   faulty, imperfect

identical   same, alike, exactly like, duplicate   different

identify   recognize, know, place, distinguish, make out,
name, tell, label, tag, designate (*Slang* — spot, nail, peg)
IDENTIFICATION, IDENTITY

idiot   simpleton, imbecile, moron, half-wit, fool (*Slang* —
nitwit, dimwit, simp)   IDIOTIC

idle   1. inactive, unoccupied, at leisure   busy, 2. lazy, loafing
ambitious, 3. useless, vain, futile, worthless   worthwhile, 4.
unwarranted, groundless, unfounded   IDLER

idol   1. god, 2. favorite, darling   IDOLIZE

igloo   ice hut, Eskimo hut

ignite   burn, set afire, light, kindle, stoke   IGNITION

ignoble   mean, base, low, without honor, shameful, disgraceful   noble

ignorant unintelligent, foolish, uninformed, unaware, uneducated (*Slang* — dumb) smart, knowledgeable
IGNORANCE

ignore disregard, overlook, snub, slight, avoid mind, heed

ill 1. sick, ailing, unwell, indisposed, out of sorts, below par, under the weather, rocky healthy, 2. evil, bad, wrong good ILLNESS

illegal unlawful, criminal, illegitimate legal

illegible unclear, indistinct, unreadable legible, clear

illiterate uneducated, uncultured, unlearned, ignorant learned, educated

ill-natured cross, disagreeable, bad-tempered pleasant

illogical unreasonable, senseless, unsound, unscientific logical

illuminate 1. light, brighten, spotlight, 2. clarify, explain, simplify, show, illustrate ILLUMINATION

illusion deception, delusion, trick, misconception

illustrate 1. clarify, explain, show, demonstrate, 2. represent, picture, portray ILLUSTRATION

illustrious famous, great, outstanding, splendid, radiant, bright, shining, glorious

image likeness, representation, picture, reflection, resemblance, vision, appearance

imagine 1. envision, fancy, conceive, dream, 2. suppose, guess, assume, presume, gather
IMAGINABLE, IMAGINARY, IMAGINATION, IMAGINATIVE

imbecile simpleton, idiot, moron, half-wit, fool (*Slang* — nitwit, dimwit, simp)

imbed enclose, fix, inset, inlay

imitate   copy, act like, repeat, mirror, reflect, echo, emulate
IMITATION

immaculate   pure, clean, spotless   dirty

immature   undeveloped, unripe, inexperienced, green, childish   mature

immeasurable   great, boundless, endless, unlimited, infinite   limited

immediately   instantly, at once, without delay, now, promptly, straightaway, forthwith, quickly, swiftly, directly (*Slang* — pronto)   later

immense   huge, large, vast, great, stupendous, enormous, monumental, mammoth, gigantic, giant   tiny
IMMENSELY, IMMENSITY

immerse   1. submerge, plunge, sink, dip, inundate, drown, dunk, 2. absorb, engross, occupy, engage, grip, hold, fascinate, enthrall

immigrate   enter, come into   leave
IMMIGRANT, IMMIGRATION

imminent   forthcoming, approaching, nearing, impending (*Slang* — in the cards)

immoral   wrong, wicked, evil, bad, sinful   moral

immortal   everlasting, undying, eternal   IMMORTALITY

immovable   fixed, firm, steadfast, stable, stationary   movable

immune   resistant, exempt, clear, excused, spared, let off   subject to   IMMUNITY, IMMUNIZE

imp   1. pixie, sprite, elf, little devil, gremlin, 2. brat, whipper-snapper, mischief-maker (*Slang* — cutup)

impact   collision, crash, bump, clash, shock, brunt

impair   damage, harm, weaken, hurt, make worse, break   improve

impartial fair, neutral, unprejudiced, unbiased, uninfluenced, indifferent prejudiced

impassable unapproachable, inaccessible passable

impassioned emotional, ardent, passionate, fervent, earnest, sincere, serious, excited indifferent

impassive unmoved, unfeeling, unemotional, unresponsive, unsympathetic emotional

impatient restless, anxious, eager, intolerant patient
IMPATIENCE

impeach accuse, charge, indict, arraign, denounce, reproach (*Slang* — pin on, put the finger on, hang something on)

impede hinder, obstruct, curb, inhibit, arrest, check, interrupt, retard, delay, limit, confine, cramp, hamper
facilitate IMPEDIMENT

impel drive, force, cause, push, move, propel, stimulate, compel, make

impenetrable 1. unapproachable, inaccessible, impassable, dense open, passable, 2. obscure, unclear, vague, unintelligible clear

imperative urgent, necessary, compulsory, compelling, pressing, crucial, critical, mandatory unnecessary

imperceptible slight, vague, unclear noticeable

imperfect defective, faulty, incomplete, inadequate, deficient, impaired, blemished, marred perfect
IMPERFECTION

imperial supreme, majestic, magnificent, regal, royal

imperious 1. haughty, arrogant, domineering, overbearing, 2. urgent, necessary, compelling, pressing, crucial, critical, imperative unnecessary

impersonal impartial, neutral, unbiased, detached, unprejudiced biased

impertinence insolence, impudence, rudeness, brazenness, cockiness (*Slang* — brass, freshness, gall, crust, nerve) respectfulness, courtesy IMPERTINENT

impetuous hasty, rash, sudden, abrupt, impulsive, unexpected, reckless restrained, careful, thoughtful

impetus driving force, momentum, thrust, push

implement 1. carry out, get done, bring about, complete neglect, 2. tool, utensil, instrument, apparatus, device, appliance, contraption (*Slang* — gimmick)

implore beg, plead, appeal, entreat, beseech, pray

imply suggest, hint, intimate, infer, insinuate

impolite rude, discourteous, disrespectful, ill-mannered, insolent polite

import 1. bring in, receive, take in, admit, introduce export, 2. meaning, significance, implication, substance, effect, importance IMPORTATION

important meaningful, valuable, influential, significant, substantial, prominent, outstanding unimportant IMPORTANCE

impose put, place, set, charge, levy, tax, burden with, force

imposing impressive, dramatic, spectacular, grand, magnificent, splendid, noble, glorious, proud, stately, majestic, elegant unimpressive

impossible inconceivable, unimaginable, absurd, unthinkable (*Slang* — no go) possible IMPOSSIBILITY

impostor pretender, deceiver, cheat, impersonator, fraud, faker (*Slang* — phony)

impoverish make poor, ruin, break, bankrupt, exhaust, deplete enrich

impractical unfeasible, unworkable, unrealistic practical IMPRACTICABLE

impregnable   resistant, strong, unconquerable, unassailable, invincible   vulnerable

impress   1. affect, strike, 2. fix, establish, root, plant, stamp, 3. mark, imprint, engrave   IMPRESSION, IMPRESSIVE

imprint   mark, engrave, impress, stamp

imprison   jail, confine, lock up   free, release
IMPRISONMENT

improbable   unlikely, doubtful, questionable   probable

improper   1. wrong, incorrect, unsuitable, inappropriate, unfit, bad, 2. indecent, unbecoming   proper

improve   better, perfect, progress, mend, develop, advance
worsen   IMPROVEMENT

improvise   invent, make up, devise, originate, dream up, dash off, ad-lib

imprudent   rash, indiscreet, overconfident, unwise, unsound, unreasonable, unintelligent, ill-advised   careful, prudent
IMPRUDENCE

impudent   forward, bold, immodest, pert, impertinent, rude, disrespectful, brash, saucy (*Slang* — flip, cocky, cheeky, smart, smart-alecky, fresh, crusty, nervy)
polite, courteous   IMPUDENCE

impulse   1. thrust, push, urge, pressure, compulsion, 2. notion, sudden thought, fancy, flash, inspiration
IMPULSIVE

impure   1. dirty, unclean, polluted, contaminated, infected clean, pure, 2. bad, corrupt, indecent, obscene, foul, filthy, nasty   clean, decent   IMPURITY

inability   incapability, ineptitude, incompetence
ability

inaccessible   unreachable, out-of-the-way, unapproachable, out of reach   accessible

inaccurate   incorrect, inexact   accurate   INACCURACY

inactive   idle, sluggish, motionless, still, calm   active

inadequate   deficient, lacking, wanting, short of, insufficient, unsatisfactory   enough, adequate

inadvisable   unwise, imprudent, ill-advised, ill-considered wise, advisable

inappropriate   unfitting, unsuitable, improper   appropriate

inattentive   unmindful, heedless, unobserving, distracted, negligent, wandering   attentive

inaugurate   begin, install, introduce, launch, admit, initiate, instate   INAUGURAL

inborn   natural, innate, hereditary, instinctive

incapable   unable, incompetent, unqualified, unfit   capable

incense   1. provoke, anger, annoy, irritate, vex, exasperate, ruffle, pique (*Slang* — aggravate, peeve, miff, rile), 2. fragrance, perfume, aroma, scent

incentive   motive, stimulus, encouragement, inducement

incessant   continual, uninterrupted, unbroken, constant, ceaseless, endless, nonstop, infinite, perpetual, steady interrupted

incident   happening, event, occurrence, experience, adventure   INCIDENTAL, INCIDENTALLY

incinerator   furnace, burner

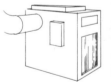

incipient   beginning, initial, introductory   final

incite   stir, urge, rouse, agitate, excite, inflame, provoke, instigate

inclement   rough, stormy, cold, harsh, severe, cruel pleasant

incline   1. tend, be willing, be game, 2. influence, affect, sway, move, induce, persuade, 3. lean, bend, bow, tilt, tip, 4. slope, hill, grade   INCLINATION, INCLINED

include   contain, comprise, cover, enclose   exclude
INCLUSION, INCLUSIVE

income   receipts, returns, profits, earnings, proceeds, wages, payment

incomparable   matchless, unequaled   comparable

incompetent   unable, incapable, unqualified, unfit
competent, able

incomplete   unfinished, deficient, wanting, lacking, imperfect, partial   complete

incomprehensible   unintelligible, hard to understand, difficult, vague, obscure   understandable

inconceivable   unbelievable, unthinkable, unconvincing, incredible   believable

inconsiderate   thoughtless, unmindful   considerate

inconsistent   disagreeing, illogical, unreasonable, senseless, invalid   consistent

inconspicuous   unseen, unnoticed, unapparent
conspicuous

inconvenient   untimely, inappropriate, unfavorable, troublesome, bothersome, awkward   convenient, timely
INCONVENIENCE

incorporate   join, unite, combine, unify, merge

incorrect   wrong, faulty, inaccurate, improper
correct, right

increase   enlarge, extend, add to, expand, advance, raise
decrease   INCREASINGLY

incredible   unbelievable, doubtful, questionable, unconvincing, staggering, preposterous, absurd, ridiculous   believable
INCREDIBLY, INCREDULOUS

incur   contract, bring on, catch (*Slang* — come down with)

incurable   hopeless, beyond remedy   curable

indebted   owing, obliged, involved

indeed   in fact, in truth, really, absolutely, positively, perfectly, certainly, definitely, surely, of course

indefinite   unclear, vague, indistinct, obscure, confused, hazy, general, broad   definite

indelible   permanent, indestructible, unforgettable, fixed

indent   dent, impress, cut, nick

independent   acting alone, unconnected, unassociated, self-reliant   dependent   INDEPENDENCE

indescribable   unexplainable, extraordinary, exceptional, remarkable   ordinary

index   list, chart, file, table, sign, symbol, guide

indicate   show, point out, exhibit, demonstrate, display, present, express, suggest, hint, imply, signify INDICATION, INDICATOR

indifferent   unbiased, impartial, detached, disinterested, cool, neutral, impersonal, unconcerned   concerned INDIFFERENCE, INDIFFERENTLY

indigenous   native, original, natural to   foreign

indignant   angry, irate (*Slang* — mad, sore, worked up, riled up)   INDIGNATION

indignity   insult, affront, offense, injury   respect

indirect   devious, roundabout, out-of-the-way   direct

indiscreet   unwise, imprudent, unsound, unreasonable, ill-advised   careful

indispensable   essential, necessary, needed, required, vital unnecessary

indisposed   1. ill, sick, ailing (*Slang* — under the weather, out of sorts, rocky)   well, 2. unwilling, forced   willing

indistinct unclear, confused, dim, obscure, vague, cloudy, hazy, blurred clear, distinct

individual 1. single, separate, one, personal, special, 2. human, man, being
INDIVIDUALITY, INDIVIDUALLY

indivisible inseparable, solid divisible

indolent lazy, shiftless, do-nothing, unenterprising, slothful ambitious INDOLENCE

indomitable unconquerable, unyielding, invincible, unbeatable, uncontrollable, unruly, unmanageable
yielding, controllable

induce influence, persuade, lead on, cause, elicit, evoke, prompt, move, sway INDUCEMENT

induct introduce, bring in, install, place, inaugurate, enlist, enroll, draft

indulge humor, favor, oblige, please, gratify, satisfy, cater to, pamper, coddle, spoil
INDULGENCE, INDULGENT

industrious hard-working, diligent, energetic, tireless lazy

industry trade, business, manufacture, labor, work, concern, dealings INDUSTRIAL

inedible uneatable edible

ineffectual useless, ineffective, powerless, unsuccessful effective

inefficient unable, incapable, incompetent, unfit, inept, unskillful efficient INEFFICIENCY

inequality unevenness, irregularity, imbalance equality

inert lifeless, slow, sluggish, motionless, inactive, stagnant, listless active

inevitable destined, fated, doomed, unavoidable, sure, certain, inescapable

inexact vague, indefinite, broad, general, unclear, obscure, inaccurate, incorrect   exact

inexcusable unpardonable, unforgivable, unjustifiable excusable

inexhaustible 1. tireless, 2. endless, unlimited, infinite limited

inexpensive cheap, low-priced, reasonable   expensive

inexperienced unpracticed, untried, green, unfamiliar, ignorant, immature, undeveloped   experienced

inexplicable unexplainable, mysterious   understandable

infallible reliable, sure, unerring, right   unreliable

infamous wicked, bad, disgraceful, evil, base, low, shameful, notorious, terrible, scandalous, outrageous
virtuous, good, moral   INFAMY

infancy beginning, babyhood   maturity
INFANT, INFANTILE

infantry army, foot soldiers

infect 1. disease, contaminate, communicate, pollute, corrupt, poison, 2. influence   INFECTION, INFECTIOUS

infer 1. conclude, reason, deduce, gather, derive, assume, presume, suppose, expect, reckon, calculate, imagine, 2. indicate, imply, suggest, hint   INFERENCE

inferior lower, worse, subordinate, secondary, lesser
superior   INFERIORITY

infernal hellish

infest overrun, crawl with, plague, beset

infidel unbeliever, skeptic   believer

infinite limitless, boundless, endless, immeasurable, perpetual, everlasting, eternal, ceaseless   limited
INFINITELY

infirm weak, feeble, unstable, sickly, unsound, frail
strong, healthy INFIRMITY

inflame 1. excite, stir, move, affect, provoke, arouse, incite,
anger soothe, calm, 2. redden, swell, irritate
INFLAMMABLE, INFLAMMATION

inflate swell, puff out, expand, broaden, enlarge, stretch,
increase, blow up deflate
INFLATION

inflexible stiff, rigid, firm, unbending, unyielding, stubborn,
inelastic flexible

inflict give, cause, impose, effect, produce, bring about,
wreak

influence sway, affect, move, induce, persuade, prejudice
INFLUENTIAL

inform 1. tell, communicate, advise, enlighten, instruct,
notify, report, 2. accuse, tattle, blab, snitch, squeal, betray
INFORMATION

infrequent rare, scarce, sparse, scattered, occasional,
uncommon, irregular frequent

infringe violate, break, trespass, overstep

infuriate enrage, anger, madden, antagonize, provoke,
irritate, incite, agitate soothe, calm

infuse 1. put in, instill, 2. inspire, lift, infect, animate,
3. drench, saturate, bathe

ingenious clever, skillful, proficient, masterful, inventive,
original, creative, imaginative, productive, inspired
unoriginal, dull INGENUITY

ingenuous 1. frank, open, sincere, candid, straightforward
secretive, 2. simple, natural, innocent, plain, unsophisticated
sophisticated

ingredient part, element, factor, component

inhabit live, dwell, occupy, reside, lodge, stay, room
INHABITANT

inhale breathe in, gasp, sniff, smell   exhale

inherent internal, natural, implanted, existing, belonging, instinctive

inherit receive, come into   INHERITANCE

inhospitable uncordial, unfriendly, unreceptive, ungracious, unneighborly   friendly, hospitable

inhuman unfeeling, cruel, brutal, ruthless, uncivilized   kind

iniquity injustice, evil, sin, wrong, crime, outrage   justice

initial 1. first, earliest, beginning, primary, introductory final, 2. letter

initiate 1. start, begin, originate, pioneer, lead, head, institute, introduce, launch, break the ice, 2. admit, receive, take in, install, let in   expel, 3. instruct, introduce, educate INITIATION, INITIATIVE

inject force into, fill, insert   extract   INJECTION

injure damage, harm, hurt, wound, wrong, impair   heal, correct   INJURIOUS, INJURY

injustice inequity, unfairness, unjustness   justice

inkling hint, suggestion, notion, indication, glimmer, clue, suspicion, impression, idea

inlaid embedded, inset, lined

inlet entrance, entry, opening, passageway

inmate occupant, resident, tenant, inhabitant

inmost 1. deepest, farthest in, 2. private, secret

inn hotel, tavern, roadhouse, lodge

innocent 1. guiltless, faultless, blameless, sinless   guilty
2. harmless   harmful   INNOCENCE

innovate introduce, change, modernize INNOVATION

innumerable countless, many, infinite, unlimited few

inoculate immunize, vaccinate INOCULATION

inoffensive harmless, unobjectionable offensive

inquire ask, question INQUIRY

inquisitive curious, prying, snooping, meddlesome

inroad raid, attack, invasion, foray

insane crazy, foolish, mad, unbalanced, deranged (*Slang —* nutty, screwy, wacky, goofy) sane INSANITY

insatiable greedy, unquenchable, covetous

inscribe write, engrave, mark, imprint, impress, stamp INSCRIPTION

insensible unfeeling, unaware, unconscious, numb, unknowing sensitive, aware INSENSITIVE

inseparable indivisible, solid, joined separable

insert put in, enter, introduce, inject, set in extract INSERTION

inside 1. in, into, within, 2. interior, innermost

insight wisdom, perception, intuition

insignia emblems, badges, symbols

insignificant unimportant, meaningless, negligible, small, little, slight significant, meaningful

insincere dishonest, false, superficial, artificial sincere

insinuate hint, suggest, imply, intimate, indicate

insist urge, press, maintain, stress, demand INSISTENCE, INSISTENT

insolent rude, insulting, impudent, arrogant, haughty, defiant, bold polite INSOLENCE

insoluble   unexplainable, unsolvable   solvable

inspect   examine, observe, study, contemplate
INSPECTION, INSPECTOR

inspire   influence, cause, prompt, encourage   discourage
INSPIRATION

install   1. admit, establish, let in, inaugurate, instate, receive,
2. place, put in, fix, plant, set   INSTALLMENT

instance   example, case, occasion, circumstance

instant   1. immediate, pressing, urgent, prompt, quick, 2.
moment, second   INSTANTANEOUS, INSTANTLY

instead   in place of, rather than, in lieu of

instinct   natural feeling, natural tendency
INSTINCTIVE

institute   1. establish, begin, set up, create, organize, form,
launch (*Slang* — start the ball rolling), 2. society, organization, school, establishment, foundation   INSTITUTION

instruct   1. teach, educate, show, guide, 2. inform, direct,
tell, command, order, dictate, advise
INSTRUCTION, INSTRUCTIVE, INSTRUCTOR

instrument   tool, device, means, implement, utensil, apparatus, gadget, appliance, contraption (*Slang* — gimmick)
INSTRUMENTAL

insufferable   unbearable, intolerable   tolerable, bearable

insufficient   inadequate, not enough, unsatisfactory, deficient   enough

insulate   isolate, separate   INSULATION, INSULATOR

insult   offend, affront, humiliate

insure   1. protect, safeguard, defend, shelter, cover, 2.
guarantee, warrant, assure, endorse, certify, sponsor, back,
3. make sure, affirm, vouch, determine   INSURANCE

insurgent rebel, rioter, revolter, agitator, ringleader, troublemaker, instigator, rabble-rouser

insurrection revolt, rebellion, mutiny, riot, uprising obedience, compliance

intact untouched, whole, uninjured, undamaged, unchanged, complete

intake 1. input, entry, 2. income, earnings, revenue, receipts, proceeds, profits outgo

intangible untouchable, unsubstantial tangible

integrate 1. equalize, balance, coordinate, proportion, 2. amass, form a whole segregate INTEGRATION

integrity 1. honesty, sincerity, uprightness, honor, respectability dishonesty, 2. wholeness, completeness, entirety, totality incompleteness

intelligent sensible, bright, knowing, understanding, rational, aware, perceptive ignorant
INTELLECT, INTELLECTUAL, INTELLIGENCE, INTELLIGIBLE

intemperate excessive, extreme, unreasonable, unrestrained
INTEMPERANCE

intend mean, plan, propose, aim, have in mind, contemplate
INTENT, INTENTION, INTENTIONAL

intense 1. great, considerable, extreme, drastic, 2. forceful, strong, dynamic, fierce, severe, rigorous (*Slang* — snappy, zippy, peppy) moderate

inter bury, entomb

intercede go between, interfere, intervene, mediate, negotiate, arbitrate, umpire, referee

intercept interrupt, check, stop, arrest, hold up

interchange exchange, change, switch, trade, substitute

intercourse 1. communication, dealings, 2. sexual relations, copulation

interest 1. concern, curiosity, intrigue unconcern, apathy, 2. share, portion, part, percentage (*Slang* — divvy, cut), 3. premium, rate, profit, 4. business, affair, matters

interesting arousing, provocative, inviting, entertaining, thought-provoking, fascinating, absorbing, gripping, engrossing, enthralling, spellbinding, captivating, intriguing, attractive, appealing uninteresting, dull

interfere 1. intervene, intercede, mediate, arbitrate, umpire, referee, 2. meddle, intrude, encroach, interrupt (*Slang* — barge in, cut in, butt in, horn in, crash)
INTERFERENCE

interior inside, inner, middle, heart, core, nucleus exterior, outside

interject insert, put between, implant, interpose

interlace weave, intertwine, braid

interlock join, link, connect, mesh, engage separate

interlude intermission, interval, interim, respite, break, pause, recess, interruption

intermediate in between, intervening, middle

interminable endless, long, lengthy, infinite, perpetual

intermingle mix, blend, merge, combine, mingle separate

intermission pause, interruption, interlude, interval, interim, respite, break, recess

intermittent periodic, recurrent, sporadic, irregular, broken, unsteady regular, continual

internal inner, inside, interior, innermost external, outer

interpret explain, clarify, translate, analyze
INTERPRETATION

interrogate question, examine, quiz, test, inquire of, grill, cross-examine INTERROGATION

interrupt break in, hinder, stop, intrude, interfere INTERRUPTION

intertwine interlace, weave, braid

interval interruption, intermission, interlude, interim, respite, break, pause, recess

intervention interference, intrusion, infringement, meddling INTERVENE

interview question, interrogate, quiz, test, examine

1. intimate 1. close, familiar, 2. innermost, private, secret

2. intimate hint, suggest, imply, indicate, insinuate

intimidate frighten, threaten, menace, cow, browbeat, bully, harass, terrorize

intolerable unbearable, insufferable tolerable, bearable

intolerant impatient, unsympathetic, bigoted, prejudiced tolerant, understanding

intoxicated 1. drunk, inebriated (*Slang*— plastered, pickled, soused, crocked, tight, high) sober, 2. excited, impassioned, moved, touched, impressed, affected unmoved INTOXICATE

intrepid fearless, dauntless, brave, courageous, bold, valiant, heroic timid, afraid

intricate complicated, perplexing, entangled, complex, confused, involved simple

intrigue 1. plot, scheme, conspiracy, 2. love affair, romance, amour

intriguing fascinating, alluring, captivating, charming, enchanting, enthralling, attractive, interesting, appealing, enticing, inviting, tantalizing, thrilling, tempting, provocative unappealing, dull

introduce 1. bring in, inaugurate, institute, launch, innovate, 2. present, acquaint with INTRODUCTION

intrude interfere, infringe, encroach, trespass, meddle, overstep (*Slang* — barge in, cut in, butt in, horn in, crash) INTRUSION

inundate flood, overflow, run over, cascade, deluge, drench

invade intrude, overrun, encroach, trespass, advance upon, infringe, raid, attack INVASION

invalid 1. sickly, weak, unhealthy, infirm, frail, debilitated, 2. void, without value, ineffective valid

invaluable priceless, precious, dear, worthwhile worthless

invariable unchanging, constant, permanent, unalterable, uniform, steady, consistent changing

invent originate, make up, devise, develop, contrive, concoct INVENTION, INVENTOR

inventory stock, collection, list

invert turn around, reverse

invest 1. venture, stake, 2. empower, place, provide, endow INVESTMENT, INVESTOR

investigate search, explore, examine, inspect, study, scrutinize, review, probe INVESTIGATION, INVESTIGATOR

invigorating stimulating, exhilarating, energizing, refreshing, bracing debilitating, weakening

invincible unbeatable, unconquerable, invulnerable, impregnable vulnerable

invite 1. ask, request, call, summon, 2. attract, tempt, interest, appeal INVITATION

invoke pray, beseech, entreat, beg, implore, appeal, plead INVOCATION

involuntary 1. unwilling, forced, 2. instinctive, automatic, mechanical, spontaneous, reflex, unconscious, compulsive, unthinking, unintentional voluntary

involve 1. include, concern, affect, entail, implicate, encompass, envelop, 2. complicate, tangle, confuse, confound, 3. occupy, absorb, engross INVOLVEMENT

irate angry, mad, indignant, infuriated

irksome tiresome, tedious, wearisome, troublesome, bothersome, trying, annoying, irritating

irregular 1. unnatural, abnormal, 2. uneven, erratic, distorted, rough regular

irrelevant unfitting, inappropriate, unrelated, far-fetched relevant

irresistible compelling, moving

irresolute hesitating, uncertain, unsure, indecisive, fickle resolute, definite

irreverent disrespectful, discourteous, insolent, impudent, impious respectful

irritable impatient, cross, cranky, irascible, testy pleasant, agreeable

irritate 1. annoy, vex, incite, agitate, stir up, provoke, instigate, foment, infuriate, madden, anger, 2. make sore, pain, hurt, wound, chafe, rub, grate soothe IRRITATION

isolate separate, segregate, set apart, quarantine, seclude ISOLATION

issue 1. cause, principle, campaign, problem, topic, subject, theme, text, question, point, 2. publication, edition, copy

itch 1. prickly feeling, 2. desire, craving

item 1. part, segment, portion, subdivision, component, piece, article, 2. notation, entry

itemize list, sum up, total, summarize

J

jab   poke, push, thrust, nudge, prod

jagged   pointy, ragged, notched, serrated   smooth

jail   imprison, lock up, hold captive, incarcerate

jam   1. crowd, stuff, load, cram, press, squeeze, push, crush, heap, 2. jelly, marmalade, preserve

jar   1. shake, rattle, jolt, bounce, 2. glass container

jaunt   trip, journey, excursion, tour, voyage, outing, expedition (*Slang* — whirl, jump, hop)   JAUNTY

jealous   envious, desirous of, covetous   JEALOUSY

jeer   make fun of, taunt, scoff, mock

jeopardize   risk, endanger, imperil, hazard, expose (*Slang* — put on the spot)   JEOPARDY

jerk   pull suddenly, twist suddenly, jolt, yank

jest   joke, fun, mock, tease (*Slang* — ride, josh, kid, rib, razz)   JESTER

jetty   breakwater, pier, buttress, bulwark

jewel   stone, gem, ornament   JEWELRY

jingle   ring, chime, tinkle

job   work, business, employment, task, assignment, duty, position

jog   run, trot, gait, sprint, lope

join   connect, fasten, clasp, unite, combine, couple, link, put together, attach, annex
separate, part, detach, disconnect, disjoin

joke   jest, quip, banter, tease (*Slang* — ride, josh, rib, kid, razz, wisecrack)   JOKER

jolly   merry, cheerful, pleasant, joyful, jovial, gleeful
sad, solemn, grim, serious, glum

jolt   jerk, jar, shake, startle, jounce

jostle push, shove, thrust, bump

jot write, mark down, note, record

jounce jolt, bounce, bump

journal 1. daily record, account, log, diary, chronicle, 2. newspaper, magazine JOURNALISM, JOURNALIST

journey trip, voyage, tour, expedition, excursion, jaunt, outing, junket

jovial kindly, good-natured, merry, good-hearted, good-humored, joyful, gleeful, jolly sad, solemn, grim, serious, glum

joyful glad, happy, cheerful, blissful, merry, jovial, gleeful sad, solemn, grim, serious, glum JOY, JOYOUS

jubilant rejoicing, exulting, triumphant, overjoyed, gay, delighted, elated dejected JUBILATION, JUBILEE

judge 1. decide, consider, form an opinion, 2. mediate, referee, umpire JUDGMENT, JUDICIAL

judicious wise, sensible, thoughtful, well-advised ignorant

jumble mix, confuse, scramble, muddle (*Slang* — foul up, ball up, snafu) compose, arrange, organize

jumbo big, huge, enormous, immense, colossal, giant, gigantic, mammoth, monstrous, tremendous small, little, dwarf, midget, mini

jump spring, leap, bound, vault, hurdle, hop

junction joining, connection, union, linking, coupling, meeting, hookup, tie-up separation JUNCTURE

junior 1. younger, 2. lower, lesser, secondary, subordinate, minor senior

junk 1. rubbish, trash, scrap, litter, debris, 2. Chinese sailing ship

just 1. exact, precise, 2. only, merely, 3. righteous, fair, proper, good, moral, virtuous corrupt, unjust JUSTICE

jut stick out, project, stand out, protrude recess, indent

juvenile young, youthful old, mature, aged

K

keen 1. sharp, cutting, fine, acute, 2. quick, exact, smart, bright, clever, sharp-witted (*Slang* — quick on the trigger, sharp as a tack)
dull

keep have, hold, maintain, preserve, conserve, save, tend, protect, guard discard, lose
KEEPER, KEEPING, KEPT

kennel doghouse, pound

key 1. opener, 2. clue, answer, explanation, lead, 3. tone, pitch, note

kid 1. tease, joke, fool, jest (*Slang* — ride, josh, rib, razz), 2. child, tot, 3. young goat

kidnap snatch, carry off, abduct, shanghai

kill slay, slaughter, murder, destroy, end, finish, annihilate, execute

kin family, relatives, relations, folks KINDRED

kind 1. friendly, gentle, decent, generous, considerate, warm-hearted, tender, sympathetic, thoughtful mean, cruel, unkind, 2. sort, type, variety, species, nature, make
KINDNESS

kindle 1. set afire, light, ignite extinguish, 2. arouse, stir up, start, trigger, move, provoke calm, pacify

king ruler, sovereign, monarch, chief, potentate

kink 1. curl, twist, 2. complication, 3. quirk, mental twist, queer idea

kiss touch with lips, osculate, buss (*Slang* — smack, smooch)

kit equipment, set, outfit, furnishings, gear, rig

knack skill, talent, art, know-how

knave rascal, tricky man, rogue, scoundrel, villain
KNAVERY

knead mix, blend, combine, massage

knife blade, sword

knit join, grow together, fasten, connect, unite

knock hit, strike, punch, jab, pound, beat, hammer, rap, bang (*Slang* — bat, crack, wallop, clout, belt, clobber, bash, paste, clip, swat, sock, conk)

know understand, comprehend, perceive, recognize, identify, be sure of, be aware KNOWLEDGE

L

label name, title, tag

labor work, toil, employment, industry (*Slang* — grind)
LABORER, LABORIOUS

labyrinth maze, complex, tangle

lacerate tear roughly, mangle, wound

lack want, need, require, fall short

lacquer varnish, polish, gild

lad boy, youth LADDIE

laden loaded, burdened, weighted

ladle dipper, scoop

lady woman, matron

lag linger, loiter, dawdle, poke, dillydally, delay, tarry

lament mourn, sorrow, grieve, bewail, bemoan
rejoice, celebrate LAMENTATION

lance pierce, cut, puncture, stab, perforate, knife, impale

land   1. ground, soil, sod, shore, surface, earth, 2. descend, arrive, touch down, alight   LANDING

landmark   point, milestone

lane   path, road, narrow way, pass, aisle, alley, avenue, channel, artery

language   speech, words, tongue, talk (*Slang* — lingo, patter)

languid   weak, drooping, feeble, debilitated, listless, lethargic, dull, sluggish   energetic, vigorous   LANGUISH

lank   slender, thin, lean, skinny, gaunt, scrawny   stocky, chunky

lap   1. lick, drink, 2. wrap around, fold over

lapse   sink, decline, slump, go down

larceny   theft, stealing, robbery

lard   fat, grease

large   big, sizable, great, grand, huge, vast, immense, enormous, colossal, giant, gigantic, mammoth, massive   small, little

lariat   rope, lasso

lark   fun, fling, joke, spree, celebration, revel

lash   strike, blow, beat, hit, whip, flog

lass   girl, youth   LASSIE

lasso   rope, lariat

last   latest, end, final, conclusive, ultimate   first, beginning

latch   hook, clasp, lock, fastener, catch, closing, seal

late   behind, slow, tardy

latent   hidden, concealed, covered, obscured, underlying

lather   soap, foam, suds, froth

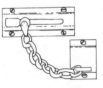

latter   later, more recent   former

laud   praise, commend, glorify, compliment, extol
belittle, criticize

laugh   giggle, chuckle, smile, grin, titter, snicker, guffaw,
howl, roar   (*Slang* — be in stitches)
LAUGHABLE, LAUGHTER

launch   start, set afloat, introduce, fire, set going, spring

launder   wash, bathe, scour, scrub   LAUNDRY

lavatory   bathroom, toilet, latrine, washroom

lavish   free, abundant, liberal, plentiful, ample, extravagant,
generous, prodigal   stingy, sparing, skimpy

law   rule, principle, standard, formula, ordinance, regulation, act, decree, proclamation, edict
LAWFUL, LAWYER

lax   loose, slack, careless, lenient, vague, lazy   rigid, firm
LAXITY

lay   put, place, set, rest, deposit, arrange

lazy   lax, inactive, indolent   active, ambitious

lea   meadow, pasture, grassy field

lead   come first, head, escort, guide, conduct, direct, run
LEADER, LEADERSHIP

league   union, alliance, association, society, federation,
group, band

leak   drip, dribble, run out

lean   1. thin, scant, spare, lanky, meager, slight, slim,
slender, narrow, skinny, scrawny   bulky, fat, 2. bend, rest,
slope, slant, incline, tip

leap   jump, spring, vault, hop, bound, hurdle, dive, plunge,
pounce

learn   memorize, gain knowledge, discover, find out

lease rent, hire, let, charter

leash strap, chain, rein, collar, shackle

least fewest, smallest, minimum most, maximum

leave go, depart, quit, abandon, withdraw, vacate, exit
arrive, stay

lecture speech, talk, sermon, address, recitation, discourse,
oration

ledge shelf, ridge, edge, rim

legal lawful, legitimate, authorized, permitted, allowed,
admissible, valid, sound, just illegal

legend story, fiction, fairy tale, myth, fable, folklore
LEGENDARY

legible readable, plain, clear illegible

legion unit, outfit, regiment, troop, battalion, company,
squad, team, division, army, force

legislation lawmaking, resolution, regulation, ruling, enactment, decree, ordinance, statute
LEGISLATE, LEGISLATIVE, LEGISLATURE

legitimate lawful, rightful, allowed, legal, authorized,
permitted, admissible, valid, sound, just illegitimate

leisure freedom, spare time

lend give, loan, advance

length extent, measure, span, reach, stretch, distance
LENGTHEN

lenient mild, gentle, merciful, lax, loose, relaxed, unrestrained, soft, easy harsh, strict

less smaller, fewer, reduced more

lesson teaching, instruction, assignment, exercise, course,
study

let 1. allow, permit, leave, consent, grant, admit   deny, 2. rent, lease, hire out, charter, contract

letter 1. alphabet sign, character, symbol, 2. message, note, communication, dispatch

level flat, even, equal, uniform, constant, steady, smooth   uneven

liable 1. likely, probable, apt, 2. responsible, accountable, answerable

liar fibber, falsifier, fabricator, perjurer, storyteller

liberal 1. generous, plentiful, abundant, ample, extravagant, lavish, extensive, unselfish   stingy, 2. tolerant, broad-minded, freethinking, progressive   conservative

liberty freedom, independence, autonomy, emancipation

license permit, warrant, consent, authorization, sanction, approval

lick lap, taste

lid cover, top, cap, stopper

lie 1. fib, falsify, fabricate, exaggerate, 2. recline, repose

life existence, being

lift raise, pick up, elevate, hoist

light 1. bright, clear, open, lucid   dark, 2. weightless, airy, delicate   heavy

like prefer, care for, be fond of, fancy, enjoy, appreciate (*Slang* — have eyes for, go for, get a kick out of)   dislike   LIKING

likeness similarity, resemblance   difference

likewise similarly, also, moreover, too, as well

limber flexible, bending, pliable, elastic   stiff, inflexible

limit end, boundary, restriction, extreme, tip, confine

limp weak, drooping, sagging, flimsy, loose, soft, floppy stiff

limpid clear, transparent, lucid, translucent cloudy

line 1. rope, cord, wire, string, 2. mark, stroke, stripe, streak, dash, 3. edge, boundary, limit, confine, 4. row, arrangement, series, sequence, 5. type, kind, brand, sort, make

lineage race, family, ancestry

linger stay, wait, delay, remain, tarry, loiter, dawdle, dillydally, lag (*Slang* — take one's own sweet time, hang around, hold on, sit tight, stick around, wait a second)

link unite, connect, join, combine, couple, put together, bridge separate

liquid fluid solid

liquor whiskey, drink, alcohol, spirits (*Slang* — booze)

list 1. enumeration, schedule, record, register, inventory, line-up, 2. tilt, tip, slant, slope, lean

listen hear, eavesdrop (*Slang* — be all ears)

listless tired, uninterested, unconcerned, lethargic, apathetic active

literally exactly, actually, really, word-for-word

literate learned, scholarly, cultured, educated illiterate

literature writings, books, publications

lithe bending, supple, elastic, flexible, pliable, plastic, limber stiff

litter clutter, rubbish, trash, scrap, rubble, debris, junk

little small, short, tiny, bit, minimum, slight, miniature, mini, puny, teeny, wee big

live 1. be alive, exist die, 2. reside, occupy, dwell, stay, house, room, inhabit (*Slang* — hang out)

livelihood   support, keep, maintenance, sustenance, sub-sistence   LIVING

lively   exciting, bright, cheerful, vivid, vigorous, gay, active, energetic, interesting, spirited, animated, vivacious, spry (*Slang* — zippy, snappy, chipper, full of life, peppy) dull   LIVELIER, LIVELIEST

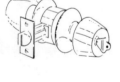

livestock   cattle, animals

livid   1. pale, grayish, 2. very angry, furious, enraged (*Slang* — sore, riled up, fit to be tied)

load   1. burden, pack, cargo, freight, 2. fill, stuff unload, empty

loaf   idle, lounge, loiter, lie around

loan   lend, advance, give

loath   unwilling, reluctant

loathe   hate, dislike, abhor, detest, abominate, despise   love

lobby   entrance, passageway, vestibule, foyer

local   regional, limited, particular, restricted

location   position, place, region, area, zone, territory, district, section, neighborhood, spot, site, situation LOCATE, LOCALITY

lock   fasten, close, hook, clasp, latch, shut, seal unlock, open

locomotion   travel, movement, motion, transit

lodge   live, reside, inhabit, occupy, dwell, room, stay LODGER, LODGING

lofty   high, grand, dignified, proud, haughty, eminent, prominent, elevated, soaring, towering

log   1. wood, lumber, timber, board, 2. record, register, account, scrapbook, album, catalog, journal

logical   reasonable, sensible, sound, sane, rational
illogical, unreasonable   LOGIC

loiter   linger, idle, stop, dillydally, wait, delay, stay, tarry, dawdle (*Slang* — hang around, stick around)

loll   droop, hang, sprawl, repose, recline, relax (*Slang* — take it easy)

lonely   alone, solitary, isolated, unaccompanied, friendless, desolate   LONE, LONELINESS, LONESOME

long   lengthy, extensive, far-reaching   short

look   1. see, search, hunt, explore, stare, glance, peek, peer, gaze, gape, gawk (*Slang* — gander), 2. seem, appear

loom   appear, emerge, come in sight, show up

loose   1. limp, drooping, slack, unfastened, untied   tight, 2. vague, free, unclear, confused, hazy, inexact   definite

loot   rob, plunder, burglarize (*Slang* — hold up, stick up)

lope   run, sprint, bound, race, gallop

lord   owner, ruler, master, boss, proprietor

lose   1. fail, flop, be unsuccessful, forfeit, sacrifice
win, succeed, 2. misplace, mislay   find   LOSS, LOST

lot   1. many, bunch, group, cluster, clump   few, 2. quantity, amount, sum, number, portion, 3. fate, fortune, chance, luck, destiny, end (*Slang* — break), 4. field, plot, tract

lotion   ointment, salve, cream, balm

lottery   raffle, drawing

loud   noisy, thunderous, roaring, resounding   soft, low

lounge   rest, relax, loaf, lie down, repose, laze, sit around, take it easy

love   adore, like, care for, be fond of, fancy, idolize, cherish (*Slang* — have eyes for, be set on, dig, go for, have a case on)

lovely delightful, exquisite, charming, appealing, enchanting, beautiful, pretty, attractive, fetching (*Slang* — out of this world) LOVELINESS

low 1. inferior, lesser, short high, 2. mean, coarse, vulgar, base, wicked, evil, bad, sinful, vile

loyal true, faithful, obedient, dutiful, devoted, trustworthy disloyal LOYALTY

lubricate grease, oil, anoint LUBRICANT

lucid 1. clear, shining, light, transparent, translucent, 2. understandable, plain, distinct, clear-cut, explicit unclear, cloudy

luck chance, fortune, fate, lot, fortuity LUCKY

ludicrous ridiculous, absurd (*Slang* — way-out)

lug drag, pull, haul, tug

luggage baggage, bags, valises

lull quiet, calm, hush, silence, stillness, pause, rest, break, recess, intermission, respite, lapse, letup

lumber timber, logs, wood

luminous light, shining, radiant, beaming, gleaming, glowing, bright, clear

lump swelling, bump, mass, hunk, chunk

lunge thrust, attack, push

lurch sway, topple, tip, rock, roll, toss, tumble, pitch

lure pull, attract, draw on, entice, seduce (*Slang* — give the come-on, rope in)

lurid terrible, sensational, startling, melodramatic

lurk hide, sneak, slink, prowl, creep

luscious delicious, savory, pleasing, tasty

luster   shine, brightness, brilliance, sheen, glow, gleam, gloss
LUSTROUS

lusty   strong, healthy, vigorous, powerful, mighty, sturdy, rugged, strapping, robust, hardy, hale, husky, hefty   weak

luxury   extravagance, frills, prosperity, elegance, comfort, well-being, magnificence, grandeur, splendor, swankiness
poverty   LUXURIOUS

lyrical   musical, poetic   LYRIC

M

mad   1. crazy, insane, wild, foolish, lunatic, daft, demented, deranged, unbalanced, touched (*Slang* — cracked, not all there) sane, 2. angry, annoyed, irritated, exasperated, disgruntled, enraged, furious, cross, irritable, ornery, raging, disagreeable (*Slang* — sore, riled up, fit to be tied)   peaceful
MADDEN

magazine   journal, periodical, publication

magic   witchcraft, wizardry, sorcery, voodoo
MAGICIAN

magistrate   judge

magnetic   attractive, pulling, drawing, alluring
MAGNET, MAGNETISM

magnificent   splendid, grand, stately, majestic, superb, exquisite, marvelous, wonderful, grandiose, glorious, imposing, elaborate, impressive (*Slang* — divine, terrific, sensational, out of this world, swell)

magnify   exaggerate, increase, intensify, expand, enhance, enlarge, extend, broaden, stretch, inflate (*Slang* — step up, lay it on, talk big, jazz up, boost)   minimize

maid   servant, helper, domestic, housekeeper

mail 1. send, dispatch, post, 2. letters, correspondence

maim cripple, disable, injure, hurt, wound

main chief, most important, principal, foremost, leading, dominant, primary, first secondary MAINLY

maintain keep, uphold, possess, support, bear, sustain, preserve, save, guard, protect, retain MAINTENANCE

majestic grand, stately, noble, great, kingly, dignified, high, prominent, eminent, regal, royal, imperial, sovereign, grandiose, magnificent, impressive, elegant, imposing, proud MAJESTY

major larger, greater, superior, higher, senior minor MAJORITY

make 1. build, form, shape, compose, create, assemble, manufacture, fashion, fabricate, construct, produce, do, execute destroy, 2. cause, force, compel, 3. kind, brand, type, line, sort

malady sickness, illness, disease, ailment, disorder, infirmity

male manly, masculine female

malice spite, ill will, meanness MALICIOUS

malign slur, slander, speak evil of, defame, smear .

malignant deadly, harmful, destructive, killing, fatal, mortal, lethal harmless, benign MALIGNANCY

malleable yielding, adaptable, changeable, pliant, flexible, plastic, elastic, bendable, supple stubborn, unyielding, rigid

maltreat abuse, mistreat

mammoth huge, gigantic, immense, vast, enormous, giant, colossal, titanic, monumental (*Slang* — whopping) microscopic, miniature

man   1. human being, person, Homo sapiens, folk, society, mortal, individual, soul, 2. male, fellow, gentleman (*Slang* — chap, guy)   woman   MANKIND

manage   control, conduct, handle, direct, operate, work, regulate, govern, lead, supervise, administer, run (*Slang* — mastermind)   MANAGEMENT, MANAGER

mandate   command, order, dictate, injunction, referendum

maneuver   operate, work, run, conduct, handle, drive, manipulate, engineer, plot, scheme, intrigue, conspire, plan

mangle   cut, tear apart, lacerate, mutilate, maim, injure, hurt, wound

manhood   manliness, maturity, adulthood   youth

mania   craze, insanity, madness, infatuation, enthusiasm, desire (*Slang* — bug)

manifest   apparent, clear, plain, visible, open, exposed, perceptible, discernible, evident, obvious, open-and-shut   hidden, obscure   MANIFESTATION

manifold   many, various, multiple   few

manipulate   handle, manage, touch, feel, operate, work, conduct, maneuver

man-made   artificial, not natural   natural

manner   way, kind, mode, style, fashion, form, nature, character, means, method

manor   estate, land, property, domain, mansion, large house, palace, castle, villa, chateau

manslaughter   killing, homicide, murder, assassination, elimination

mantle   cloak, cover, coat, robe, wrap

manual   1. guidebook, directory, handbook, 2. by hand

manufacture make, invent, create, fashion, construct, build, erect, compose, prepare, devise, fabricate

manuscript writing, copy, composition, work, paper, document

many numerous, various, multitudinous, myriad, several, considerable (*Slang* — zillion) few

map chart

mar damage, injure, blemish, disfigure, scar, deform, spoil, ruin

marathon race, relay, contest

march walk, hike, parade, tramp

margin border, edge, rim, leeway, room

mariner sailor, seaman, navigator, tar, salt

marionette puppet, doll

mark 1. line, sign, evidence, indication, manifestation, 2. grade, rating

marked noticeable, plain, evident, noted, apparent, decided

market store, shop, mart

marriage union, joining, coupling, linking, wedding, matrimony, nuptials MARRY

marshal arrange, lead, conduct, escort, guide, usher, squire

mart market, shop, store

martial militant, warlike, military, combative, belligerent, aggressive, hostile peaceful

martyr sufferer, victim, tortured

marvelous wonderful, extraordinary, miraculous, astounding, superb, magnificent, glorious, divine, exceptional, remarkable MARVEL

masculine manly, strong, vigorous, virile

mash   crush, mix, soften, crumble, grind, grate, granulate, pulverize

mask   disguise, cover, camouflage

masquerade   disguise, pretend, impersonate, pose

mass   bulk, lump, quantity, load, amount, measure, volume, accumulation, hunk, chunk, lots, pile, stack, heap, slew, batch (*Slang* — gobs, scads, oodles)

massacre   slaughter, killing, butchery, carnage, pogrom

massage   rub, knead, stroke

massive   big, large, heavy, solid, sturdy, strong, clumsy, ponderous, thick, coarse   little

master   director, commander, ruler, head, controller, chief MASTERY

masterly   expert, skillful, proficient, adept, handy, clever (*Slang* — crackerjack)

mat   rug, cover

match   1. lighter, 2. contest, battle, engagement, encounter, game, sport, play, 3. duplicate, twin, double, companion, mate, fellow, counterpart, complement, equivalent, equal

mate   pair, couple, team

material   substance, fabric, stuff, matter, composition, goods

maternal   motherly   paternal, fatherly

mathematics   numbers, measurements, figures, calculation, computations   MATHEMATICAL, MATHEMATICIAN

matrimony   marriage, wedding, nuptials

matron   woman, lady

matter   1. material, substance, composition, content, 2. affair, business, concern, transaction, activity

mature   ripe, full-grown, developed, mellow, adult, ready immature   MATURITY

maul   bruise, batter, abuse

mausoleum   tomb, vault, crypt, shrine

maxim   proverb, rule, law, code, regulation, principle, adage, saying

maximum   largest, highest, greatest, uppermost, head, chief minimum

may   be able, can, be allowed

maybe   possibly, perhaps, conceivably, perchance

maze   network, complex, tangle, labyrinth, confusion, muddle

meadow   grassland, pasture, range, field

meager   poor, scanty, thin, lean, sparse, skimpy generous, abundant

meal   repast, spread

mean   1. signify, intend, denote, imply, indicate, suggest, connote, 2. petty, unkind, malicious, ill-humored, cross, irritable, testy pleasant, 3. average, medium, normal, middle   MEANING

meander   wander, wind, twist, stray

measure   size, grade, rank, compare, assess, appraise, estimate, rate   MEASUREMENT

mechanic   machinist, repairman, craftsman, technician MECHANICAL, MECHANISM

medal   award, honor, reward, medallion, prize

meddle   interfere, busybody, intrude, interrupt, intervene, trespass (*Slang* — barge in, butt in, horn in) MEDDLESOME

media   instruments, tools, agents, implements

mediate   make peace, settle, negotiate, intercede, intervene, referee, umpire, arbitrate   MEDIATION

medicinal healing, helping, relieving, remedial, corrective, therapeutic MEDICAL, MEDICINE

mediocre average, ordinary, fair, moderate, adequate, satisfactory, acceptable, passable, so-so MEDIOCRITY

meditate think, reflect, consider, contemplate, study, ponder, weigh, brood, deliberate MEDITATION

medium 1. middle, average, mean, halfway, mediocre, fair, 2. instrument, tool, agent, implement

medley mixture, hodgepodge, conglomeration, assortment, combination

meek mild, patient, submissive, gentle, tame, subdued, uncomplaining, passive, modest, unassuming, unpretentious aggressive

meet join, unite, connect, come together, assemble, gather, encounter, converge separate MEETING

melancholy sad, gloomy, blue, pensive, wistful, depressing, dismal cheerful

mellow mature, ripe, developed, full-grown, soft

melody tune, song MELODIOUS

melt dissolve, change, soften, liquefy solidify

member part, offshoot, branch, organ MEMBERSHIP

membrane covering, tissue, layer

memorable notable, rememberable

memorandum note, letter, report, reminder, memo

memorize learn by heart, remember MEMORY

menace threat

menagerie zoo, collection, kennel

mend repair, improve, fix, service, patch up, heal break, impair

mental intellectual, thinking, rational MENTALITY

mention   remark, comment, observe, say, note, state, name, specify, stipulate, designate

menu   list, account, bill of fare, line-up

merchandise   goods, wares, commodities, products
MERCHANT

mercy   kindness, compassion, pity, sympathy, charity
MERCIFUL

merely   simply, only, purely, barely   MERE

merge   absorb, swallow, combine, unite, mix, blend, fuse, join, mingle, scramble   separate   MERGER

merit   quality, value, worth, goodness, excellence, fineness

merry   gay, joyful, jolly, jovial, gleeful, mirthful, festive   sad, downcast   MERRILY, MERRIMENT

mesh   net, screen, web, complex

mess   dirty, disfigure, contaminate, pollute, corrupt

message   word, communication, dispatch, letter, epistle, note

mete   distribute, share, give, allot, grant, present, dispense, measure, deal out, dole out, hand out (*Slang* — dish out)

meteoric   swift, flashing, brief, blazing
METEOR, METEORITE

meter   measure, record, gauge

method   system, way, manner, means, mode, fashion, style, procedure, process, form, course, plan, scheme, design, arrangement   METHODICAL

metropolitan   city, civic, urban, municipal
METROPOLIS

mettle   spirit, courage, nerve, stamina, pluck, spunk (*Slang* — backbone, guts)

microscopic   infinitesimal, tiny, minute   huge
MICROSCOPE

middle   center, heart, core, nucleus, hub

midget   dwarf, pygmy, runt   giant

mien   manner, way, conduct, behavior, semblance

might   be able, can, be allowed

mighty   strong, powerful, great, grand, potent, powerful, forceful, vigorous, stout, sturdy, rugged, robust, hearty weak   MIGHT, MIGHTILY

migrant   roving, traveling, wandering, roaming, rambling, meandering, drifting, straying, transient   stationary MIGRATE, MIGRATION

mild   gentle, kind, calm, warm, temperate, moderate, lenient, good-natured, good-humored   harsh, violent

militant   fighting, warlike, combative, belligerent, aggressive, hostile, antagonistic, contentious, pugnacious, bellicose (*Slang* — scrappy)   peaceful

military   army, troops, soldiers, armed forces, service

mimic   imitate, copy, ape, mock, mime, parrot, copycat (*Slang* — take off on)

mince   chop, shatter, crush, smash, fragment

mind   1. brain, intelligence, mental ability, intellect, 2. obey, heed, regard, comply, listen to   ignore, 3. attend, watch, observe, notice, look after

mine   1. excavate, dig, scoop out, 2. blow up, blast

mingle   mix, associate, blend, combine

miniature   small, tiny, minute

minimum   least, lowest, smallest   maximum

minister   clergyman, spiritual guide, pastor, chaplain

minor   1. smaller, lesser, inferior, secondary, lower   major, 2. underage, immature

minstrel   musician, bard, troubadour

minus less, lacking, without, excepting, missing, absent

1. minute instant, moment, twinkling (*Slang* — jiffy, sec, half a shake)

2. minute small, tiny, miniature, slight, negligible, insignificant   large, significant

miraculous wonderful, marvelous, remarkable, extraordinary, phenomenal, incredible, awesome   MIRACLE

mire mud, slush, muck, slime

mirror reflect, echo, copy, imitate

mirth fun, laughter, merriment, joy, glee, levity, amusement   gloom, sadness

misbehave behave badly, act up (*Slang* — carry on, cut up)   behave

miscellaneous mixed, combined, blended, conglomerate, scrambled, jumbled

mischievous naughty, harmful, devilish, impish, playful, prankish, elfish   MISCHIEF

miser moneygrubber (*Slang* — scrimp, penny pincher)   spendthrift

miserable poor, mean, wretched, unhappy, pitiful, shabby, woeful, sorry   happy   MISERY

misfortune difficulty, trouble, distress, hardship, ruin, mishap, disaster, catastrophe, calamity, tragedy, accident   fortune, good luck

misgiving doubt, suspicion, anxiety, question, skepticism, qualm, concern, uneasiness

mishap misfortune, difficulty, trouble, distress, hardship, ruin, disaster, catastrophe, calamity, tragedy, accident   good luck, fortune

misjudge mistake, err, slip up, miscalculate

mislay   lose, miss, misplace   find

mislead   deceive, misdirect, misinform (*Slang* — give a bum steer)

misplace   mislay, lose, miss   find

miss   fail, lose, forfeit, sacrifice   get, succeed

misshapen   deformed, disfigured, grotesque

missile   rocket, projectile

missing   lacking, wanting, lost, absent, nonexistent, vanished, gone

mission   errand, business, purpose, task, work, stint, job, assignment, chore, charge, duty

mist   cloud, fog, vapor, haze, film, dimness, blur   MISTY

mistake   error, blunder, fault, slip, oversight, faux pas (*Slang* — boo-boo, boner)

mistreat   abuse, ill-treat, molest, bruise

mistress   woman, matron, housekeeper

mistrust   doubt, be skeptical, suspect, distrust, question, challenge, dispute   trust

misunderstanding   disagreement, difficulty, difference, misinterpretation, mistake, error   understanding

misuse   mishandle, treat badly

mitt   glove

mix   stir, join, blend, combine, fuse, mingle, merge   separate   MIXTURE

moan   wail, groan, howl, cry, bawl, suffer, agonize, complain

moat   trench, fortification, channel, ditch, entrenchment

mob   crowd, mass, throng, multitude, horde, pack, bunch

mobile   movable, changeable, fluid   immobile

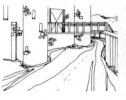

mock mimic, imitate, ape, ridicule, scoff, jeer, taunt, deride, laugh at (*Slang* — ride, pan, razz) MOCKERY

mode manner, way, style, fashion, form, vogue, custom, method

model copy, shape, design, reproduction, duplicate, replica, standard, prototype, image, likeness

moderate calm, fair, medium, mild, conservative, temperate, gentle, restrained, lenient extreme, harsh

modern contemporary, up-to-date, progressive, forward-looking archaic

modest humble, bashful, shy, quiet, unpretentious, plain, simple showy MODESTY

modify change, alter, vary, diversify, qualify, adjust, fix MODIFICATION

moist wet, damp, humid, dank, watery dry MOISTEN, MOISTURE

mold 1. shape, form, sculpture, carve, model, 2. decay, rot, spoil, deteriorate, disintegrate, crumble, go bad

molest trouble, injure, harm, hurt, damage, wrong, disturb, mistreat, annoy, abuse, torment, harass, badger, pester, plague

moment instant, minute, twinkling (*Slang* — jiffy, sec, half a shake) MOMENTARILY, MOMENTARY

momentous important, great, outstanding, considerable, eventful, stirring, influential, powerful, effective unimportant

momentum force, impetus, thrust, push

monarch ruler, sovereign, head, emperor, king, queen, chief

money currency, legal tender, cash, dollars (*Slang* — dough, jack, beans, wampum)

mongrel crossbreed, hybrid

monitor 1. helper, assistant, 2. recorder, clerk, 3. adviser, informant, counselor, reporter, announcer

monogram signature, mark, seal, stamp

monopoly control, corner, possession

monotonous boring, humdrum, repetitious, tedious, dreary, dull interesting MONOTONY

monsoon rains, storm, winds

monstrous horrible, dreadful, shocking, grotesque, deformed, disfigured MONSTER

monument tower, memorial, shrine, pillar

monumental important, weighty, great, vast, immense, stupendous, enormous, huge, notable, remarkable, memorable, extraordinary, exceptional, special (*Slang*—tremendous, terrific, whacking, thumping, rousing) insignificant

mood feeling, temperament, humor, disposition, nature, frame of mind, phase

moody gloomy, sullen, glum, mopish, morose, sulky cheerful

moor anchor, fasten, secure, dock, tie

mop wipe, wash, scrub, scour, swab

mope sulk, grieve, sorrow, brood over, fret rejoice

moral right, just, ethical, honorable, reputable, upstanding, respectable, law-abiding, virtuous, good, righteous immoral MORALS, MORALITY, MORALLY

morale spirit, enthusiasm

morass swamp, marsh, bog, mire

morbid 1. unhealthy, sickly, diseased, unwholesome healthy, 2. ghastly, horrible, dreadful, awful, shocking, appalling pleasant

more greater, further, farther, in addition, extra, another less

moreover   besides, also, furthermore, as well, too

morose   gloomy, sullen, sulky, moody, glum   cheerful

morsel   piece, fragment, particle, bit, crumb, scrap, shred

mortal   1. man, human being, person, soul, individual, body, 2. deadly, fatal, lethal, killing, destructive, malignant

mortify   wound, humiliate, shame, embarrass, disgrace
MORTIFICATION

most   greatest, extreme, maximum, supreme, highest, majority   least

mostly   mainly, chiefly, almost all, nearly

mother   1. originate, produce, cause, bring about, breed, 2. female parent, mommy, mama, mom   father, 3. care for, attend to, look after, watch, mind, foster, nurse, nurture
MOTHERHOOD, MOTHERLY

motion   1. movement, stir, activity, proceedings, doings, 2. suggestion, proposal, legislation, resolution, proposition

motive   reason, cause, ground, basis, motivation, prompting

motley   mixture, varied, assorted, diversified, various, several, many

motor   engine, machine

mottled   spotted, streaked, dappled, speckled, flecked, piebald

motto   saying, maxim, proverb, adage

mound   heap, hill, swell, pile, stack

mount   1. rise, get on, ascend, go up, climb, board   descend, 2. increase, gain, grow, advance   decrease, 3. position, place, fix, set   remove

mountain   1. hill, elevation, 2. large amount, quantity, volume, mass, abundance, much (*Slang* — heap, pile, stack, slew, batch, oodles, gobs, scads)

mourn   grieve, sorrow, lament, bewail, bemoan   rejoice
MOURNFUL

move   1. change, budge, stir, stimulate, impel, motivate, animate, 2. influence, sway, affect, persuade, induce, arouse, prompt, convince   MOVABLE, MOVEMENT

mow   cut, clip, crop, prune, shear, shave

much   quantity, abundance, volume, mass

mucilage   glue, adhesive, cement, paste

muck   dirt, filth, rot, slime, mire

mud   mire, muck, slush, slime, dirt

muddle   mess, disorder, confusion, chaos (*Slang* — mix-up, foul-up, snafu, hassle)

muff   bungle, blunder, fumble, botch, spoil, mess (*Slang* — foul up, louse up, goof up, gum up)

muffle   silence, mute, dull, soften, deaden, cushion, smother, stifle, suppress   MUFFLER

muggy   warm, damp, close, stuffy, humid, dank, sticky

mulish   stubborn, obstinate, willful, headstrong, tenacious, unyielding, inflexible, rigid, adamant

multiply   increase, advance, gain, grow, rise, procreate

mum   silent, mute, speechless, quiet

mumble   mutter, speak indistinctly   shout

municipal   civic, urban, metropolitan

murder   1. kill, assassinate, eliminate, purge, liquidate, slaughter, massacre, 2. spoil, ruin, botch, muff, mar, butcher, make a mess (*Slang* — foul up, louse up, goof up, gum up)
MURDERER, MURDEROUS

murky   dark, gloomy   light, cheerful   MURK

murmur mutter, whisper shout

muscle strength, brawn (*Slang* — beefiness) MUSCULAR

muse dream, think, envision, ponder, contemplate, reflect, deliberate, consider

musical melodious, tuneful, lyrical, dulcet, harmonious MUSIC, MUSICIAN

muss rumple, mess, disarrange, disorganize, disarray, litter, clutter arrange, fix

must should, ought to, be obliged to, have to, need to, be forced to

muster assemble, gather, collect, summon, cluster, accumulate, amass, group, compile, recruit scatter, disperse

musty moldy, mildewed

mute silent, dumb, voiceless, speechless

mutilate cut, tear, break off, amputate, clip, lacerate

mutiny rebellion, revolt, riot, insurrection, uprising, insurgence MUTINEER, MUTINOUS

mutter mumble, complain, grumble, murmur, whisper

mutual reciprocal, joint, common

muzzle silence, restrain, gag, bind, bridle

myriad many, numerous, multitudinous, considerable (*Slang* — quite some, zillion)

mysterious secret, hidden, profound, mystical, recondite, occult MYSTERY

mystify bewilder, puzzle, perplex, baffle, confound (*Slang* — bamboozle, stick, stump, floor, get, beat, throw, lick)

myth legend, story, fiction, fantasy, fable, fairy tale, falsehood, fabrication truth MYTHICAL, MYTHOLOGY

N

nag 1. pester, annoy, bother, pick on (*Slang* — bug), 2. horse, pony

nail 1. fasten, hold, fix, secure, 2. catch, seize, hook, snare, trap, capture, apprehend (*Slang* — land, rope, collar, grab) release

naked uncovered, exposed, nude, bare, undressed (*Slang* — in the buff, in the altogether, in the raw)   covered

name title, label, tag, appellation   (*Slang* — moniker, handle)

nap sleep, doze, drowse, siesta (*Slang* — snooze)

narcotics drugs, opiates, tranquilizers, sedatives, barbiturates (*Slang* — dope, junk, pot, goofballs)

narrate tell, relate, recount, report, recite, review, describe NARRATIVE, NARRATOR

narrow slender, close, tight, restricted, cramped, confined, meager, limited   wide

nasty unpleasant, revolting, disgusting, repulsive, offensive, foul, vile, sickening, nauseating, filthy, odious, obnoxious, dirty (*Slang* — icky, ugly)

nation country, land, society, community NATIONAL, NATIONALITY

native natural, original, indigenous   foreign

natural genuine, typical, real, authentic, legitimate, honest, pure, original, true, characteristic, normal   unnatural, false NATURE

naturally of course, plainly, certainly, surely, indeed (*Slang* — you bet, you bet your life, you bet your boots)

naught nothing, zero, nil

naughty bad, disobedient, misbehaving, disorderly, evil, wrong

navigate sail, steer, cruise, guide
NAVIGATION, NAVIGATOR

near close, imminent, at hand far

nearly almost, close to, just about, approximately

neat 1. clean, orderly, trim, tidy, shipshape, well-kept disorderly, sloppy, 2. skillful, clever, apt, adept, proficient, handy, expert, masterful, well-done (*Slang* — cute, crack, crackerjack)

necessary required, compulsory, urgent, important, imperative, obligatory, compelling, needed, essential, exigent unnecessary

need want, lack, require NEEDY

neglect overlook, disregard, ignore, pass over, slight, be inattentive, be careless, be thoughtless, be inconsiderate care

negligent careless, indifferent, neglectful, inattentive, remiss careful NEGLIGENCE

negotiate arrange, talk over, settle, mediate, intervene, umpire, arbitrate, referee (*Slang* — deal)

neighboring near, bordering, next to, adjoining, adjacent, surrounding NEIGHBOR, NEIGHBORHOOD

neighborly friendly, kind, amiable, congenial, cordial, warm, amicable unfriendly

nerve strength, courage, stamina, daring, bravado, mettle (*Slang* — spunk, cheek, backbone, guts, gall, crust)

nervous excited, upset, restless, disturbed, ruffled, shaken, flustered, agitated, perturbed, high-strung, tense, strained, edgy, jittery calm, composed

nestle snuggle, cuddle, hold closely

net 1. trap, snare, 2. lacelike cloth, mesh, web, 3. gain, earn, acquire, get, obtain, secure

nettle irritate, provoke, annoy, vex, anger, disturb

neutral impartial, detached, unprejudiced, cool, independent, indifferent involved

nevertheless however, notwithstanding, although, but, regardless, anyway

new fresh, modern, recent, original, young, unused, firsthand old

news tidings, information, word, story

next following, nearest, closest, succeeding, successive, subsequent

nibble chew, munch

nice pleasing, agreeable, satisfactory, enjoyable, desirable, gratifying, good, fine

niche nook, corner, cranny, recess, alcove

nick notch, cut, dash, indentation

niggardly stingy, cheap, miserly (*Slang* — tight, penny-pinching)

nimble light, quick, active, fast, swift, speedy, agile (*Slang* — quick on the trigger, snappy) slow

nip 1. pinch, bite, squeeze, 2. cold, chill, crispness, 3. small drink, sip (*Slang* — swig)

noble great, grand, majestic, distinguished, lofty, eminent, prominent, important, grandiose, magnificent, stately, dignified, aristocratic common NOBILITY

nocturnal nightly

nod bow, bob, tip, bend, signal

noise sounds, racket, clamor, din, clatter, uproar, tumult,

bedlam, hubbub, commotion, ballyhoo, rumpus (*Slang* — ruckus) quiet NOISILY, NOISY

nomad wanderer, traveler, rover, roamer, vagrant, migrant

nomination naming, appointment, selection, choice, designation NOMINATE

nonchalant indifferent, unconcerned, cool, blasé, lackadaisical, easygoing, devil-may-care, casual

nonsense foolishness, ridiculousness, folly, absurdity, stupidity, rubbish, poppycock (*Slang* — bunk, hooey, baloney)

nook corner, niche, cranny, recess, alcove

noose rope, snare, lasso

normal usual, regular, average, standard, ordinary, typical, characteristic, true to form abnormal, unusual

notable striking, important, remarkable, noteworthy, memorable, special, extraordinary, exceptional, rare, famous, distinguished, renowned, celebrated, well-known, prominent, popular, notorious

notch nick, cut, gash, indentation

note 1. write, record, inscribe, list, mark down, jot down, indicate, mark, comment, 2. observe, heed, regard, notice

notice note, observe, heed, regard, see NOTICEABLE

notify announce to, inform, advise, report, tell, instruct, remind, warn (*Slang* — post, tip, tattle, squeal, snitch, blabber)

notion idea, understanding, opinion, view, belief, thought, impression, sentiment

notorious famous, renowned, celebrated, popular, well-known, infamous

nourish feed, nurture, nurse, strengthen, sustain, maintain NOURISHMENT

novel   new, original, fresh, unique, firsthand, different, unusual   NOVELTY

novice   beginner, newcomer, tyro, greenhorn, freshman (*Slang* — rookie)

now   1. at once, immediately, right away   later, 2. presently, today, at this time

noxious   harmful, poisonous, damaging, detrimental, toxic   harmless

nucleus   middle, core, heart, kernel, hub, focus

nudge   push, prod, shove, poke, jab, prompt

nugget   lump, clump, mass, wad, hunk, chunk

nuisance   annoyance, pest, bother, trouble, irritation (*Slang* — headache, pain in the neck)

numb   dull, unfeeling, deadened, insensitive

number   1. quantity, sum, count, collection, amount, measure, bulk, portion, multitude, 2. numeral, figure, digit, symbol

numeral   number, figure, digit, symbol

numerous   many, multitudinous, several, abundant, various, myriad, considerable (*Slang* — zillion)   few

nurse   nurture, nourish, foster, feed, sustain, care for, tend to, mind

nurture   rear, bring up, foster, train, care for, raise, feed, tend, mind, nurse, nourish

nutrition   food, nourishment   NUTRITIOUS

O

oaf   lummox, clown, clod, lout, fool, dunce, blockhead (*Slang* — dope, jerk)

oath   promise, pledge, vow, agreement, commitment, bond

obey   yield, submit, comply, mind, heed, listen to
disobey, resist   OBEDIENCE, OBEDIENT

object   1. thing, article, 2. purpose, end, goal, target, intent, aim

objection   protest, challenge, dissent, disapproval, complaint, criticism (*Slang* — kick, squawk, howl)   approval

obligate   require, oblige, bind, pledge, compel, force
OBLIGATION

obliging   helpful, considerate, thoughtful, accommodating, well-meaning   discourteous

obliterate   destroy, erase, blot out, wipe out, demolish, delete

oblivious   unconscious, senseless, preoccupied, forgetful
mindful, aware   OBLIVION

obnoxious   offensive, disagreeable, hateful, nasty, repulsive, disgusting, loathsome, vile, terrible, dreadful, deplorable, wretched, abominable, detestable, despicable, contemptible (*Slang* — awful, atrocious, impossible)   pleasant

obscene   dirty, smutty, filthy, lewd, bawdy, pornographic, unclean, indecent   decent, clean

obscure   indistinct, unclear, indefinite, faint, dim, vague, dark, shadowy, blurred, fuzzy, hazy   clear   OBSCURITY

observe   1. see, note, examine, study, perceive, behold, inspect, scrutinize, contemplate, review, 2. celebrate, commemorate, 3. keep, practice, obey, comply with, heed, follow   neglect, ignore
OBSERVANCE, OBSERVANT, OBSERVATION

obsolete   extinct, passé, old-fashioned, dated, outmoded, discontinued, antiquated (*Slang* — old hat, has-been)
recent, stylish

obstacle barrier, obstruction, block, stoppage, hindrance, deterrent, impediment, hitch, snag, catch

obstinate stubborn, willful, headstrong, bullheaded, pig-headed, unyielding, unbending, inflexible, adamant, firm, stiff, rigid   flexible

obstruct block, hinder, clog, bar, impede, delay   aid, help OBSTRUCTION

obtain get, acquire, gain, secure, procure, earn, receive   lose

obtuse 1. slow, stupid, dense, slow-witted   bright, quick, 2. blunt, dull, unsharpened   sharp

obvious plain, understandable, apparent, clear, evident, manifest, explicit, distinct   hidden

occasionally sometimes, now and then, once in a while, from time to time   OCCASION, OCCASIONAL

occupant tenant, resident, lodger, inhabitant, dweller, boarder   OCCUPANCY

occupation 1. business, employment, trade, work, activity, affair, matter, concern, interest, capacity, role, function, duty, task, stint, job, 2. possession, holding, ownership OCCUPY

occur happen, take place, transpire, come about OCCURRENCE

odd 1. strange, peculiar, queer, unusual, curious, unique, eccentric, weird, bizarre (*Slang* — funny, screwy, nutty, wacky) usual, ordinary, 2. extra, left over, remaining, spare ODDITY, ODDLY

odious hateful, offensive, displeasing, revolting, repulsive, disgusting, vile, foul, obnoxious, horrible, terrible, dreadful, wretched (*Slang* — awful, beastly, impossible, atrocious) pleasant

odor smell, fragrance, scent, essence, aroma

offend displease, hurt, pain, grieve, wound, disgust, sicken, horrify, affront, insult   please
OFFENDER, OFFENSE, OFFENSIVE

offer present, propose, suggest, submit, try, attempt
OFFERING

office 1. position, duty, task, job, work, function, capacity, role, post, 2. room, workplace, headquarters, studio, department (*Slang* — shop)

offset balance, cushion, compensate, counteract, soften, neutralize

offshoot addition, branch, byproduct, outgrowth, appendage, supplement, accessory

offspring child, descendant, young (*Slang* — kid)

often repeatedly, many times, frequently   seldom

ogre monster, fiend, demon, devil

old 1. aged, ancient, antique, elderly, mature   young, new, 2. former, obsolete, abandoned, discontinued, stale, outworn, discarded   recent

omen sign, indication, warning, portent

ominous threatening, unfavorable, sinister, menacing

omit neglect, exclude, leave out, bar, miss, skip   include
OMISSION

omnipotent almighty, all-powerful, divine

one-sided partial, unfair, prejudiced, biased
neutral, impartial

onlooker spectator, observer, watcher, bystander, witness

only just, merely, simply

onset 1. beginning, commencement, start, opening   end, 2. attack, assault, offense, charge, drive, onslaught (*Slang* — push)

onslaught attack, assault, onset, offense, charge, drive, push

onward further, forward, ahead backward

ooze leak, seep, filter, drip, flow

opaque dark, dull, filmy, cloudy, obtuse, murky, obscure, vague, unclear, indistinct clear, transparent

open 1. begin, start, launch, initiate, unfold, establish, originate close, 2. expose, uncover, disclose, reveal, show, bare cover OPENING

openly frankly, sincerely, freely secretly

operate work, run, manage, conduct, carry on, handle, function, perform, act OPERATION, OPERATOR

opinion belief, judgment, estimate, impression, feeling, sentiment, attitude, view, theory, conception, thought, idea, outlook, conviction

opponent enemy, foe, adversary, competitor, rival, combatant, contender ally, friend

opportunity chance, occasion, time, opening, turn, spell

oppose fight, struggle, resist, hinder, contradict, conflict with, counteract, refute, dispute, cross agree OPPOSITE, OPPOSITION

oppressive harsh, severe, unjust, burdensome, overbearing, domineering, dictatorial, tyrannical OPPRESS, OPPRESSION, OPPRESSOR

optical visual, seeing

optimistic cheerful, happy, bright, pleasant, radiant, glad, lighthearted, jaunty, carefree pessimistic

optional voluntary, elective required OPTION

oral spoken, voiced, vocalized, sounded, articulated, verbal, uttered, said ORALLY

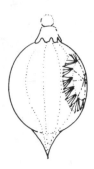

orb sphere, globe, ball

orbit path, circuit, circle, revolution, route

orchestra band, ensemble

ordain order, decide, decree, command, dictate, direct, instruct, bid, rule, authorize, sanction ORDINANCE

ordeal experience, test, trial, tribulation

order 1. arrangement, condition, state, manner, mode, way, disposition, formation, system, 2. command, bid, direction, instruction ORDERLY

ordinary 1. usual, common, normal, average, regular, every-day, standard unusual, special, 2. mediocre, inferior, poor, so-so outstanding, exceptional ORDINARILY

organize arrange, classify, systematize, categorize, sort, group, set up, establish, orient ORGANIZATION

origin 1. beginning, start, infancy, birth, inception, 2. source, parentage, derivation, root
ORIGINAL, ORIGINALITY, ORIGINALLY
ORIGINATE

ornament decoration, adornment, embellishment, garnish, trimming ORNAMENTAL, ORNATE

ornery unruly, disobedient, rebellious, contrary, obstinate, stubborn, willful, headstrong, firm, stiff, rigid, adamant, difficult, mean, malicious, disagreeable, cross, irritable, cranky pleasant

orthodox usual, customary, conventional, traditional, accepted, proper, correct unorthodox, different

ostentatious showy, flashy, pretentious, overdone, garish, fancy, swanky (*Slang* — classy, ritzy)

other different, distinct, additional, extra, supplementary, further, fresh, new

ought should, be obliged, must, need to, have to

outbreak revolt, riot, disturbance, uprising, rebellion, eruption, outburst, torrent

outburst eruption, outbreak, torrent, discharge, ejection

outcast homeless, friendless, abandoned, deserted, forlorn, forsaken, derelict, rejected, disowned

outcome result, consequence, effect, upshot, fruit, conclusion

outcry noise, clamor, uproar

outdated old, old-fashioned, outmoded, unfashionable
stylish

outdo surpass, excel, outshine, defeat, beat (*Slang* — lick, whip, trim) OUTDID, OUTDONE

outfit equip, furnish, prepare, rig, fit

outgrowth product, result, effect, consequence, outcome, fruit, upshot, byproduct

outing trip, journey, jaunt, excursion

outlandish odd, queer, peculiar, curious, strange, weird (*Slang* — funny)

outlaw outcast, exile, criminal, convict (*Slang* — crook, gangster)

outlay spending, expense, costs

outline 1. plan, sketch, diagram, chart, draft, pattern, drawing, 2. profile, contour, skeleton

outlook view, attitude, position

outlying remote, external, outer

outnumber exceed

output yield, production, proceeds, crop, harvest

outrageous shocking, insulting, absurd, nonsensical, ridiculous, foolish, crazy, preposterous, bizarre, excessive, extreme, exorbitant, disgraceful, shameful, scandalous, unwarranted OUTRAGE

outright altogether, entirely, completely, thoroughly, wholly, fully, totally, quite, freely, openly, downright

outset start, beginning, commencement, opening

outspoken frank, unreserved, unrestrained, open, vocal, candid, straightforward, direct, forthright shy, reserved

outstanding important, well-known, great, eminent, famous, prominent, distinguished, conspicuous, significant, noticeable, striking, bold unimportant, insignificant

outwit outmaneuver, outdo, outsmart

overbearing masterful, domineering, dictatorial, autocratic, arbitrary, arrogant, bossy humble

overcast cloudy, dark, gloomy, dismal, somber, bleak, hazy, misty clear, bright

overcome conquer, defeat, upset, overpower, surmount (*Slang* — smear, clobber, shellac)

overdo exaggerate, stretch, magnify, enlarge, carry too far, go to extremes

overflow flood, run over, cascade, spill, inundate

overhaul repair, service, mend, fix, condition

overhead 1. above, high, aloft, 2. costs, expenses

overjoyed delighted, enchanted, ecstatic, elated, enraptured, jubilant depressed

overlook 1. neglect, ignore, disregard, pass over, skip, let slip, miss note, notice, 2. face, view, watch

overpass bridge, span, viaduct

overpower master, overwhelm, surmount, defeat, conquer, crush, vanquish (*Slang* — lick, smear, clobber, shellac)

overrun exceed, spread, infest, beset, abound, flood

oversee   supervise, manage, direct, superintend, administer, preside, boss

oversight   error, slip, negligence, omission

overstep   exceed, go beyond, surpass, transcend, trespass

overthrow   defeat, destroy, overcome, overpower, overturn, upset, unseat, dethrone

overture   1. proposal, offer, bid, 2. prelude, introduction finale

overwhelm   1. crush, overcome, defeat, surmount, conquer, vanquish (*Slang* — lick, smear, clobber, shellac), 2. astonish, surprise, amaze, astound, bewilder, startle, dumbfound, flabbergast

owe   be indebted, be obliged, be liable

own   have, possess, hold, maintain, monopolize
OWNER, OWNERSHIP

P

pace   1. rate, speed, 2. stride, gait, step, walk, tread

pacify   quiet, calm, tranquilize, soothe, appease, placate, mollify   anger, provoke   PACIFIC, PACIFICATION

pack   fill, load, stuff, cram, stow, box   unpack, empty
PACKAGE

pact   agreement, contract, understanding, bargain, treaty, alliance

pad   1. cushion, pillow, wadding, 2. notebook, tablet, ledger, album

paddle   1. spank, whip, beat, lick, wallop, 2. oar

padlock   bolt, bar, lock

page 1. paper, sheet, leaf, 2. attendant, usher, errand boy, servant

pageant show, spectacle, pomp, display, entertainment, exhibition, presentation, parade, review

pail bucket

pain suffering, hurt, discomfort, distress, ache, pang, soreness, irritation PAINFUL

painstaking careful, particular, thorough, elaborate, diligent, exacting, meticulous, scrupulous, precise, accurate careless

paint 1. coat, color, cover, decorate, trim, garnish, 2. draw, sketch, picture, depict, draft, portray, represent PAINTING

pair set, two, couple, both, twins, mates, team, duo

pal friend, playmate, companion, fellow, comrade, associate, colleague, partner, crony (*Slang* — buddy, chum, sidekick)

palace castle, mansion, villa, chateau

palatable delicious, luscious, delectable, savory, tasty (*Slang* — scrumptious, yummy)

pale dim, colorless, faint, weak, vague, indistinct, lifeless, pallid, wan, sallow, whitish bright, vivid

palpitate tremble, quiver, beat, throb, pulsate, flutter

paltry trifling, petty, worthless, poor, miserable, cheap

pamper humor, favor, indulge, cater to, oblige, coddle, spoil

pamphlet booklet, brochure, leaflet, folder

panel 1. group, forum, board, 2. partition, wall, division, separation, barrier

pang pain, hurt, discomfort, distress, ache, soreness, irritation

panic fear, fright, scare, alarm, dread, awe, terror, phobia

panorama   scene, vista, lookout, sight

pant   breathe, puff, gasp, wheeze

pants   trousers, breeches

par   average, normal

parade   procession, show, display, review, promenade, march, exhibition, pageant

paradise   heaven, bliss, glory, ecstasy, elation, enchantment

paralyze   deaden, numb, desensitize, disable, cripple

paramount   most important, chief, foremost, principal, main, leading, dominant, primary, top, uppermost, maximum

parcel   package, bundle, pack, lot

parched   thirsty, dry, dehydrated

pardon   forgive, excuse, absolve, exonerate, exculpate, acquit, vindicate

pare   peel, trim, skin, strip, scrape

park   1. land, reservation, sanctuary, 2. settle, place, put, set, station

parry   avoid, evade, dodge, hedge, ward off, sidestep (*Slang* — duck)

part   1. portion, segment, fraction, share, division, section, component, cut, 2. role

partake   share, participate, contribute, join in (*Slang* — get into the act)

partial   partly, fractional, fragmentary, limited

participate   partake, contribute, take part in, have a hand in, enter into, join in PARTICIPANT

particular   1. special, unusual, different ordinary, 2. meticulous, critical, discriminating, fastidious, finicky, exacting, fussy

parting   departure, going away, leaving, exit, withdrawal   arriving

partition   separation, division, wall

partner   companion, mate, collaborator, assistant, participant, comrade, colleague (*Slang* — sidekick)
PARTNERSHIP

party   1. group, company, gang, crew, body, band, faction, 2. person, individual, fellow, 3. festival, fete, affair, ball, celebration (*Slang* — blowout, jamboree, shindig)

pass   1. succeed, do well   fail, 2. spend, use, employ, 3. deliver, hand over, transfer, 4. go, travel, move, progress
PASSING

passage   1. corridor, hallway, arcade, entranceway, opening, lane, channel, artery, passageway, 2. section, paragraph, chapter, excerpt, selection, extract, 3. voyage, cruise, crossing, trip, trek

passageway   passage, corridor, hallway, arcade, entranceway, opening, lane, channel, artery

passion   1. emotion, strong feeling, fervor, craze, enthusiasm, 2. rage, anger, fury, violence, 3. love, affection, fondness, ardor, lust, desire   PASSIONATE

passive   inactive, dormant, submissive, unresisting, compliant, yielding, docile, mild, gentle   forceful

past   ended, gone by, former, over, previous, preceding   future

paste   glue, adhesive, cement, mucilage

pastel   pale, soft, light, fair

pastime   recreation, amusement, enjoyment, diversion, relaxation

pasture   grassland, meadow, range

pat   tap, stroke, rap

patch mend, repair, fix, service

paternal fatherly maternal, motherly

path route, track, way, trail, road, line

pathetic pitiful, touching, moving, sad, distressing

patience tolerance, endurance, indulgence, perseverance, persistence (*Slang* — stick-to-it-iveness) impatience PATIENT

patriotic loyal, nationalistic, chauvinistic PATRIOT, PATRIOTISM

patrol watch, guard, protect, keep vigil, police

patronize 1. deal with, trade with, 2. back, sponsor, finance, promote, support PATRON, PATRONAGE

patter 1. drum, beat, pound, throb, 2. chatter, chat, prattle, babble, jabber, blab

pattern 1. arrangement, design, illustration, picture, print, 2. model, example, standard, prototype, paragon

pauper poor man

pause wait, stop, rest, recess, cease (*Slang* — take time out, knock off)

pave cover, floor PAVEMENT

pavilion building, structure, edifice

paw handle, touch, feel

pawn pledge, deposit (*Slang* — hock)

pay give, remunerate, compensate PAYMENT

peaceful quiet, calm, still, tranquil, placid, untroubled, pacific, serene, cool troubled PEACE, PEACEABLE

peak top, crest, hilltop, summit, pinnacle, crown, tip, apex, acme, zenith

peal ring, chime, toll

peculiar 1. strange, odd, unusual, queer, curious ordinary, 2. special, distinctive, characteristic, typical, representative PECULIARITY

pedal drive, push, roll

peddle vend, sell, hawk PEDDLER

pedestrian walker, hiker (*Slang* — hoofer)

peek glance, glimpse, peep, look slyly

peel strip, pare, skin

peep peek, glance, glimpse, look slyly

peer 1. equal, match, equivalent, like, 2. look, peek, peep

peevish cross, complaining, fretful, petulant

pell-mell headlong, tumultuous, hastily, hurriedly, quickly, swiftly, speedily

pelt 1. attack, strike, pound, beat, knock, hammer, rap, bang, whip, thrash, wallop, 2. skin, hide, fur

pen 1. write, inscribe, record, 2. enclose, confine, shut in, surround, coop up

penalize punish, chastise, discipline, castigate PENALTY

pending waiting, until, during

penetrate 1. pierce, enter, puncture, bore, perforate, 2. understand, perceive, see through PENETRATION

penitence sorrow, repentance, penance

penmanship handwriting, script, calligraphy

pennant flag, banner, streamer, ensign, standard, colors

penniless poor, destitute, down-and-out, bankrupt (*Slang* — broke, busted, flat, strapped)

pension allowance, aid, assistance, help, subsidy, grant, stipend

pensive thoughtful, contemplative, reflective, meditative, deliberating, absorbed, engrossed, melancholy, serious, wistful

people persons, folks, community, society, public, human beings, men

pep spirit, energy, vim, vigor, verve, punch, dash, drive, animation, life, vivacity   apathy

perceive sense, observe, feel, experience, detect, recognize, distinguish, make out   PERCEPTION

percentage proportion, part, ratio, rate, quota (*Slang* — cut, divvy)

perch rest, sit, settle, straddle

perchance perhaps, possibly, maybe, conceivably

perennial continuous, constant, perpetual, steady, regular

perfect faultless, flawless, ideal, correct, accurate, right imperfect, faulty   PERFECTION

perforate pierce, penetrate, puncture, enter, bore PERFORATION

perform do, act, execute, transact, carry out, accomplish, achieve   PERFORMANCE, PERFORMER

perhaps possibly, maybe, conceivably

peril danger, harm, jeopardy, hazard, risk, endangerment PERILOUS

period interval, span, time

periodical magazine, journal, gazette

perish die, decease, succumb, disappear, vanish, decay PERISHABLE

permanent lasting, durable, enduring, long-lasting, unchanging, constant, stable, steady   temporary PERMANENCE

permeate penetrate, spread through, pervade, saturate, soak

permit allow, consent, let, grant, admit PERMISSION

pernicious harmful, hurtful, damaging, injurious, detrimental, malignant, deadly, destructive, fatal, mortal harmless

perpendicular upright, vertical

perpetrate commit, effect, achieve (*Slang* — pull off)

perpetual eternal, lasting, continuous, unceasing, permanent, infinite, endless, incessant, constant short-lived, brief PERPETUATE

perplex puzzle, bewilder, baffle, confound, mystify (*Slang* — bamboozle, stump, floor, get, beat, buffalo, throw) PERPLEXITY

persecute harm, oppress, torment, harass, molest, torture, antagonize, badger

persevere persist, endure, continue, carry on, keep on PERSEVERANCE

persist last, stay, continue, endure, prevail, go on, persevere (*Slang* — stick with it) PERSISTENCE, PERSISTENT

person individual, soul, somebody, someone

personal private, special, individual, specific, particular impersonal PERSONALLY

personality identity, individuality

perspire sweat PERSPIRATION

persuade convince, convict, convert, win over, induce (*Slang* — sell) dissuade PERSUASION, PERSUASIVE

pert bold, saucy, flippant, forward, impudent, impertinent, brazen, perky, flip, cocky, cheeky (*Slang* — smart-alecky, fresh, crusty, nervy, sassy) courteous, polite

pertain belong, relate, be appropriate, be connected, refer, apply, concern PERTINENT

perturb disturb, trouble, distress, bother, agitate, upset

peruse examine, study, inspect, review, read carefully

pervade fill, permeate, penetrate, overrun

perverse 1. stubborn, contrary, willful, difficult, obstinate, 2. wrong, incorrect, untrue, false, erroneous, 3. wicked, corrupt PERVERSION

perverted distorted, twisted, warped, contorted normal

pessimistic unhappy, cheerless, joyless, gloomy, cynical optimistic, cheerful PESSIMISM, PESSIMIST

pester annoy, vex, trouble, torment, molest, bother, harass, badger, tease, nag (*Slang* — pick on, ride) PEST

pestilence plague, epidemic, disease

pet stroke, pat, caress, fondle

petite little, small, slight, tiny big

petition request, demand, requisition, appeal, plea

petrify 1. terrify, horrify, shock, appall, frighten, stun, 2. harden, solidify, become stone

petty 1. unimportant, small, trivial, puny, minor, inferior important, 2. mean, base, low, wretched, miserable, despicable, contemptible

petulant irritable, peevish, fretful, grouchy

phantom illusion, fantasy, apparition, specter, ghost, spirit, vision, spook

pharmacist druggist, chemist PHARMACY

phase stage, state, aspect

phenomenal extraordinary, exceptional, remarkable, wonderful, marvelous, miraculous PHENOMENON

philanthropic charitable, kindly, benevolent, bighearted, generous, giving, humanitarian selfish, stingy
PHILANTHROPIST, PHILANTHROPY

philosophical wise, reasonable, calm
PHILOSOPHER, PHILOSOPHY

photograph snap, film, take a picture (*Slang* — shoot, mug)
PHOTOGRAPHER, PHOTOGRAPHY

phrase clause, part, section, passage

physician doctor, medic

physique figure, form, shape, build, body, frame

pick choose, select, harvest, gather, cull

picket 1. strike, boycott, revolt, 2. bar, fence, wall, enclose

pickle preserve, marinate

pickpocket rob

picnic feast, outing, festivity

picture represent, illustrate, portray, depict, describe, characterize

piece part, bit, portion, division, segment, section, share (*Slang* — cut)

pier dock, wharf, breakwater

pierce penetrate, puncture, perforate, stab, bore

pigment coloring, shade, stain, dye

pile heap, stack, mound, collection, slew, batch

pilfer steal, thieve, take, filch, rob (*Slang* — lift, cop, pinch)

pilgrimage journey, trip, trek, expedition, crusade
PILGRIM

pillage plunder, rob, loot, burglarize (*Slang* — hold up, stick up)

pillar column, support, shaft, monument, post

pillow   cushion, headrest, bolster

pilot   operator, driver, engineer, conductor

pimple   swelling, bump, boil

pin   clasp, fasten, hook, clip

pinch   squeeze, press, tweak, nip

pinnacle   peak, high point, crest, top, spire, summit, crown, apex, acme, zenith   bottom, base

pioneer   settler, leader, colonist, forerunner

pious   religious, devout, reverent, faithful, believing atheistic   PIETY

pipe   tube, reed, hose

pique   arouse, stir, incite, instigate, agitate, inflame, invoke, excite, foment, infuriate, exasperate, annoy, anger, disturb, aggravate, peeve, rile   soothe, calm

piracy   stealing, pillaging, plundering, looting, thievery PIRATE

pistol   gun, firearm, revolver (*Slang* — shooting iron, gat, rod)

pit   hole, cavity, crater, hollow

pitch   1. throw, fling, hurl, toss, sling, cast, heave, 2. sway, fall, topple, flounder, stagger, rock, roll, reel, lurch

pitfall   trap, snare

pity   sympathy, sorrow, compassion, mercy PITEOUS, PITIABLE, PITIFUL

pivot   turn, swivel, swing, rotate, wheel, gyrate

placard   poster, notice, sign, billboard

place   arrange, fix, compose, put, locate, situate, set, station

placid   calm, peaceful, quiet, still, tranquil, smooth, pacific, untroubled

plague 1. disease, epidemic, pestilence, 2. annoy, vex, bother, torment, molest, trouble, harass, badger, worry, pester, haunt soothe, comfort

plain 1. clear, understandable, simple, distinct, obvious, evident complex, involved, 2. homely, ordinary, unattractive pretty

plan propose, intend, design, mean, aim, think, devise, arrange, plot, scheme, maneuver, project

plane 1. flat, level, horizontal, even, smooth uneven, 2. airplane, aircraft

plank board, wood

plant establish, fix, root, settle, sow

plastic changeable, variable, mobile, fluid, flexible, pliant, supple rigid, fixed

platform 1. stage, rostrum, balcony, 2. policy, program, plan, course

plausible reasonable, logical, sound, sensible, believable unbelievable

playful frisky, sportive, gay, spirited, lively, animated, vivacious, frolicsome, impish, mischievous, devilish
serious, solemn PLAY

plaza square

plea 1. request, appeal, petition, asking, 2. excuse, defense
PLEAD

pleasant pleasing, enjoyable, likable, desirable, agreeable, gratifying, delightful, charming, appealing, enchanting, cheerful, genial, happy, satisfying unpleasant, displeasing
PLEASURE

pleat fold, crease, tuck

pledge promise, vow, oath, assurance, guarantee, word

plentiful ample, enough, abundant, generous, sufficient, lavish scarce, insufficient PLENTY

pliable flexible, supple, plastic, elastic, yielding, limber, suggestible, compliant rigid PLIANT

plight predicament, pinch, complication, muddle, difficulty, dilemma (*Slang* — pickle, spot, jam, hole, hot water, mess, stew)

plod trudge, lumber (*Slang* — plug away, grind)

plot 1. plan, scheme, intrigue, conspire, contrive, maneuver, concoct, 2. outline, sketch, graph, map, chart, blueprint, diagram

plow cultivate, work, till, furrow

pluck pull, pick, jerk, tug, yank

plucky courageous, spirited, brave, bold, valiant, gallant, heroic, resolute, game, mettlesome, spunky, nervy
fearful, timid

plug block, clog, stop, obstruct, stuff, jam, congest

plump fat, round, stuffed, stout, obese, fleshy, corpulent, pudgy, chubby, stocky, chunky, tubby thin

plunder rob, steal, loot, pillage, fleece

plunge dive, plummet, drop, fall, swoop down

plush luxurious, sumptuous, elegant, elaborate, grand, magnificent, glorious, impressive, majestic (*Slang* — swell)
poor

pocket load, pack, stow, take in, accept, receive, take, get, acquire

poetry verse, rhyme, lyric, ode POEM, POET, POETIC

point direct, aim, show, indicate

poised composed, collected, balanced, confident, assured
upset

poisonous toxic, deadly, destructive, noxious, harmful, malignant, venomous POISON

poke thrust, push, shove, ram, jab, goad, spur

pole bar, rod, shaft, post, beam, stick

police guard, watch, patrol, shield

policy plan, program, procedure, course, principles, line, platform

polish shine, burnish, gloss, rub, buff, glaze, wax, furbish

polite refined, courteous, civil, gracious, respectful, well-mannered, tactful rude

poll canvass, survey, vote, questionnaire

pollute contaminate, infect, taint, tarnish, defile, foul, poison POLLUTION

pomp spectacle, display, sight, exhibition, show, pageant, ostentation, magnificence modesty POMPOUS

ponder consider, contemplate, study, reflect, deliberate, meditate, think over, muse, brood

ponderous heavy, clumsy, bulky, massive, weighty, cumbersome, unwieldy light, airy

pool 1. lake, pond, puddle, reservoir, 2. contribute, combine

poor 1. needy, penniless, impoverished, destitute (*Slang* — broke, busted, strapped) rich, 2. pitiful, unfortunate, wretched, miserable fortunate POVERTY

pop shoot, burst, bang, fire, crack, explode, detonate

popular 1. common, usual, regular, customary, ordinary, everyday, prevalent, conventional, traditional unusual, 2. well-liked, dear, beloved, adored, admired, cherished, favorite, pet unpopular, disliked POPULARITY

population inhabitants, people

port   harbor, dock, wharf, pier

portable   movable, transferable, conveyable

portal   door, gate, entrance, threshold

portent   forewarning, omen, sign, premonition

portion   part, share, division, segment, section, fraction, fragment, piece (*Slang* — cut, divvy)   whole

portly   1. stout, fat, obese, plump, pudgy, stocky, chubby, heavyset   thin, 2. dignified, stately, imposing, grand, noble, majestic

portray   represent, picture, depict, illustrate, characterize, impersonate, describe   PORTRAIT, PORTRAYAL

pose   1. posture, position, bearing, carriage, 2. pretense

position   1. place, location, situation, spot, 2. job, duty, function, role, office, capacity, situation, post

positive   sure, definite, certain, absolute, convinced, assured

possess   own, have, hold, control, maintain, occupy   POSSESSION, POSSESSIVE, POSSESSOR

possible   likely, conceivable, imaginable, feasible, probable, credible, achievable, attainable, plausible   impossible   POSSIBILITY, POSSIBLY

post   1. list, schedule, notify, inform, 2. position, situation, office, duty, job

postpone   delay, put off, defer, suspend, hold over, table, shelve, stall, procrastinate

posture   position, carriage, bearing

potent   powerful, strong, forceful, mighty   weak, puny

potential   possible, promising, hidden, likely, conceivable

potion   drink, dose (*Slang* — swig)

pouch   sack, bag

pounce jump, swoop, leap, spring, hop, bound, hurdle, vault, plunge, dive

pound beat, strike, knock, hit, hammer, rap, bang, batter, drum

pour drain, flow out, spew, spill, stream

pout sulk, mope, fret, frown, scowl

powder sprinkle, dust, spatter

power strength, might, force, vigor, energy, potency, authority, right, control, influence, command, mastery, dominion
POWERFUL

practically 1. usefully, profitably, advantageously, 2. almost, nearly, really, essentially, fundamentally, basically, about PRACTICAL

practice train, drill, exercise, prepare, condition, rehearse, repeat

praise compliment, commend, laud, approve of, extol, glorify, flatter (*Slang* — butter up, soft-soap)

prance stroll, saunter, strut, promenade, bounce, swagger, romp (*Slang* — sashay)

prank mischief, trick, caprice, whim, antic, caper (*Slang* — monkeyshine, shenanigan)

prattle babble, chatter, jabber, blab

pray appeal, plead, petition, beg, entreat, implore, beseech

preach lecture, sermonize, advise, urge, expound
PREACHER

precarious dangerous, unsafe, uncertain, hazardous, critical, ticklish, touchy, delicate, unsure, unsound, shaky
sure, safe

precaution forewarning, notification

precede lead, head, come first, forerun follow, succeed
PRECEDENT, PRECEDING

precept   rule, saying, belief, axiom, principle, proposition

precinct   district, boundary, limit, community, vicinity, neighborhood

precious   valuable, expensive, costly, dear, loved, priceless, adored, cherished, admired, prized, special   cheap

precipice   bluff, cliff, slope, palisade   PRECIPITOUS

precipitation   1. rain, snow, moisture, 2. haste, speed, impetuousness, impulsiveness, rashness   PRECIPITATE

precise   exact, accurate, definite, careful, strict, positive, absolute, meticulous, detailed, explicit, clear-cut
PRECISION

preclude   bar, exclude, prevent, deter, shut out, prohibit, forbid   allow

precocious   advanced, forward, premature

predecessor   leader, forerunner

predicament   mess, complication, plight, embarrassment, pinch, dilemma (*Slang* — pickle, spot, squeeze, jam, hole, hot water, stew)   comfort

predict   foresee, foretell, prophesy, divine, forecast, portend
PREDICTION

predominant   chief, superior, main, principal, leading, foremost

preface   introduction, preamble, foreward, preliminary

prefer   choose, favor, rather, desire, fancy, pick, select
PREFERABLE, PREFERENCE

pregnant   productive, fertile, full

prejudiced   biased, opinionated, partial, influenced
impartial   PREJUDICE

preliminary   prior, preceding

premature   early, advanced, forward, too soon, hasty
late, delayed

premeditated planned, forethought, intended, plotted, calculated, meant, deliberate spontaneous, accidental

prepare ready, fix, arrange, provide, concoct, compose, equip, rig, plan PREPARATION, PREPARATORY

preposterous absurd, senseless, foolish, ridiculous, nonsensical, crazy, outrageous, unreasonable, silly

prescribe order, direct, assign, advise, recommend, suggest, advocate PRESCRIPTION

presence attendance, being, existence, occurrence, appearance PRESENT

present give, offer, tender, submit, extend, donate, bestow, award, grant, deliver, hand over (*Slang* — dish out, slip, shell out, fork over, kick in, come across with) PRESENTATION

presently shortly, soon, directly, before long

preserve protect, keep, maintain, guard, defend, save, shelter, shield, screen, harbor, uphold, support, reserve, conserve, sustain, retain destroy, neglect PRESERVATION, PRESERVER

preside direct, administer, officiate, govern PRESIDENCY, PRESIDENT

press 1. push, force, squeeze, clasp, tighten, 2. urge, insist, coax, goad, prod, stress, 3. iron, smooth

pressing urgent, compelling, crucial, necessary, driving

pressure 1. weight, force, load, burden, 2. influence, power, effect, domination

prestige importance, greatness, distinction, prominence, significance, superiority, mastery, power, influence, authority

presume suppose, assume, surmise, guess, think, imagine, fancy, imply, infer PRESUMABLE, PRESUMPTION

presumptuous daring, bold, arrogant, insolent, brazen (*Slang* — nervy) modest, humble

pretend make-believe, act, feign, bluff, sham, fake
PRETENSE

pretentious showy, ostentatious, flashy, fancy, affected
modest

pretext pretense, excuse, cover, sham

pretty attractive, lovely, beautiful, handsome, good-looking
(*Slang* — cute) ugly, homely

prevalent widespread, common, fashionable, popular,
customary, current, standard, usual, well-known, general,
universal uncommon
PREVAIL, PREVAILING, PREVALENCE

prevent prohibit, forbid, deter, keep from, preclude, stop,
block, thwart, inhibit, hinder (*Slang* — foul up, louse up,
gum up) allow, permit PREVENTION, PREVENTIVE

previous prior, earlier, former, one-time, preceding
following, succeeding PREVIOUSLY

price cost, value, amount, rate, charge, worth, expense
(*Slang* — tab, damage, score)

priceless valuable, invaluable, precious, dear, expensive,
costly (*Slang* — stiff, steep)

prickly sharp, stinging, tingly

pride self-respect, self-esteem, dignity, vanity, egotism

prim neat, proper, precise, prudish, overmodest, strait-laced,
puritanical, formal, stiff, stuffy casual

primary first, important, chief, main, principal, leading,
dominant, essential, basic, fundamental, foremost, paramount secondary PRIME

primitive 1. ancient, original, prehistoric, uncivilized, barbarous, native modern, 2. simple, basic, fundamental,
elementary, beginning advanced, sophisticated

principal chief, main, important, leading, dominant, fore-

most, primary, head, prominent, essential secondary
PRINCIPALLY

principle rule, law, standard, belief, dogma, doctrine, truth, proposition, precept

print 1. stamp, impress, mark, etch, engrave, 2. publish, issue, put out, publicize

prior earlier, before, previous, former after, later
PRIORITY

prison jail, penal institution, penitentiary, reformatory (*Slang* — clink, jug, cooler, stir, can) PRISONER

privacy secrecy, seclusion, intimacy, retreat, hideaway, sanctum, cloister, withdrawal, isolation, solitude
PRIVATE

privilege advantage, license, favor, liberty, freedom, grant
PRIVILEGED

prize 1. reward, award, treasure, 2. value, appreciate, hold dear, cherish, adore, idolize, worship, respect, revere

probable likely, liable, apt, presumable, promising, hopeful improbable PROBABILITY, PROBABLY

probation test, trial, try, check

probe examine, investigate, search, explore

problem issue, question, mystery, enigma, puzzle, perplexity, conundrum

procedure process, course, measure, custom, practice, rule, policy, plan, method, way, manner, means

proceed progress, advance, go forward, go ahead

proceeds receipts, income, profits, earnings, returns

process operation, procedure, course, step, act, way, manner, means, mode

proclaim declare, announce, herald, publicize, voice, advertise PROCLAMATION

procure obtain, get, acquire, secure, purchase, buy

prod poke, jab, goad, stir, thrust, ram, drive, butt

prodigal wasteful, lavish, extravagant, spendthrift, squandering

prodigious 1. great, huge, vast, immense, stupendous, enormous, colossal, mammoth, gigantic (*Slang* — tremendous, terrific, whopping, whaling, whacking, rousing, roaring, thundering), 2. wonderful, marvelous, miraculous, extraordinary, remarkable, exceptional ordinary

prodigy marvel, wonder, miracle, phenomenon, rarity, curiosity, first-rater, genius

productive fruitful, fertile, yielding, prolific, creative, inventive, gainful, profitable sterile
PRODUCE, PRODUCT, PRODUCTION

profanity swearing, cursing PROFANE

profess claim, allege, maintain, contend

professional occupational, vocational PROFESSION

proficient skilled, expert, adept, apt, clever, masterful, ingenious, deft, effective, competent, crack
inefficient, clumsy

profit gain, benefit, advantage, earnings, returns, receipts, proceeds loss PROFITABLE

profound deep, great, extreme, intense, serious shallow

profuse lavish, extravagant, abundant, generous, liberal, free, unsparing, bountiful, bighearted, magnanimous, prodigal scarce PROFUSION

program schedule, plan, list, prospectus, bill, calendar, agenda, roster, register, line-up

progress advance, proceed, go ahead, move
PROGRESSIVE

prohibit forbid, bar, ban, disallow, veto, deny, prevent, deter, thwart, restrict, foil   allow   PROHIBITION

1. project plan, scheme, proposal, plot, design, intention, undertaking, enterprise, venture

2. project 1. protrude, stick out, bulge   recede, 2. show, screen   PROJECTION

prolific productive, rich, plentiful, fruitful, creative   sterile

prolong extend, stretch, lengthen, elongate, drag out   shorten

prominent well-known, important, outstanding, distinguished, great, eminent, famous, popular, celebrated   unknown   PROMINENCE

promiscuous indiscriminate, uncritical, loose, mixed, combined, scrambled, unorganized, haphazard, random   selective

promising hopeful, encouraging, favorable, probable, likely   hopeless   PROMISE

promotion advancement, forwarding, improvement, lift, rise, betterment, progress   PROMOTE

prompt 1. punctual, quick, instant, immediate, ready   slow, late, 2. remind, hint, suggest, coach   PROMPTLY

prone 1. inclined, liable, willing, ready   unwilling, 2. flat, level, horizontal, prostrate, reclining, reposing   vertical, standing

pronounce sound, utter, articulate, voice, enunciate, express   PRONUNCIATION

pronounced distinct, marked, decided, plain, clear, obvious, evident, definite, clear-cut, visible, downright, absolute, conspicuous, noticeable, prominent, bold, striking, outstanding, flagrant, glaring   unnoticeable, vague

prop support, bolster, hold up, brace

propagate   produce, increase, breed, multiply, generate, procreate

propel   drive, push, shove, move, impel, motivate, stimulate
PROPULSION, PROPELLER

proper   correct, right, fitting, decent, respectful, accurate, perfect, faultless, tasteful   improper, unsuitable
PROPERLY

property   possession, holdings, belongings   PROPRIETOR

prophesy   predict, foretell, forecast, divine, foresee, soothsay
PROPHECY, PROPHET

proportion   ratio, measure, amount, balance, portion, share, interest, part, percentage

proposal   plan, scheme, suggestion, offer, intent, project, design, motion   PROPOSE, PROPOSITION

prosecute   1. complete, carry out, fulfill, discharge, execute, transact, practice, exercise, pursue, follow, 2. bring suit, take action against   PROSECUTION

prospective   expected, anticipated, awaited, coming, promised, due, future, eventual   PROSPECT

prosperous   successful, thriving, fortunate, triumphant, comfortable, flourishing, well-off, wealthy, rich, opulent, affluent   unsuccessful, poor   PROSPER, PROSPERITY

prostrate   1. helpless, overcome, defenseless, powerless, fallen   strong, proud, 2. prone, horizontal, flat, lying, reclining   upright, vertical

protect   defend, guard, shield, safeguard, shelter, screen, cover, ensure, harbor
PROTECTION, PROTECTIVE, PROTECTOR

protest   object, squawk, dispute, challenge, dissent (*Slang —* kick)   agree

protrude   project, stick out, bulge   recede
PROTRUSION

proud 1. boastful, dignified, elated, pleased, satisfied, gratified, delighted, 2. arrogant, haughty, vain, lofty, conceited, bragging (*Slang* — stuck-up, cocky, uppish)
humble, modest

prove show, verify, check, confirm, justify, certify, establish, substantiate, demonstrate, document   PROOF

proverb maxim, adage, saying

provide supply, give, furnish   PROVISION

province 1. division, department, part, field, sphere, domain, 2. region, area, zone, territory, district, quarter, place, neighborhood, kingdom, empire, principality

provoke anger, vex, excite, stir, irritate, annoy, incense, exasperate, pique, ruffle, enrage, infuriate, antagonize, irk, nettle, disturb, arouse, taunt, aggravate, peeve, rile
pacify, soothe   PROVOCATION, PROVOCATIVE

prowess daring, courage, valor, gallantry, heroism, boldness, skill   fear, cowardice

prowl sneak, slink, lurk, steal, creep, rove

proxy agent, substitute, deputy, alternate, replacement, representative, surrogate

prudent careful, sensible, discreet, cautious, guarded, judicious   careless   PRUDENCE

pry 1. meddle, mix, busybody, peek, peep, search, grope, snoop, 2. loosen, jimmy, wrench

public people, populace, society, persons, population, inhabitants

publish divulge, reveal, make known, circulate, broadcast, spread, advertise, print, issue

pucker wrinkle, fold, crumple

puffy swollen, inflated, bloated, distended, dilated
deflated   PUFF

pull   1. tug, draw, heave, haul, tow, drag, yank, jerk, strain, stretch   push, 2. attract, lure, influence

pulsate   beat, throb, palpitate, drum, pound

pulverize   crumble, granulate, powder, crush, mash, smash, grind, grate

pummel   beat, punch, thrash, flog, strike, pound, hammer, rap, bang, batter, wallop

punch   pummel, beat, thrash, flog, strike, pound, hammer, rap, bang, batter, wallop

punctual   prompt, quick, immediate, speedy, exact, precise late

puncture   pierce, perforate, penetrate, stab, bore, impale

pungent   sharp, biting, bitter, acid, stinging, tangy, spicy tasteless, bland

punish   discipline, chastise, correct, castigate, penalize
PUNISHMENT

puny   1. weak, meager, slight, little, small, frail, delicate, fragile   strong, sturdy, 2. petty, unimportant, trivial important

pupil   student, scholar, schoolchild

purchase   buy, shop

purify   cleanse, clarify, clean, clear, refine, filter   soil, pollute
PURE, PURITY

purpose   plan, aim, intention, design, object, goal, target, resolution, determination, will
PURPOSEFUL, PURPOSELY

pursue   chase, follow, seek, go after, shadow, trail, heel, hunt, quest (*Slang* — tail, tag along, string along)
PURSUIT

push   1. press, thrust, shove, force, drive, propel, nudge pull, 2. urge, encourage, prod, coax, spur, goad   discourage

put   place, lay, set, arrange, deposit   remove

putrid   rotten, foul, bad, decayed, spoiled, stinking, smelly, rancid, reeking, awful, atrocious (*Slang* — lousy, punk) clean, pure

puzzle   perplexity, quandary, dilemma, confusion, bewilderment, mystery, enigma, problem, conundrum

pygmy   dwarf, midget

Q

quack   imposter, pretender, charlatan, fake

quaff   drink, sip, imbibe, guzzle

quaint   odd, curious, old-fashioned

quake   shake, tremble, vibrate, quiver, shiver, shudder

qualified   competent, fit, capable, efficient, able, suited, eligible   unfit, unsuitable   QUALIFICATION, QUALIFY

quality   nature, kind, characteristic, constitution, trait, feature, mark, type, property

qualm   uneasiness, doubt, skepticism, misgiving, question, suspicion, apprehension, anxiety

quandary   dilemma, perplexity, predicament, confusion, puzzle, uncertainty (*Slang* — pickle)

quantity   amount, number, sum, measure, portion, volume, mass, multitude

quarantine   separate, segregate, isolate, confine, seclude

quarrelsome   argumentative, cranky, cross, irritable, peevish, belligerent, grouchy (*Slang* — scrappy)   peaceful   QUARREL

quaver   shake, tremble, vibrate, quiver, shiver, quake

queer 1. odd, strange, peculiar, curious, eccentric, weird (*Slang* — funny, screwy, nutty, wacky) normal, 2. homosexual, deviant

quell calm, subdue, quiet, pacify, appease, cool, hush, mollify, lull, smother, crush, reduce, suppress, extinguish, stifle incite

quench stop, extinguish, put out, stifle, suppress, quell, squelch

query question, ask, inquire, demand, interrogate, quiz answer

quest search, hunt, pursue, seek, explore

question inquire, ask, query, demand, interrogate, quiz answer

questionable doubtful, uncertain, dubious, improbable, unlikely, implausible certain, sure

quick 1. fast, swift, hasty, brisk, lively, speedy, rapid, fleet, expeditious (*Slang* — snappy), 2. alert, attentive, smart, bright, keen, sharp
slow QUICKLY

quiet still, silent, hushed, peaceful, serene, tranquil, calm noisy

quip joke, witticism, pleasantry, jibe (*Slang* — wisecrack)

quit stop, leave, cease, discontinue, end, halt, desist, refrain, depart, withdraw, retreat, abandon, resign, vacate (*Slang* — skip, cut, lay off) continue, remain

quite completely, absolutely, entirely, really, truly, rather, very, exceedingly (*Slang* — real, jolly, mighty)

quiver shake, shiver, tremble, vibrate, quake, quaver, shudder

quiz test, examine, interrogate, question, query

quota ratio, share, proportion, percentage, allotment

quote cite, illustrate, refer to, repeat, echo QUOTATION

R

race 1. run, speed, rush, tear, dash, dart, hurry, hasten, scoot, scamper, scurry, sprint, bound, bolt, quicken, accelerate, chase (*Slang* — hotfoot, skedaddle), 2. people, folk, clan, tribe, nation, breed, culture, lineage

rack 1. hurt, torture, pain, torment, agonize, punish, harass, distress, strain soothe, comfort, 2. framework, shelf

racket 1. noise, din, commotion, tumult, uproar, disturbance, hubbub, fracas, ado, fuss, rumpus, stir, row (*Slang* — to-do, ruckus) peace, quiet, 2. fraud, swindle, dishonesty (*Slang* — gyp)

radiant shining, bright, beaming, luminous, gleaming, glowing, lustrous dull, dim RADIANCE, RADIATE

radical extreme, greatest, utmost moderate

radio broadcast, transmit

rage 1. anger, passion, violence, storm, frenzy, furor, fit, delirium, mania, craze, excitement calm, serenity, 2. fad, fashion, style

ragged torn, worn, shabby, shoddy, tattered, frayed, frazzled, seedy neat RAG

raid attack, invade, assault, plunder, pillage, loot, seize

rain precipitate, shower, pour, sprinkle, drizzle

raise 1. lift, increase, elevate, hoist, boost lower, 2. produce, rear, build, create, construct destroy

rally 1. assemble, meet, gather, congregate, collect, throng, crowd, cluster, convene disperse, 2. improve, recover, recuperate, mend, revive

ram strike, push, thrust, shove, press, bear, drive, prod, goad

ramble wander, roam, rove, gad, drift, stray, meander

rampage racket, commotion, hubbub, tumult, uproar, disturbance, fracas, ado, fuss, rumpus, stir, row (*Slang* — to-do, ruckus)   peace, quiet

ranch   farm, range, plantation, homestead

random   haphazard, aimless, irregular, unorganized planned

range   limit, extent, distance, reach, length, scope

rank   1. grade, class, position, rate, value, evaluate, gauge, appraise, classify, arrange, group, categorize, 2. offensive, repulsive, disgusting, revolting, foul, vile, odious, repugnant, obnoxious, sickening, nasty, putrid, rotten   fresh, wholesome

rankle   pain, distress, inflame, irritate, fester, ache, hurt

ransack   search, rummage, forage, pillage, plunder, loot, raid, rifle

ransom   redeem, reclaim, recover, retrieve, regain

rap   knock, tap, hammer, bang

rapid   quick, swift, fast, speedy, fleet, hasty, expeditious (*Slang* — snappy)   slow

rapture   joy, delight, ecstasy, bliss, elation, enchantment, glee, happiness   distress, sorrow   RAPT

rare   scarce, sparse, uncommon, infrequent, peculiar, unusual   common, ordinary   RARELY, RARITY

rascal   rogue, scoundrel, devil, scamp, trickster

rash   1. hasty, careless, reckless, impetuous, impulsive, sudden, imprudent, brash   careful, cautious, 2. inflammation, breaking-out

rate   grade, classify, position, rank, value, evaluate, appraise, group, categorize, estimate, measure

ratify   confirm, approve, validate, certify, support, uphold, authenticate, substantiate, endorse, accept, pass, O.K. veto, refuse   RATIFICATION

ratio   proportion, comparison, percentage

ration   allowance, portion, share, quota, allotment, budget, measure, supply, amount

rational   sensible, reasonable, thinking, logical, sound, level-headed   irrational, foolish   RATIONALIZE

rattle   1. clatter, patter, 2. confuse, disturb, upset, fluster, ruffle, unsettle   calm

raucous   harsh, hoarse, husky, gruff, coarse
melodious, sweet

ravage   damage, destroy, devastate, ruin, wreck
restore, build

ravenous   1. hungry, starved, famished, empty, 2. greedy, grasping, piggish, hoggish, vulturous, gluttonous
satisfied

ravishing   enchanting, delightful, lovely, appealing, charming, beautiful, stunning, dazzling, gorgeous, alluring, enticing, fascinating   unattractive, plain   RAVISH

raw   1. immature, inexperienced, green, undeveloped, callow, crude   developed, experienced, 2. cold, wind-swept, nippy, wintry, freezing, piercing, bitter   warm, mild, 3. uncooked
cooked

ray   light, gleam, beam, stream

raze   destroy, tear down, level, flatten, demolish
build, construct

reach   1. arrive at, come to, approach, land, 2. extend, stretch

react   respond, answer   REACTION

ready   prepared, set, fit   unprepared

real   actual, true, genuine, authentic, substantial, certain, legitimate, bona fide, sincere, honest, pure   untrue, fake
REALITY, REALLY

realize   understand, grasp, conceive, comprehend, follow, appreciate (*Slang* — catch on, get)   REALIZATION

realm   region, range, extent, sphere, field, province, domain

reap   gather, acquire, gain, obtain, get, earn, glean

rear   1. back, hind, posterior front, 2. raise, produce, create, nurse, foster, train

reason   cause, motive, explanation, logic, sense, ground, justification, basis

reasonable   sensible, fair, logical, just, sound, sane, rational, practical, realistic, justifiable unreasonable

rebel   revolt, rise up, defy, riot, mutiny, disobey, disregard obey REBELLION, REBELLIOUS

rebuff   reject, renounce, deny, repudiate, disown, disclaim, spurn, scorn, disdain, snub accept, welcome

rebuke   scold, disapprove, reprove, reprimand, lecture, correct, chide, berate (*Slang* — tell off, give it to, dress down, bawl out, chew out, give what-for) praise, approve

recall   1. remember, recollect, review, reminisce forget, 2. summon, call back

recede   retreat, withdraw, regress advance

receive   take in, get, gain, admit, accept, obtain, secure give

recent   new, late, modern, up-to-date RECENTLY

reception   party, entertainment, social, festivity

recess   1. pause, hesitate, rest, adjourn, 2. indent, notch, set back

recipe   formula, instructions, directions, prescription

recite   narrate, tell, relate, recount, rehearse, review, repeat RECITAL, RECITATION

reckless   rash, careless, heedless, thoughtless, inconsiderate, hasty, unmindful, impetuous cautious, careful

reckon   1. think, consider, judge, suppose, hold, regard, deem, imagine, fancy, believe, 2. count, calculate, compute, estimate, figure, evaluate, appraise

recline lie down, repose, lounge, rest

recluse hermit, shut-in, isolationist

recognize 1. acknowledge, see, behold, know, 2. realize, appreciate, understand, admit, allow, accept RECOGNITION

recollect remember, recall, reminisce, review, reflect RECOLLECTION

recommend advise, suggest, advocate, instruct, guide, direct, urge RECOMMENDATION

recompense pay, reward, compensate

reconcile settle, harmonize, bring together, mend, fix up RECONCILIATION

record write, inscribe, register, enroll, list, mark down, note, post, enter, log, tabulate, chronicle

recount recite, narrate, tell, relate, review

recover 1. regain, retrieve, get back, reclaim, rescue lose, 2. recuperate, get better, rally, revive, heal, improve, come around, make a comeback, get back in shape RECOVERY

recreation play, amusement, entertainment, pleasure, enjoyment, diversion, relaxation, pastime, fun, sport work, toil

recruit enlist, draft, sign up, enroll, muster

rectify adjust, remedy, fix, regulate, set right, amend, correct

recur repeat, return, come again

redeem fulfill, pay off, deliver, make good, recover, rescue REDEMPTION

redress repair, remedy, rectify, correct, right, mend, fix, relieve

reduce lessen, lower, decrease, diminish, cut, moderate increase REDUCTION

reek smell, stink

reel 1. sway, rock, swing, lurch, roll, wobble, stagger, pitch, flounder, 2. spool, roller

refer direct, point, recommend, send, allude
REFERENCE

referee judge, moderator, umpire, arbitrator, mediator

refine perfect, develop, improve, purify, cultivate, polish

reflect 1. mirror, send back, 2. think, ponder, study, deliberate, consider, contemplate, meditate, muse, mull over
REFLECTION, REFLECTOR

reform change, improve, convert, revise

refrain avoid, abstain, forego, shun indulge

refrigerate cool, chill REFRIGERATOR

refuge shelter, protection, asylum, retreat, haven, port, harbor, sanctuary

refund repay, reimburse, pay back

1. refuse decline, reject, say no, rebuff (*Slang* — turn down, not buy) accept, allow

2. refuse waste, garbage, rubbish, rubble, trash, litter, junk

refute argue, dispute, contradict agree

regal 1. royal, majestic, sovereign, imperial, 2. dignified, stately, splendid, magnificent, imposing

regard consider, think of, judge

regardless notwithstanding, despite

region place, space, area, location, district, zone, territory, section, vicinity

register record, inscribe, write, enroll, list, post, enter, log, indicate REGISTRATION

regret bemoan, bewail, be sorry for, rue

regular 1. usual, customary, steady, habitual, everyday, common, typical, normal, routine, 2. uniform, even, orderly, balanced, symmetrical irregular

regulate 1. manage, govern, handle, direct, rule, control, organize, run, command, 2. adjust, remedy, rectify, correct
REGULATION

rehearse practice, repeat, train, drill, exercise, prepare
REHEARSAL

reign rule, prevail

reinforce strengthen, fortify, brace, intensify weaken
REINFORCEMENT

reiterate repeat, recount, retell, review

reject exclude, bar, eliminate, expel, discard, throw away, dispose of, cast off, refuse, decline (*Slang* — turn down) accept REJECTION

rejoice cheer, gladden, encourage, hearten, inspire, celebrate, glory, delight grieve

relapse return, revert, regress, reverse, slip back advance

relate tell, report, state, declare, recite, narrate, recount

related associated, connected, affiliated, allied, akin
RELATIONSHIP, RELATIVE

relax rest, ease up, loosen (*Slang* — knock off, take five)
RELAXATION

relay carry, deliver, pass, transfer, hand on, impart

release free, let go, relieve, dismiss, discharge, expel, fire, sack, can, bump, retire, relinquish, liberate hold

relent yield, bend, give, relax, submit, give in

relentless harsh, without pity, merciless, unsympathetic, ruthless, heartless, cruel, strict, firm, rigid, inflexible, unyielding, uncompromising, persevering, persistent, steadfast, hard lenient, sympathetic

relevant   pertinent, applicable, apropos, suitable, connected, fitting   unconnected, irrelevant

reliable   trustworthy, dependable, faithful, steadfast, loyal, true, devoted, safe, sure, stable   undependable, unreliable RELIANCE

relic   memento, remembrance, token, souvenir, trophy, keepsake

relief   1. freedom, ease, alleviation, release, help, assistance, aid, 2. change, substitution, replacement, alternate, proxy (*Slang* — pinch hitter)   RELIEVE

religious   pious, devout, reverent, faithful   RELIGION

relinquish   give up, surrender, yield, waive, forego, abandon, release, sacrifice   hold, keep

relish   enjoy, like, appreciate, savor   dislike

reluctant   unwilling, grudging, disinclined, loath   willing

rely   depend on, trust, confide, count on   RELIABLE

remain   continue, endure, persist, stay, last, keep on leave, depart   REMAINDER

remark   comment, speak, state, say, observe, note, mention

remarkable   unusual, noteworthy, extraordinary, exceptional, wonderful, marvelous, great, striking, notable, special, rare   ordinary

remedy   cure, correct, fix, rectify, heal, treat, doctor

remember   remind, recall, recollect, recognize   forget

remind   prompt, suggest to   REMINDER

remnant   leftover, remains, residue, balance

remorse   regret, sorrow, grief

remote   far, distant, removed, secluded, isolated, hidden near, close

remove take away, withdraw, extract, eject, expel, oust, deduct, subtract, eliminate, dispose of, doff, discard (*Slang* — bounce) keep REMOVAL

render 1. cause, make, do, effect, 2. give, present, grant, allow, allot

rendezvous meeting, appointment, session, get-together

renounce give up, relinquish, surrender, yield, waive, abandon, release, reject, deny, disclaim, discard, spurn, scorn keep

renovate recondition, redo, remake

renowned famous, celebrated, popular, distinguished, notable, notorious, well-known

rent hire, lease, charter, let RENTAL

repair mend, fix, service, overhaul, patch up, restore break, destroy

repast meal, food, refreshment

repeal withdraw, abolish, take back, revoke, recall, cancel, annul, invalidate, rescind, overrule

repeat say again, recite, reiterate, duplicate, echo (*Slang* — come again) REPETITION

repel 1. drive back, rebuff, hold off, 2. repulse, offend, revolt, disgust, nauseate, sicken please

repent regret, be sorry REPENTANCE, REPENTANT

replenish fill again, provide, supply, furnish

replica copy, reproduction, duplicate, double

reply answer, respond, retort, acknowledge, react

report describe, tell, repeat, relate, narrate REPORTER

repose rest, sleep, recline, lounge (*Slang* — take it easy)

represent 1. portray, depict, illustrate, stand for, symbolize,

characterize, express, describe, 2. exhibit, show, demonstrate, display, manifest, present, reveal, disclose
REPRESENTATION, REPRESENTATIVE

repress keep down, restrain, suppress, quell, crush, squash, smother, stifle, hush up, censor, muffle, squelch (*Slang* — sit on, put the lid on) REPRESSION

reproach blame, accuse, denounce, condemn (*Slang* — knock, pan, slam, rap) absolve

reprove scold, blame, lecture, reprimand, chide, rebuke (*Slang* — dress down, tell off, jump on, bawl out, chew out, give what-for) REPROOF

repudiate reject, renounce, deny, disclaim, disown, discard, spurn, scorn, disdain, exclude

repulsive ugly, repelling, horrible, hideous, horrid, frightful, disgusting, dreadful, terrible, repugnant, offensive, ghastly, revolting, gruesome (*Slang* — awful) pleasing
REPULSE

reputable honorable, respectable, well-thought-of, upstanding, upright, principled, moral, honest dishonest
REPUTATION, REPUTE

request ask, requisition, apply for

require 1. need, necessitate, lack, want, 2. demand, order, command, oblige REQUIREMENT, REQUISITION

rescue save, free, recover, redeem, salvage, retrieve, release, liberate, extricate

research investigate, inquire, hunt, explore, look into, search, dig, delve

resemblance likeness, similarity, sameness RESEMBLE

resentment displeasure, irritation, annoyance, vexation, bitterness, wrath, anger, indignation
RESENT, RESENTFUL

reserve keep, hold, save, store, preserve, put aside
RESERVATION

reside live, dwell, inhabit, occupy
RESIDENCE, RESIDENT, RESIDENTIAL

residue remains, leftovers, rest, dregs, sediment, balance

resign give up, relinquish, surrender, yield, waive, forego, renounce, abandon, retire, quit, vacate, abdicate
RESIGNATION

resist oppose, withstand, counteract   comply, yield
RESISTANCE, RESISTANT

resolute firm, bold, resolved, decided, persevering, obstinate, willful, unyielding, unbending, adamant, game, spirited (*Slang* — nervy, spunky) wavering RESOLUTION

resolve determine, decide, settle

resourceful skillful, clever, deft, adept, ingenious, smart, cunning RESOURCE

respect admire, regard, esteem, appreciate, value, revere, honor, idolize, adore RESPECTABLE, RESPECTFUL

respective particular, individual, special, specific, personal
RESPECTIVELY

respiration breathing, inhalation, exhalation
RESPIRATORY

respite rest, relief, lull, pause, recess, break, interruption, intermission, breather, reprieve

resplendent bright, shining, splendid, brilliant, vivid, dazzling, glorious, flamboyant, gorgeous (*Slang* — devastating, stunning)

respond answer, reply, retort, acknowledge, react
RESPONSE, RESPONSIVE

responsible 1. accountable, answerable, liable exempt, 2. trustworthy, reliable, dependable, faithful, loyal
irresponsible, undependable RESPONSIBILITY

rest   1. repose, pause, recess, recline, lounge (*Slang* — take it easy), 2. remains, residue, leftovers, balance

restless   uneasy, disturbed, troubled, agitated, excited, disquieted, fidgety, impatient, anxious   calm, composed

restore   put back, replace, reinstate, repair, mend, fix, overhaul, renew, renovate   RESTORATION

restrain   hold back, keep down, control, check, arrest, inhibit, curb, suppress, smother, stifle, retard, impede, limit, confine, restrict (*Slang* — squelch)   RESTRAINT

restrict   confine, limit, restrain, bound, cramp, hamper, impede   free, liberate   RESTRICTION

result   consequence, end, effect, outcome, upshot, fruit, product, conclusion

resume   continue, return to, go on with   RESUMPTION

retain   keep, hold, maintain, preserve, save   relinquish

retaliate   reciprocate, retort, strike back, revenge, avenge (*Slang* — get back at)

retard   delay, hinder, detain, keep back, impede, inhibit, curb, check, arrest (*Slang* — hold up)   accelerate

retire   1. resign, quit, vacate, relinquish, abdicate, 2. withdraw, discharge, dismiss, expel, remove, suspend, 3. retreat, recede, 4. go to bed (*Slang* — turn in, hit the hay) RETIREMENT

retiring   shy, modest, reserved, timid, bashful, restrained, distant   outgoing, aggressive

retort   reply, answer, respond, retaliate

retract   withdraw, repeal, revoke, rescind, recall, cancel, annul, invalidate

retreat   withdraw, fall back, retire, reverse   advance

retrieve   recover, regain, recoup, get back, reclaim, repossess, retake, salvage, rescue, redeem, save

return   1. go back, come back, revert, revisit, 2. give back, repay, reimburse

reunion   gathering, assembly, meeting, get-together, social, reception   REUNITE

reveal   show, display, open, disclose, expose, manifest, exhibit, demonstrate, present, bare, divulge   hide, conceal   REVELATION

revenge   retaliate, get even with

revenue   income, earnings, receipts, profits, returns, proceeds

reverberate   echo, resound, reflect

revere   love, respect, honor, admire, value, idolize, adore, esteem, cherish, worship, prize   despise, scorn   REVERENCE, REVERENT

reverse   revert, regress, return, back up   advance

revert   regress, change back, reverse, return

review   1. study, remember, recall, learn, 2. examine, inspect, survey, observe, look at, consider, criticize, size up

revise   correct, change, improve, alter, rewrite, amend

revive   restore, refresh, bring back, renew, regenerate, resurrect, resuscitate   REVIVAL

revoke   repeal, cancel, withdraw, rescind, retract, recall, abolish, annul, invalidate, over rule

revolt   1. rebel, mutiny, rise up, riot, revolutionize, 2. offend, repel, sicken, nauseate, disgust, horrify, appall   please, delight

revolution   1. change, revolt, overthrow, rebellion, riot, uprising, 2. circle, circuit, cycle, orbit, turning

revolve   turn, go around, circle

reward   compensate, pay, remunerate, award

rhythm   beat, swing, tempo, meter

rich   1. abounding, fertile, productive, prolific   sterile, 2. wealthy, affluent, well-to-do, prosperous, opulent, comfortable   poor, 3. valuable, costly, elegant, priceless, expensive   cheap, 4. flavorful   tasteless

rickety   weak, shaky, unsteady   steady

rid   clear, free, do away with

riddle   puzzle, enigma, conundrum

ridicule   mock, deride, laugh at, scoff, jeer, taunt, sneer at (*Slang* — ride, pan, razz)

ridiculous   nonsensical, foolish, crazy, preposterous, outrageous, bizarre, unbelievable, ludicrous
sensible, believable

rifle   rob, ransack, steal, plunder, loot, pillage

rift   1. split, break, crack, cleft, fracture, fissure, gap, crevice, 2. falling-out, estrangement, difference, parting, breach, alienation, separation

rig   fit, equip, outfit, furnish, prepare

right   1. good, just, lawful, fitting, suitable, proper, valid, sound, 2. correct, true, exact, accurate, perfect, faultless
wrong

righteous   virtuous, just, proper, good, moral, pure, worthy
immoral, corrupt

rigid   1. stiff, firm, unbending, unchanging, hard, 2. stubborn, unyielding, adamant, strict, taut, tense
flexible

rigorous   harsh, strict, severe, rigid, relentless, hard
lenient, flimsy   RIGOR

rim   edge, border, margin, fringe

ring   1. sound, peal, toll, chime, tinkle, jingle, clamor, 2. circle, band

riot revolt, rebel, rise up, mutiny, brawl RIOTOUS

rip tear, break, cut

ripe developed, ready, mature, full-grown unripe, green

rise 1. get up, stand go down, 2. go up, advance, ascend, mount descend, 3. increase, grow, gain decrease, 4. originate, begin, start, appear end, 4. revolt, rebel, riot, mutiny

risk chance, hazard, gamble, venture, endanger, imperil, jeopardize, expose RISKY

ritual ceremony, formality, service, exercise, rite

rival match, compete with, vie with RIVALRY

road path, track, trail, thoroughfare, lane

roam wander, rove, gad, drift, stray, meander, ramble

roar thunder, boom, clamor

rob steal, burglarize, loot, sack, pillage, plunder, thieve, pilfer, filch (*Slang* — hold up, lift, swipe, cop, pinch, stick up) ROBBERY

robust strong, sturdy, healthy, mighty, powerful, potent, stalwart, rugged, hardy, vigorous, husky, heavy weak

rock 1. sway, swing, reel, lurch, roll, bob, flounder, tumble, pitch, toss, 2. stone

rogue rascal, scamp, scoundrel, mischief-maker, imp, elf, pixie, villain ROGUISH

role capacity, character, part, position, function

roll turn, move, rotate, pivot, swivel, gyrate, wheel

romp play, frolic, caper, carry on (*Slang* — cut up, horse around)

room 1. space, scope, margin, latitude, leeway, 2. chamber

root   cause, source, origin, derivation

rosy   bright, cheerful, sunny, optimistic, favorable, encouraging

rot   decay, spoil, disintegrate, go bad, crumble   ROTTEN

rotate   spin, turn, gyrate, swivel, pivot   ROTATION

rough   1. coarse, unsmooth, bumpy, choppy, shaggy, broken, uneven, irregular   smooth, 2. harsh, rowdy, severe, fierce, difficult, gruff, brusque, rude, crude, curt, surly, blunt, tough, snippy   gentle

round   circular, globular, rotund, spherical

rouse   stir, excite, arouse, awaken, move, provoke, pique, kindle, inflame, foment, stimulate, agitate, disturb, shake

rout   defeat, conquer, crush, overcome, beat, scatter (*Slang* — lick)

route   course, circuit, path, rounds, itinerary

routine   habit, method, system, arrangement, order

rove   wander, roam, gad, drift, stray, meander, ramble, tramp

1. row   1. line, file, string, train, series, sequence, succession, column, 2. paddle

2. row   quarrel, noise, fracas, brawl, dispute, squabble, rumpus (*Slang* — ruckus, run-in, scrap, rumble, hassle)

rowdy   rough, disorderly, naughty, bad, misbehaving, boisterous, rambunctious   well-mannered

royal   majestic, noble, dignified, stately, grand, regal, imperial, aristocratic   ROYALTY

rub   massage, scrub, scour, buff, stroke

rubbish   1. waste, trash, garbage, refuse, scrap, debris, litter, junk, 2. nonsense, silliness, absurdity, poppycock (*Slang* — baloney, hogwash, malarkey, bunk, hooey)

rude impolite, rough, coarse, discourteous, uncivil, disrespectful, insolent, ill-mannered, ill-behaved, vulgar, boorish, gruff, brusque, curt, blunt, harsh, surly, impudent, impertinent, saucy, crude, crass, flip, cocky, cheeky (*Slang* — smart-alecky, fresh, crusty, nervy)   polite, well-mannered

rudiment foundation, basis, groundwork, beginning, origin, seed   RUDIMENTARY

rue regret, repent, deplore, bemoan, bewail, be sorry for (*Slang* — kick oneself)

ruffian rowdy, rogue, cad, tough, bully, brute, hoodlum (*Slang* — hooligan)

ruffle 1. disturb, annoy, provoke, irk, vex, excite, fluster, upset, shake, trouble, perturb, agitate, rattle, rile, 2. fold, crease, wrinkle, furrow

rug carpet, mat, covering

rugged 1. rough, uneven, jagged, ragged, rocky, snaggy   smooth, 2. sturdy, vigorous, strong, powerful, potent, stalwart, hardy, robust, muscular, athletic, brawny, well-built, healthy, hale, husky, hefty, beefy   weak, feeble

ruin destroy, spoil, mar, upset, wreck, devastate, ravage, demolish (*Slang* — mess up, foul up, louse up, gum up)

rule 1. govern, control, reign, dominate, regulate, command, head, lead, direct, manage, supervise, administer, decree, dictate, order, instruct, prevail, guide, influence, 2. measure, mark off

rumble roar, thunder, boom, roll

rummage search, ransack, scour, comb

rumor gossip, broadcast, circulate, spread word

rumple crumple, crush, wrinkle, crease, dishevel, muss up

rumpus noise, uproar, disturbance, commotion, hubbub, tumult, racket, fracas, ado, fuss, pandemonium, din, clamor, row (*Slang* — ruckus, rumble)

run   1. hasten, hurry, speed, sprint, bound, flee, bolt, race (*Slang* — hotfoot, step lively) slow up, 2. go, move, operate, work, 3. stretch, extend, reach, range, lie, spread, 4. flow, stream, pour, gush, discharge, 5. continue, last, endure, persist stop, 6. campaign, electioneer, stump, politic, 7. conduct, manage, direct, regulate, handle, govern, administer, lead, head, guide, steer, pilot, supervise, oversee, boss (*Slang* — mastermind), 8. tear, ravel, 9. span, period, time, spell

runway   path, track, road

rupture   break, burst, fracture, crack

rural   countrified, rustic, provincial, bucolic

ruse   trick, device, hoax, deception, fraud, subterfuge (*Slang* — gimmick)

rush   1. speed, hasten, hurry, dash, dart, scurry, race, run, expedite, accelerate slow up, 2. pressure, push, attack, charge, besiege, drive, assault, storm

rustic   1. rural, countrified, provincial, bucolic, 2. simple, plain sophisticated

rusty   1. corroded, eroded, worn, old, 2. unpracticed

rut   habit, routine

ruthless   cruel, merciless, heartless, cold, unfeeling, brutal, savage, inhumane kind

S

sack   1. plunder, steal, pillage, loot, rob, fleece, 2. bag, pack

sacred   religious, holy, spiritual

sacrifice   give up, relinquish, release, surrender, yield, waive, forego, lose, forfeit

sad sorrowful, unhappy, dejected, depressed, blue, melancholy, downcast, discouraged, gloomy, somber, glum, morose, sullen, grievous, miserable, pathetic, unfortunate, forlorn   happy, glad   SADNESS

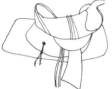

saddle 1. harness, yoke, hitch up, 2. burden, load, encumber, oppress, weigh down   relieve

safe secure, unharmed, protected, guarded, sheltered, shielded   endangered, unsafe   SAFETY

safeguard shield, screen, bulwark, precaution

sag droop, sink, hang, dangle, slump

saga story, tale, yarn, epic, account, anecdote, narrative

sage wise, knowing, learned, profound   ignorant, dull
SAGACIOUS

sail glide, coast, skim, navigate, cruise, float   SAILOR

salary pay, wages, remuneration, compensation

salutary beneficial, healthful, advantageous, wholesome
harmful, unhealthful

salutation greeting, hail, hello   SALUTE

salvage save, rescue, recover, redeem, retrieve   lose
SALVATION

salve ointment, lotion, cream, balm, pomade

same identical, alike, equivalent   different

sample test, experiment, try

sanction permit, approve, allow, authorize, support, license, accept, O.K.   deny

sanctuary refuge, asylum, haven

sand scrape, smooth, file, grind

sane sensible, sound, rational, logical (*Slang* — all there)
SANITY

sanguine   hopeful, expectant, confident, cheerful, optimistic
pessimistic

sanitarium   infirmary, hospital, clinic

sanitary   clean, hygienic, sterile, pure, prophylactic, spotless,
healthful   dirty, unsanitary   SANITATION

sap   weaken, debilitate

sarcastic   sneering, cutting, stinging, bitter, sharp, caustic
SARCASM

satisfy   1. please, gratify, content, benefit, suit, appease
deny, 2. convince, persuade, assure, comfort, relieve
SATISFACTION, SATISFACTORY

saturate   fill, load, stuff, pack, cram, gorge, soak, drench
empty

saucy   rude, impudent, impertinent, pert, disrespectful, flippant, cocky, flip, cheeky (*Slang* — smart-alecky, fresh,
nervy, crusty)   polite

saunter   stroll, ramble, wander, meander

savage   uncivilized, barbarous, fierce, cruel, wild, untamed,
ruthless, inhumane   civilized, gentle   SAVAGERY

save   1. store, economize, scrimp, preserve, conserve, keep,
maintain, reserve, accumulate, gather   spend, discard, 2.
rescue, protect, salvage, recover, redeem, retrieve

savor   relish, enjoy, like   SAVORY

say   1. speak, declare, recite, utter, voice, express, tell,
communicate, remark, comment, mention, assert, relate,
2. power, authority, right, prerogative

scald   burn, scorch

scamp   rascal, rogue, scoundrel, devil, mischief-maker

scamper   scurry, rush, tear, dash, dart, run, scoot, race,
hasten, hurry, scuttle, hustle

scan examine, inspect, scrutinize, look at, study, review

scandal disgrace, humiliation, shame, slander (*Slang* — dirt) SCANDALOUS

scanty meager, scarce, sparse, inconsiderable, small, slight, negligible, skimpy

scar blemish, mar, mark, wound, deface

scarce scanty, sparse, rare plentiful SCARCITY

scare frighten, alarm, startle, unnerve, terrify, horrify, appall

scatter disperse, distribute, spread, separate, part, split up, squander, strew gather, collect

scene 1. view, picture, sight, vista, lookout, landscape, setting, 2. act, 3. storm, outburst, explosion, flare-up

scent smell, odor, essence, fragrance

schedule list, index, post, enumerate, slate, program, line-up

scheme plan, plot, intrigue, conspire, connive, contrive

scholar learned man, savant, student

school educate, teach, instruct, enlighten, direct, guide

scoff mock, jeer, taunt, deride

scold blame, reprove, reprimand, chide, lecture, admonish, talk to (*Slang* — tell off, call down, bawl out, chew out, give what-for)

scoop dig, excavate, gouge, ladle

scoot dart, speed, dash, rush, tear, scamper, scurry, race, hasten, hurry, run, sprint

scope extent, degree, measure, range, sphere, space, reach

scorch burn, sear, singe, blister, parch, char

score 1. calculate, compute, figure, tally, 2. gain, earn, get, acquire, attain, win, 3. cut, mark, line, scratch, stroke

scornful mocking, disdainful, contemptuous SCORN

scoundrel villain, rascal, rogue, devil

scour clean, scrub, polish, wash, rub, buff, massage, shine

scourge whip, beat, thrash, spank, flog, lash

scout hunt, search out

scowl frown, look sullen, pout

scramble 1. mix, mingle, blend, combine, jumble, merge, fuse separate, 2. hurry, scoot, scurry, scamper, hasten, rush, tear, dart, hustle, scuttle, bustle

scrap 1. fight, quarrel, struggle, squabble, tiff, spat, bicker, row, 2. small amount, shred, snatch, speck, particle, 3. waste, litter, debris, trash, rubbish, junk

scrape 1. rub, brush, skim, graze, grate, 2. trouble, predicament, plight, pinch, strait, mess, complication, muddle, embarrassment (*Slang* — pickle, spot, jam, hole, hot water, stew)

scratch scrape, mark, cut, graze, score, scar, engrave

scrawl scribble, scratch

scrawny lean, thin, skinny, spare, gaunt, lanky, bony, spindly husky, chubby

scream yell, cry, shout, howl, shriek, screech, wail, squall, bawl, shout

screech shriek, scream, squeal, yell, cry, shout, howl

screen 1. shelter, protect, hide, cover, cloak, veil, shade, safeguard, 2. sift, strain, filter, refine, sort, separate, 3. inspect, analyze, check

screw fasten, tighten, twist, rotate, turn

scribble scrawl, scratch

scrimmage struggle, fight, encounter, battle, fray, clash, tussle, scuffle, melee, hassle (*Slang* — ruckus, scrap)

script writing, penmanship

scrub scour, clean, polish, wash, rub, buff, massage, shine

scrupulous careful, meticulous, exacting, particular, precise, fussy, fastidious (*Slang* — picky)   careless

scrutinize inspect, examine, look at, observe, study, contemplate, review   SCRUTINY

scuffle struggle, fight, tussle, melee (*Slang* — scrap)

sculpture carve, form, shape, mold, model, chisel

scurry scamper, rush, tear, dash, dart, run, scoot, race, scuttle, hasten, hurry, hustle

scuttle scurry, scamper, rush, tear, dash, dart, run, scoot, race, hasten, hurry, hustle

seal 1. fasten, close, shut, lock   open, 2. endorse, sign, mark, stamp, 3. sea lion

sear burn, scorch, singe, char

search seek, look for, hunt, explore

season flavor, spice

secluded concealed, hidden, covered, obscured, secret, private, intimate, undisturbed, withdrawn, isolated, remote accessible, open   SECLUSION

secret hidden, mysterious, private, concealed, secluded (*Slang* — hush-hush)   open   SECRECY

secrete discharge, excrete, eliminate, exude   SECRETION

section divide, slice, split, partition, parcel, portion

secure 1. safe, protected, sure, sound, firm, stable   unsafe, 2. get, obtain, acquire, 3. close, fasten, shut, lock, seal, fix, attach

seduce tempt, persuade, lure, entice, lead on

seek hunt, search, look for, pursue, quest, explore

seem appear, look

seep ooze, trickle, emit, excrete

seethe burn, fume, simmer, be angry, boil, stew

segment division, section, part, portion, fraction, subdivision

seize clutch, grasp, grab, grip, clasp, snatch release
SEIZURE

seldom rarely, infrequently, hardly, not often often

select pick, choose SELECTION

self-conscious shy, timid, bashful, coy, demure

selfish egotistical, self-centered, possessive good-natured

sell market, vend, peddle buy

send dispatch, transmit, forward receive

senior elder, older junior

sensational exciting, startling, superb, exquisite, magnificent, marvelous, wonderful, glorious (*Slang* — divine, terrific, super)

sense 1. feel, perceive, understand, realize, comprehend, fathom, follow, grasp, discern, 2. intelligence, mentality, judgment

senseless 1. unconscious, lifeless, inanimate, oblivious, 2. foolish, stupid, asinine, silly, inane, idiotic (*Slang* — dizzy, soft, dumb, screwy, loony, batty, goofy, daffy, nutty) bright, sensible

sensible wise, intelligent, understanding, rational, bright, sound, sane, logical, practical, realistic senseless

sentimental emotional, tender, affectionate (*Slang* — soft, mushy, sticky)

separate   divide, part, segregate, sort, isolate, partition join, unite   SEPARATION

sequel   continuation, supplement, outcome, follow-up

sequence   succession, continuation, series, progression

serene   peaceful, calm, tranquil, quiet, untroubled, pacific disturbed, confused   SERENITY

serial   consecutive, sequential, periodic   SERIES

serious   1. thoughtful, grave, reflective, pensive, solemn, engrossed, sincere, earnest, zealous   flighty, 2. important, weighty, momentous, profound   minor, unimportant

sermon   lecture, talk, discourse, recitation

serpent   snake, viper

serve   1. supply, furnish, deliver, present, 2. work for, help, assist   SERVICE

set   place, position, arrange, fix, adjust, regulate

setting   scenery, surroundings, background

settle   1. determine, decide, resolve, fix, reconcile, mend, patch up, 2. occupy, inhabit, colonize, locate

sever   cut off, split, cleave, chop, detach, part, separate

several   some, various, assorted, diversified, many, numerous

severe   strict, stern, harsh, rough, stringent, austere (*Slang* — tough, hard-boiled)   lenient, easy

shabby   worn, ragged, shoddy, tattered, frayed, seedy (*Slang* — tacky)

shack   hut, shanty, shed, cabin

shackle   tie, bind, chain, manacle, handcuff

shaggy   rumpled, tousled, disheveled, mussed up

shake   1. vibrate, tremble, shiver, quiver, quaver, jerk, twitch, 2. jar, bump, bounce, pump, jolt, rock, sway.

shallow   1. featherbrained, simple, slow, empty profound, learned, 2. not deep   deep

sham   fraud, pretense, fake, mock, imitation, hoax (*Slang* — phony)

shambles   mess, disorder, chaos

shameful   disgraceful, humiliating, scandalous, pitiful, deplorable (*Slang* — awful, atrocious)   righteous   SHAME

shampoo   soap, lather, wash

shanty   shack, hut, shed, cabin

shape   form, fashion, mold, design, develop, adapt

share   divide, proportion, apportion, distribute, allot

sharp   1. pointy, angular   dull, 2. severe, biting, caustic, bitter, harsh, curt, gruff, brusque, blunt, snippy   charming, 3. keen, bright, smart, clever, shrewd, alert, brainy dull, stupid

shatter   destroy, smash, fragment, break

shear   cut off, clip, crop

shed   1. cast, throw off, slough, spread, radiate, 2. hut, shanty, shack

sheen   luster, shine, brightness, gloss, glow, gleam

sheepish   bashful, embarrassed, flushed, blushing, shamefaced, shy, timid

sheer   1. transparent, translucent, clear, thin, diaphanous, 2. simple, plain, pure

shelter   protect, shield, hide, guard, defend, screen, cover, harbor   expose

shield   defend, protect, guard, shelter, hide, screen, cover, cloak, harbor   expose

shift   change, substitute, alter, vary

shiftless lazy, inefficient, do-nothing, indolent, laggard
ambitious

shifty tricky, sneaky, sly, furtive, deceitful, evasive, crafty, foxy, cunning, artful, shrewd, canny (*Slang* — shady, cagey)
honest

shimmer gleam, shine, glimmer, twinkle, sparkle, glisten

shine 1. glow, gleam, glimmer, twinkle, sparkle, glisten, glare, 2. be smart, be bright

ship transport, send, dispatch, haul

shirk slack, avoid, malinger (*Slang* — goof off)

shiver shake, quiver, quaver, quake, tremble

shock startle, frighten, terrify, horrify, appall, awe (*Slang* — jar, give a turn, jolt)

shoot fire, discharge SHOT

shop market, buy, purchase

shore coast, beach, waterfront, bank

short 1. little, small, slight, puny big, 2. brief, concise, succinct, curt long

shortage lack, deficiency, want, need, deficit, absence
abundance

shortcoming fault, defect, flaw, weakness, failing, imperfection, inadequacy, deficiency

shout yell, call, cry, scream, shriek, howl, clamor

shove push, jostle, thrust, ram, bump, prod, goad, nudge

show 1. direct, point, aim, explain, clarify, demonstrate, illustrate, indicate, denote, manifest, guide, 2. display, exhibit, reveal conceal, hide

showy flashy, flaunting, ostentatious (*Slang* — jazzy, splashy) dull

shred   fragment, particle, piece, crumb, scrap

shrewd   keen, clever, sharp, smart, artful, cunning, knowing, crafty, foxy, smooth, canny (*Slang* — slick) dull, dim-witted

shriek   yell, cry, call, shout, howl, scream, screech

shrill   piercing, sharp, screechy, squeaky, harsh, grating soft

shrink   1. shrivel, wither, dwindle, become smaller, 2. withdraw, recoil, pull back, retreat, flinch, cringe

shrivel   wither, shrink, wrinkle

shroud   cover, conceal, veil, cloak, screen reveal, expose

shudder   tremble, quiver, shake, quake

shuffle   1. scrape, drag, scuff, trudge, 2. mix, combine, scramble, jumble

shun   avoid, evade, dodge, snub, slight, ignore (*Slang* — duck, pass up)

shut   close, fasten, seal, lock open

shy   bashful, timid, coy, demure aggressive

sick   ill, ailing, indisposed (*Slang* — under the weather, out of sorts, rocky) healthy, well

sift   sort, separate, divide, screen, filter, refine, strain

sight   vision, view, look, vista, scene, spectacle, display, show

sign   1. mark, endorse, seal, initial, 2. signal, gesture, motion, wave, indicate

signet   seal, insignia, label, tag, stamp, sticker, brand, hallmark

significance   meaning, connotation, implication, drift, substance, gist, effect, importance, consequence
unimportance, insignificance SIGNIFICANT, SIGNIFY

silent quiet, still, noiseless, soundless, hushed   noisy SILENCE

silhouette outline, contour, profile, configuration, shadow

silly foolish, ridiculous, inane, senseless, asinine (*Slang* — screwy, nutty, goofy, daffy, loony, batty, dizzy, wacky) sensible

similar alike, like, resembling, same SIMILARITY

simmer 1. boil, stew, cook, 2. seethe, fume, rage, storm, rant, rave

simple 1. easy, effortless   difficult, 2. bare, mere, common, ordinary, sheer, plain, 3. dull, stupid, half-witted, idiotic, moronic, ignorant (*Slang* — dumb)   bright

sin wrongdoing, misconduct, crime, vice, offense, evil, error, indiscretion SINFUL, SINNER

sincere genuine, real, honest, authentic, legitimate, bona fide, unaffected (*Slang* — straight)   insincere, phony SINCERITY

sinewy strong, powerful, tough, athletic, brawny, muscular, beefy SINEW

sing vocalize, chant, croon, hum, serenade

singe burn, scorch, sear, char

sinister bad, evil, dishonest, wrong, corrupt, fraudulent, crooked (*Slang* — fishy, shady)   righteous

sink 1. fall, go down, decline, slump, settle, lower, submerge, 2. weaken, droop, pine, fade

sip drink, taste

sire father, breed, beget, propagate, procreate, reproduce, produce

siren alarm, whistle, signal, noisemaker

sit perch, be seated

site   place, location, position, situation, whereabouts

situation   1. place, location, position, whereabouts, 2. circumstances, case, condition, terms

size   proportion, measure, extent, scope, dimensions

skillful   expert, adept, proficient, apt, handy, clever, masterful, able, capable (*Slang* — crackerjack)   unable, awkward SKILL

skim   glide, coast, sail, slide, graze, brush

skimpy   scanty, scarce, sparse, meager   generous, abundant

skinny   lean, spare, scrawny, lanky, gaunt, bony   chubby

skip   1. spring, jump, leap, 2. pass over, omit, bypass include

skirmish   argument, conflict, clash, scuffle, brush, struggle, encounter, engagement, melee (*Slang* — scrap, run-in)

skirt   border, edge, rim, margin, fringe

skulk   sneak, hide, lurk, slink, prowl, steal, creep

slack   1. loose, lax, baggy, hanging, droopy   tight, 2. slow, dull, lazy, inactive   busy

slam   close, bang, shut

slander   libel, slur, discredit, smear (*Slang* — knock)

slant   slope, incline, lean, tip, tilt

slap   hit, smack, crack

slash   cut, gash, wound, sever

slaughter   butchery, massacre, killing, carnage, genocide

slavery   bondage, servitude, serfdom   freedom   SLAVE

slay   kill, put to death, exterminate, destroy (*Slang* — croak, bump off)

sleek   smooth, glossy, slick, polished

sleep   slumber, doze, drowse, nap, rest, snooze

slender   thin, narrow, svelte, frail, slight   stout

slice   cut, sever, split, carve, slash, slit

slick   1. sleek, smooth, glossy, polished, 2. sly, tricky, cunning, shrewd, shifty, crafty, foxy (*Slang* — cagey)

slide   glide, coast, skim, skid, slip

slight   1. small, petite, puny, tiny   large, gross, 2. slender, frail, delicate, dainty, flimsy, thin, svelte   stout, 3. neglect, disregard, overlook, ignore

slim   slender, thin, svelte, slight, lean   stout

slime   mud, muck, slush, mire

sling   1. throw, cast, hurl, fling, pitch, toss, heave, flip, 2. suspend, hang, 3. bandage, support, splint

slink   sneak, lurk, prowl, steal, creep

slip   1. slide, glide, skid, 2. mistake, error, oversight, blunder

slit   cut, sever, split, cleave, tear

slogan   motto, phrase, expression, cry

slope   slant, incline, tip, lean, tilt

sloppy   1. careless, slovenly, slipshod, negligent, haphazard, messy   neat, 2. wet, slushy   dry

slothful   lazy, sluggish, do-nothing, shiftless, indolent, laggard   ambitious

slovenly   untidy, slipshod, unkempt, shabby, seedy, messy, sloppy   neat

slow   1. lingering, delaying, lackadaisical, leisurely, poking, tarrying, dillydallying   fast, 2. dull, stupid (*Slang* — dimwitted)   quick, bright

slug   1. strike, hit, knock, poke, punch, jab, smack, whack, bat, crack, clout (*Slang* — sock, clobber, paste, wallop, clip, swat), 3. token, coin

sluggish   slow-moving, inactive, lackadaisical, poky, listless, lethargic   quick, fast-moving

slumber   sleep, doze, drowse, nap, rest, snooze

slur   1. skim over, glance at, scan, 2. insult, smear, soil, slander, libel, defame, slight

sly   shrewd, underhanded, artful, cunning, shifty, smooth, crafty, canny, sneaky, clever, tricky (*Slang* — foxy, cagey, slick)

smack   1. hit, slap, crack, strike, whack (*Slang* — clobber, belt, wallop, swat), 2. kiss (*Slang* — smooch)

small   1. little, slight, puny, insignificant   big, 2. unimportant, trivial   important

smart   1. bright, clever, keen, intelligent, quick, shrewd, alert, brainy   stupid, 2. stylish, well-dressed, chic, natty, dapper, fashionable (*Slang* — sharp, nifty), 3. pain, ache, hurt

smash   1. destroy, shatter, ruin, break, crash, fragment, 2. collide, clash, bump, strike, knock, bang

smear   1. stain, mark, soil, tarnish, smudge, spot, 2. spoil, harm, blacken, defile, slander

smell   scent, odor, essence, fragrance

smile   grin, beam, laugh, smirk   frown

smog   fog, smoke, haziness, cloudiness

smooth   1. sleek, slick, glossy, polished, even, level   rough, 2. polite, pleasant, suave, chivalrous, cunning

smother   suffocate, stifle, choke, asphyxiate, muffle, suppress

smudge   smear, mark, soil, blacken, spot, stain

smug   self-satisfied, confident, vain, conceited, arrogant, boastful, egotistical   modest, humble

snag   trap, hook, catch, snatch, snare   release

snake   serpent, viper

snap   1. break, burst, split, crack, 2. snatch, seize   release

snare   trap, catch, hook

snarl   1. growl, grumble, 2. tangle, mix up, knot

snatch   1. seize, grasp, grab, clutch, hook, snag, snare, trap
release, 2. small amount, bit, scrap, shred

sneak   lurk, prowl, slink, steal, creep

sneer   mock, scoff, jeer, taunt

sniff   smell, scent, inhale

snipe   shoot at, fire at   SNIPER

snobbish   haughty, arrogant, priggish (*Slang* — stuck-up,
snooty, high-hat)   SNOB

snoop   pry, meddle, intrude, interfere (*Slang* — butt in,
horn in)

snooze   sleep, doze, nap

snub   slight, ignore, avoid, shun, spurn, rebuff

snug   1. comfortable, warm, sheltered, cozy, homelike (*Slang*
— comfy), 2. compact, close, tight   roomy

snuggle   nestle, cuddle

soak   wet, drench, saturate, steep, sop   dry

soap   lather, shampoo

soar   fly, glide, aspire, tower, hover, ascend

sob   cry, weep, bawl, blubber, snivel, wail, howl

sober   1. sensible, calm, moderate, temperate, mild, sound,
reasonable   extreme, 2. unintoxicated, uninebriated
drunk

sociable   friendly, amiable, congenial, cordial, gregarious
unfriendly, unsociable

society   1. people, folks, public, populace, community, world, 2. company, organization, association, alliance, league, union, federation, sect

sock   1. strike, hit, knock, jab, whack, bat, crack (*Slang —* belt, paste, wallop, clip, swat), 2. stocking

sod   soil, earth, dirt, ground

soft   1. delicate, tender, flexible, pliable, elastic   hard, 2. mild, kind, gentle, tender, pleasant, lenient, easygoing   harsh

soggy   damp, soaked, saturated, sopping, waterlogged   dry

soil   1. dirty, spot, stain, smudge, smear   clean, 2. slander, libel, defile, 3. ground, earth, dirt, land

sojourn   stay, stopover

solace   comfort, relieve, cheer, console, encourage, reassure, hearten

solder   cement, bind, weld, fuse, join, mend, fasten

sole   only, single, one, individual, unique

solemn   serious, grave, gloomy, dismal, somber, dreary, glum   happy, cheerful

solicit   request, appeal, ask, canvass, beg (*Slang —* mooch, bum, panhandle, touch)

solid   1. hard, firm, rigid, substantial, sturdy, strong, durable   flimsy, soft, 2. whole, entire, continuous, complete

solitary   single, individual, lone, isolated, unaccompanied

solution   1. explanation, answer, resolution, finding, outcome, result, 2. mixture

solve   answer, explain, clear up, work out, figure out, unriddle, decipher, decode

somber   dark, gloomy, dismal, dreary, melancholy, bleak, uncheerful, grave, solemn, grim   cheerful

soon   promptly, quickly, shortly, presently, directly, before long

soothe   calm, comfort, quiet, ease, pacify, relieve

sorcery   witchcraft, bewitchment, entrancement, spell, magic, wizardry, voodoo   SORCERER

sordid   dirty, filthy, slovenly, squalid

sore   1. painful, aching, tender, smarting, raw, irritated, inflamed, festering, rankling, throbbing, distressing   healed, 2. angry, offended, irate, indignant (*Slang* — mad, riled up)

sorrow   grief, sadness, regret, trouble, misfortune, suffering, woe, anguish, misery, agony, remorse   happiness

sorry   1. regretful, remorseful, repentant, apologetic, 2. sad, sympathetic, unhappy, miserable, displeased, 3. wretched, poor, pitiful

sort   arrange, separate, classify, categorize, group, divide, catalog

sound   1. make noise, utter, pronounce, voice, 2. healthy, wholesome, hearty   unhealthy, 3. strong, safe, secure, stable, substantial, firm, solid, solvent   weak, 4. correct, right, reasonable, sensible, sane, logical, rational   wrong, foolish

sour   1. spoiled, fermented, bitter, rancid   fresh, 2. disagreeable, peevish, unpleasant   pleasant

source   origin, beginning, derivation, root

souvenir   remembrance, keepsake, memento, relic, token

sovereign   supreme, greatest, regal, royal, imperial, majestic, ruling, reigning, governing

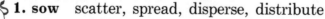

1. sow   scatter, spread, disperse, distribute

2. sow   female pig

space   extent, expanse, measure, dimension, area

spacious vast, roomy, widespread, extensive, sweeping, far-reaching, capacious confining, narrow

span 1. bridge, viaduct, 2. period, interval, spell, 3. distance, extent, reach, stretch, measure, expanse

spank slap, strike, hit, smack (*Slang* — lick, paddle) SPANKING

spar box, fight (*Slang* — scrap)

spare 1. give up, relinquish, dispense with, do without, omit, forego, part with, sacrifice, surrender, yield keep, 2. extra, surplus, remainder, balance, leftover, excess, 3. lean, skinny, thin, scrawny, lanky, bony stout

spark flash, gleam, glimmer

sparkle shine, glitter, flash, glimmer, shimmer, twinkle, glisten

sparse scanty, meager, scattered, scarce, skimpy

spasm twitch, seizure, convulsion, fit

spat quarrel, disagree, differ, dispute, fight, squabble, tiff, bicker, row (*Slang* — scrap)

spatter sprinkle, speckle, dot

speak talk, say, tell, express SPEECH, SPEAKER

spear pierce, stab, puncture, impale, lance, knife

special unusual, exceptional, particular, extraordinary, notable ordinary, usual

species group, class, kind, sort, type, variety

specific definite, precise, particular, special, fixed SPECIFICATION, SPECIFY

specimen sample, representative, type, example

speck tiny bit, particle, iota (*Slang* — dab, smidgen)

speckle spot, mottle, mark

spectacle sight, show, display, exhibition, pageant

spectacular dramatic, sensational

speculate 1. guess, theorize, conjecture, 2. gamble, risk, chance, venture, 3. reflect, meditate, consider, contemplate, study, deliberate SPECULATION

speedy fast, rapid, quick, swift, hasty, fleet, expeditious (*Slang* — snappy) SPEED

spell 1. magic power, charm, fascination, trance, 2. time, stretch, shift, period

spellbound fascinated, enchanted, interested, rapt, enthralled, gripped, engrossed, absorbed, awed, charmed, hypnotized, mesmerized bored

spend pay out, lay out, use, consume, finish off, exhaust, expend

sphere 1. ball, globe, 2. extent, realm, expanse, province, field

spice season, flavor

spike pierce, stab, puncture, impale, spear

spill overflow, run over, brim over, cascade, flood, pour

spin turn, twirl, twist, rotate, pivot, wheel, reel, swirl

spinster old maid, single woman

spiral coil, twist, twirl, kink

spirit 1. soul, heart, mind, 2. nature, disposition, temper, 3. courage, vigor, life, vivacity

spiritual religious, sacred, holy

spit saliva, drivel, dribble, drool, expectoration

spiteful annoying, malicious, hostile, vindictive, mean, ornery SPITE

splash wet, splatter, sprinkle, spatter

splatter splash, sprinkle, spatter

splendid fine, excellent, brilliant, glorious, magnificent, grand (*Slang* — great, dandy, swell, keen, hot, nifty, hunky-dory)

splendor pomp, glory, magnificence, grandeur, brilliance, brightness, radiance dullness

splice join, bind, tie, connect, attach

split separate, divide, bisect, halve, cleave, partition, sever, break, crack join, connect

spoil damage, injure, destroy, botch, impair, mar, ruin, upset, rot, decay (*Slang* — mess up, foul up, louse up, gum up)

sponsor underwriter, backer, financer, promoter, supporter (*Slang* — angel)

spontaneous instinctive, inherent, natural, automatic planned

spook ghost, specter, apparition, spirit, phantom

sport fun, play, amusement, game, contest

spot 1. stain, mark, discolor, soil, 2. pick out, recognize, know, tell, distinguish, identify, place, discern, spy, sight

spouse mate, husband, wife

spout discharge, expel, spew, eject, pour forth

sprawl spread, extend, stretch out, expand, fan out

spray sprinkle, spatter, splash

spread 1. stretch out, unfold, extend, sprawl, 2. distribute, scatter, disperse

spree gay time, escapade, celebration, fling, whirl, lark

sprig twig, branch, limb, bough, shoot, sprout

sprightly lively, gay, active, animated, spirited, vivacious, spry, energetic, nimble (*Slang* — peppy) dull, lethargic

spring leap, jump, bounce, vault, hop, bound, hurdle

sprinkle spray, spatter, splash

sprite elf, fairy, goblin, pixie, gremlin

sprout grow, develop, shoot up, flourish, thrive, bud, burgeon

spry lively, gay, sprightly, active, animated, spirited, vivacious, energetic, nimble   dull, lethargic

spunk courage, pluck, spirit, will power, nerve, grit, mettle, (*Slang* — backbone, guts)

spur urge, goad, prod, provoke (*Slang* — egg on)

spurn scorn, reject, disown, deny, repudiate, disdain, snub, rebuff

spurt flow, gush, spew, expel, erupt, jet, spout, squirt

spy see, detect, view, observe, discern, sight, spot

squabble quarrel, disagree, differ, dispute, fight, tiff, spat, bicker, row (*Slang* — scrap, hassle)

squad group, unit, company, band, gang, crew, outfit, troop, body

squalid filthy, degraded, poor, wretched, shabby, sordid, slummy   clean   SQUALOR

squall 1. cry, scream, wail, howl, moan, bawl, yell, squeal, 2. gust, gale, blizzard

squander waste, throw away, misspend, dissipate   save

square 1. adjust, settle, balance, equalize, 2. just, fair, honest, straight, equitable   crooked, 3. old-fashioned, corny, unaware, conventional   sophisticated

squash crush, press, mash, suppress, squelch

squat crouch, lie low

squawk complain, grumble, mutter (*Slang* — gripe, crab, bellyache, beef, kick, grouch, howl)

squeak   squeal, yelp

squeal   1. cry, squeak, screech, yell, 2. tattle, inform on (*Slang* — blab, snitch)

squeeze   press, crush, pinch, cram

squirm   wriggle, twist, writhe, wiggle

squirt   spew, spout, spurt, expel, pour forth, jet, gush, spray, surge, splash

stab   pierce, perforate, puncture, impale, wound

stable   1. steady, firm, unchanging, steadfast, sound, secure, settled, established   unsettled, 2. barn

stack   pile, heap, load

staff   1. group, committee, personnel, force, crew, gang, 2. stick, pole, rod, scepter

stage   1. arrange, dramatize, present, produce, perform, enact, put on, 2. period, interval, point, time, spell, 3. tier, level, layer, story, 4. platform, podium, rostrum

stagger   sway, reel, waver, flounder, tumble, lurch

stagnant   still, inactive, sluggish, inert, static, dormant   active

staid   sensible, level-headed, sober-minded, sedate, serious   flighty, unsettled

stain   spot, soil, mark, discolor

stake   1. bet, wager, gamble, risk, 2. peg, post

stale   old, worn, obsolete, musty   new, fresh

stalk   1. pursue, hunt, chase, seek, search, 2. stem

stall   1. delay, procrastinate, dillydally, dawdle, block, hinder   hurry, 2. compartment, booth, cell

stalwart   1. strong, robust, firm, potent, rugged, sturdy, powerful   weak, 2. brave, courageous, bold, valiant, gallant, heroic   cowardly

stammer   stutter, falter, stumble

stamp   1. mark, seal, label, brand, engrave, print, 2. trample, pound, crush, tread

stampede   flight, rush, panic

stand   1. rise, get up   sit, lie down, 2. endure, bear, tolerate, 3. remain, last, continue, stay, persist, 4. pedestal, base, table

standard   1. model, rule, pattern, criterion, ideal, 2. flag, banner, pennant, emblem, symbol, colors

standstill   stop, halt, pause, impasse

stanza   verse, measure, refrain

staple   1. fasten, clasp, attach, bind, connect, join, link, 2. important, principal, main

star   1. headline, excel, feature, 2. heavenly body

stare   gaze, look, gape, glare, gawk

stark   complete, entirely, downright, absolute, outright

start   1. begin, commence, set out, 2. move suddenly, jerk, jump

startle   frighten, surprise, shock, electrify, upset, alarm, unnerve (*Slang* — jar)

starve   hunger, crave food   STARVATION

state   1. tell, express, say, pose, declare, assert, relate, recite, report, expound, 2. condition, position, status, situation, circumstance, 3. nation

stately   grand, majestic, dignified, imposing, noble, grandiose, magnificent, splendid, impressive

statement   account, report, announcement, proclamation, declaration, notice

static   1. still, inactive, sluggish, inert, dormant   active, 2. electrical interference

station 1. place, post, 2. position, rank, standing, status, post

stationary fixed, immovable, immobile, firm, inflexible, motionless movable

stationery paper, writing materials

statue figure, sculpture, bust, monument

stature height, loftiness

status 1. standing, position, station, class, division, grade, rank, 2. condition, state

statute law, ordinance, rule, act, regulation, measure, dictate, decree, bill, enactment

staunch loyal, steadfast, devoted, firm, reliable, dependable, trustworthy

stay 1. remain, last, endure, continue, persist leave, 2. dwell, reside, live, occupy, inhabit, 3. delay, detain, retard, stop, hold up proceed

steady constant, fixed, inert, regular, incessant, ceaseless, perpetual changing STEADFAST

steal rob, take, thieve, pilfer, filch (*Slang* — lift, swipe, cop, pinch)

stealthy secret, sly, sneaky, underhanded, shifty open, honest

steam 1. vapor, gas, smoke, 2. power, energy, force, 3. cook, soften, freshen

steed horse, stallion, nag

steep 1. soak, drench, sop, saturate, bathe, 2. high, precipitous

steer 1. guide, direct, drive, manage, regulate, conduct, handle, lead, head, run, 2. cattle

step walk, tread, pace

sterilize   clean, sanitize, disinfect, decontaminate
STERILE

stern   severe, strict, harsh, firm, hard, exacting, austere, stringent (*Slang* — tough, hard-boiled)
lenient, easygoing

stew   1. cook, 2. fume, seethe, be angry, rage, rave, rant, storm, fret

stick   1. pierce, stab, perforate, penetrate, puncture, 2. fasten, attach, adhere, cling, 3. continue, keep on, persevere, stop, discontinue

stiff   1. rigid, firm, tense, taut, tight, inflexible, tough flexible, 2. formal, unnatural, stilted informal, 3. hard, difficult, tough easy

stifle   smother, stop, suppress, suffocate, choke

stigma   brand, slur, stain, blemish, disgrace

still   1. quiet, motionless, noiseless, calm, tranquil, peaceful, placid, smooth, untroubled noisy, 2. yet, even, until now, so far

stimulate   spur, stir, rouse, energize, invigorate, pep up, activate, motivate, move suppress, stifle
STIMULANT, STIMULUS

sting   prick, wound, pain, distress, inflame

stingy   ungenerous, miserly, cheap, closefisted (*Slang* — tight, penny-pinching) generous, liberal

stink   smell, stench, odor

stint   task, work, job, chore, duty, assignment, function, role

stir   1. mix, blend, mingle, combine, merge, scramble, jumble, 2. move, budge, mobilize, 3. excite, affect, agitate, disturb, shake, perturb, trouble, disquiet, rouse

stitch   sew, fasten, tailor

stock   supply, keep, store up, collect, accumulate, amass, stockpile, gather, hoard

stocky   sturdy, solid, fat, plump, chubby, portly, fleshy, chunky, strapping   lean, thin

stomach   1. bear, endure, take, stand, tolerate, 2. belly, abdomen

stone   rock, pebble, gem

stool   seat, chair

stoop   1. bend forward, crouch, squat, 2. porch, veranda, platform

stop   end, halt, check, stay, cease, block, discontinue, quit, arrest, prevent, conclude, terminate   start

store   1. supply, stock, keep, collect, accumulate, amass, stockpile, gather, hoard, 2. shop, mart, business
STORAGE

storm   1. attack, besiege, beset, raid, charge, assault, assail, 2. rage, be violent, rant, rave, rampage, seethe, boil, fume, 3. tempest, outburst

story   1. tale, account, chronicle, yarn, narrative, anecdote, epic, saga, 2. floor, level, tier

stout   1. fat, large, fleshy, plump, pudgy, chubby, stocky, portly   thin, 2. brave, bold, courageous, valiant, gallant, heroic, chivalrous   meek, cowardly

stow   pack, load, store

straddle   perch

straggle   wander, ramble, roam, rove, drift, stray

straight   1. direct, unswerving   crooked, 2. frank, honest, upright, square, sincere, open

strain   1. stretch, pull, extend, tug, tow, 2. sprain, wrench, injure, hurt, 3. quality, trace, streak, 4. race, descent

strand   1. abandon, desert, leave, 2. thread, string, cord, line

strange   unusual, queer, peculiar, unfamiliar, odd, curious, eccentric   ordinary, familiar   STRANGER

strangle   choke, suffocate, smother, asphyxiate

strap   1. fasten, bind, tie, wrap, lash, gird   untie, 2. whip, beat, thrash, spank, flog (*Slang* — lick, wallop), 3. belt

strapping   tall, strong, healthy, sturdy, rugged, powerful, hardy, robust, vigorous, well-built, athletic, muscular, brawny, beefy   weak

strategy   planning, management, tactics, manipulation, intrigue, maneuvering   STRATEGIC

stray   wander, roam, rove, straggle, gad, ramble, drift, meander

streak   1. mark, line, score, striate, stripe, 2. strain, element, vein, nature, quality, characteristic, tendency

stream   1. flow, pour, surge, rush, gush, flood, 2. creek, brook

street   road, thoroughfare, avenue

strength   power, force, vigor, potency, might, energy, intensity   weakness   STRENGTHEN

strenuous   1. active, energetic, vigorous, intense   inactive, 2. difficult, hard, rough, rugged, arduous, laborious (*Slang* — tough, wicked, mean)   easy

stress   1. force, strain, pressure, tension, 2. emphasis, importance, accent, insistence, urgency

stretch   extend, draw out, spread, strain, expand, distend, elongate

strew   sprinkle, scatter, disperse, distribute

strict   1. harsh, exact, precise, rigorous, severe, exacting, stringent, stern, austere (*Slang* — tough, hard-boiled) lenient, 2. perfect, complete, absolute, literal, exact, real, true

stride step, pace, walk

strife quarreling, fighting, controversy, dispute, squabble peace

strike 1. hit, knock, jab, smack, whack, bat, clout (*Slang* — sock, swat, clip, clobber, belt, bash, paste, wallop), 2. revolt, rebel

striking attractive, noticeable, obvious, conspicuous, prominent, bold, pronounced, outstanding, flagrant, glaring unattractive

string thread, connect, line up, bind, tie

strip remove, uncover, bare, peel, pare   cover

stripe line, mark, striate

strive struggle, fight, contend, battle, endeavor, labor

stroke 1. rub, caress, massage, pet, 2. feat, effort, act, deed, undertaking, attempt, 3. attack, seizure, convulsion, spasm

stroll walk, saunter, stride, strut, amble, promenade

strong powerful, vigorous, forceful, potent, mighty, sturdy, hardy, muscular, brawny   weak

stronghold fortification, bastion

structure 1. building, construction, house, edifice, 2. form, shape, figure, configuration

struggle 1. endeavor, strive, attempt, try, 2. fight, battle, contend, tussle, scuffle (*Slang* — scrap)

strut swagger, parade

stub end, tip, tail

stubborn obstinate, willful, headstrong, adamant, rigid, unyielding, inflexible   yielding, flexible

stubby stocky, chubby, squat, pudgy, chunky lanky

student pupil, scholar

studious learned, bookish, educated, scholarly, cultured, profound, erudite, diligent STUDY

stuff 1. fill, load, pack, gorge, saturate empty, 2. substance, matter, material

stuffy 1. close, stifling, airless, suffocating, oppressive airy, 2. pompous, prim, prudish, strait-laced, unimaginative, dull, staid, stodgy, old-fogyish casual, regular

stumble stagger, flounder, tumble, falter

stump 1. baffle, perplex, confound, mystify, puzzle (*Slang* — stick, flaw, get), 2. campaign, electioneer (*Slang* — whistle-stop), 3. remainder, rest, leftovers

stun daze, bewilder, shock, overwhelm, numb, stupefy

stunning 1. attractive, good-looking, beautiful, gorgeous, ravishing, glorious, dazzling, brilliant (*Slang* — devastating) unattractive, 2. bewildering, astounding, shocking, astonishing, amazing, surprising

stunt 1. shorten, abbreviate, abridge, condense, 2. feat, act, exploit, performance

stupefy stun, daze, bewilder, shock, numb

stupendous amazing, marvelous, great, huge, enormous, immense, vast, extraordinary, exceptional, remarkable, wonderful

stupid dull, unintelligent, dense, asinine, silly, foolish (*Slang* — dimwitted, dumb, thick) smart, bright

stupor unconsciousness, faint, coma, blackout, swoon, lethargy, numbness

sturdy strong, firm, powerful, rugged, hardy, robust, vigorous, well-built, athletic, muscular, brawny, sound, stable, substantial, solid, durable weak, shaky

stutter   stammer, hem, haw, falter, hesitate

stylish   fashionable, modish, voguish, smart, chic, well-dressed, natty, dapper, sporty (*Slang* — swanky, nifty, sharp)   drab   STYLE

subdue   conquer, overcome, crush, vanquish, suppress, quell, put down, squash, squelch

subject   topic, issue, problem, theme, text, question, point, plot

sublime   noble, majestic, grand, great, distinguished, lofty, prominent, eloquent, exalted

submerge   immerse, sink, dip, duck, inundate, dunk

submit   yield, surrender, comply, obey, heed, mind   SUBMISSION, SUBMISSIVE

subordinate   dependent, secondary, inferior   superior

subscribe   contribute, give to, donate to, support   SUBSCRIPTION

subsequent   following, later, coming after, succeeding, next   preceding

subside   decrease, diminish, lessen, decline   increase

subsist   live, exist, survive   SUBSISTENCE

substance   matter, material, body, stuff, essence, gist, content

substantial   1. real, actual, true, authentic   vague, 2. strong, firm, solid, stable, sound   weak, 3. wealthy, well-to-do, rich, affluent, prosperous   poor

substitute   replace, change, exchange, switch, shift   SUBSTITUTION

subtle   1. delicate, thin, fine, faint   gross, strong, 2. sly, crafty, tricky, underhanded, shrewd, cunning, foxy, clever (*Slang* — cagey, slick)   open, honest

subtract deduct, take away, remove, withdraw, discount add SUBTRACTION

successful prosperous, fortunate, well-off, thriving, flourishing, victorious, triumphant, winning, providential, booming, lucky failing, unsuccessful SUCCEED, SUCCESS

succession sequence, order, progression, series SUCCEED

succulent juicy

succumb 1. yield, give way, submit, comply, acquiesce conquer, 2. die, decease, expire, perish

suck drink, take in, absorb, draw in SUCTION

sudden unexpected, abrupt, hasty, unforeseen, impulsive, impetuous planned, deliberate SUDDENLY

sue prosecute, bring action against, litigate

suffer endure, experience, bear, stand, tolerate, undergo

sufficient enough, ample, plenty, satisfactory, adequate lacking, insufficient SUFFICIENTLY

suffocate smother, stifle, choke, muffle, suppress, asphyxiate

suffrage vote, voice, ballot

suggest hint, imply, intimate, insinuate, propose, advise SUGGESTION

suit 1. agree with, satisfy, 2. fit, become, 3. costume, dress, habit, 4. legal action, litigation, case, prosecution

suitable fitting, proper, timely, favorable, adequate, satisfactory unsuitable

sulk mope, fret (*Slang* — grump, grouch)

sullen gloomy, dismal, glum, moody, moping, morose, sulky cheerful, pleasant

sum total, whole, entirety, quantity, amount

summarize   brief, outline, abridge, capsule
expand, elaborate   SUMMARY

summit   top, peak, crest, crown, apex, acme, zenith
bottom, base

summon   call, send for, subpoena, conjure

sumptuous   rich, magnificent, costly, grandiose, grand,
splendid, imposing, impressive, stately, majestic, elegant,
elaborate, luxurious (*Slang* — swell, plush)   poor

sundown   sunset, dusk, evening, nightfall   sunrise

sundry   several, various, diversified, assorted, many

sunken   1. submerged, sunk, 2. hollow, concave

sunny   bright, cheerful, pleasant, radiant   dull

sunrise   dawn, daybreak, morning   sunset

sunset   sundown, dusk, evening, nightfall   sunrise

superb   grand, stately, magnificent, splendid, fine, excellent,
exquisite, marvelous, wonderful, grandiose, glorious, imposing, impressive, noble, majestic, sumptuous, elaborate (*Slang*
— swell)   inferior

superficial   shallow, surface, cursory   thorough, deep

superintendent   supervisor, manager, director, foreman

superior   better, greater, higher   inferior

supernatural   spiritual, superhuman, ghostly, unknown,
mysterious, mystical

supersede   displace, replace, take the place of, supplant

superstition   folklore, tradition, popular belief, old wives'
tale   SUPERSTITIOUS

supervise   direct, oversee, govern, regulate, command, head,
lead, administer, boss   SUPERVISION, SUPERVISOR

supplant   supersede, replace, displace, take the place of

supple bending, pliable, flexible, plastic, elastic, yielding, limber, lithe stiff, firm

supplement add to, complete, augment, increase, fortify, reinforce subtract

supplication prayer, request, plea, entreaty, appeal
SUPPLICATE

supply furnish, provide, stock, store

support help, aid, bolster, sustain, defend, encourage, foster

suppose believe, think, imagine, consider, assume, infer, deduce, presume

suppress restrain, repress, keep down, hold back, inhibit, curb, check, arrest, bridle, squelch, stifle, subdue, squash, restrict, limit, quell foster, encourage SUPPRESSION

supreme highest, greatest, utmost, extreme, uppermost, top, maximum, foremost, chief, paramount
SUPREMACY

sure certain, positive, absolute, definite, decided SURELY

surface outside, exterior, face interior

surge wave, gush, flow, mount, whirl, stream, rush, swell, billow

surgery operation SURGEON

surly rude, gruff, bad-tempered, brusque, curt, blunt, harsh, rough, sullen, moody pleasant, affable

surmise guess, judge, consider, regard, suppose, presume, imagine, suspect, infer, gather, conclude, deduce, think

surmount overcome, rise above, triumph over, defeat succumb

surpass excel, exceed, go beyond

surplus excess, extra, superfluous, remaining, leftover, spare, additional, supplementary lack

surprise astonish, amaze, catch unaware, astound, bewilder, awe, dumbfound

surrender give up, yield, relinquish, forego, renounce, submit, capitulate, abandon conquer

surround wrap, envelop, embrace, encircle, enclose, encompass

survey 1. examine, view, inspect, scrutinize, observe, scan, study, contemplate, peruse, review, 2. measure, gauge, assess, estimate, rate, appraise SURVEYOR

survive remain, continue, outlast, outlive SURVIVAL

susceptible pliant, suggestible, yielding, impressionable, open, pliable

suspect 1. think, guess, suppose, assume, imagine, surmise, infer, gather (*Slang* — expect, reckon), 2. doubt, distrust, question, challenge, dispute, mistrust trust

suspend 1. hang, sling, 2. postpone, delay, defer, hold over, shelve, 3. interrupt, break, arrest, halt continue
SUSPENSION

suspense anxiety, fear, concern, apprehension, distress, uneasiness, agitation, disquiet

suspicious suspecting, doubtful, questionable, wary (*Slang* — leery) SUSPICION

sustain keep up, support, bear, endure, maintain, suffer, tolerate, stand, abide succumb

swagger strut, parade

swallow 1. eat, absorb, consume, devour, gulp, ingest, 2. accept, take, believe

swamp 1. sink, overwhelm, flood, 2. marsh, bog

swap trade, deal, exchange, barter, switch

swarm crowd, throng, collect, assemble, meet, gather, cluster disperse, scatter

swat hit, strike, knock, poke, jab, whack (*Slang* — bat, clout, belt, clobber, paste, wallop, clip, sock)

sway 1. swing, reel, rock, lurch, roll, toss, pitch, 2. influence, control, rule, affect, move, persuade, prejudice

swear 1. promise, vow, vouch, 2. curse (*Slang* — cuss)

sweep 1. clean, brush, vacuum, 2. move, glide, coast, skim, slip, slide, 3. stretch, extend, range

sweet 1. sugary, saccharine bitter, 2. pleasant, agreeable, lovely, charming, adorable unpleasant

swell 1. grow bigger, increase, gain, expand, enlarge, broaden amplify, magnify, inflate, stretch, bulge, billow shrink, decrease, 2. good (*Slang* — grand, great, dandy, keen, hot, nifty, bully, ripping, hunkydory)

swelter sweat, perspire, roast

swerve dodge, sidestep, shift, turn (*Slang* — duck)

swift fast, quick, rapid, speedy, hasty, fleet, expeditious, agile, nimble (*Slang* — snappy) slow

swim bathe, float, wade SWIMMER

swindle cheat, defraud, fleece, gyp (*Slang* — beat, crook, stick, shortchange, con, chisel) SWINDLER

swine 1. hogs, pigs, 2. scoundrel, skunk (*Slang* — louse, heel, rat, stinker, bugger)

swing sway, reel, rock, roll, lurch, fluctuate, dangle, hang

swirl twist, whirl, curl, wheel, reel, spin

switch 1. whip, strike, slash, beat, thrash, bang, spank, flog, pummel, lash, strap, club, paddle (*Slang* — lick, wallop), 2. change, turn, shift, exchange, substitute, replace, trade, swap

swoon faint (*Slang* — keel over, pass out)

swoop   dive, plunge, plummet, drop, fall, pounce

sword   knife, blade

symbolize   represent, stand for, typify, illustrate
SYMBOL

symmetrical   balanced, even, orderly, regular, uniform, equal   unbalanced, uneven   SYMMETRY

sympathy   understanding, tolerance, sensitivity, pity, compassion, mercy, commiseration, condolence
SYMPATHETIC, SYMPATHIZE

symphony   concert, recital

symptom   sign, implication, token, mark, omen, indication

synthetic   man-made, artificial, mock, counterfeit, imitation, simulated   natural

system   plan, scheme, method, design, arrangement, order
SYSTEMATIC

T

table   1. list, chart, index, catalog, schedule, 2. postpone, delay, put off, shelve

tablet   1. notebook, pad, 2. pill, capsule

tack   attach, add, join, affix, fasten, clasp

tackle   1. undertake, get busy, attack, 2. seize, grapple with, 3. equipment, apparatus, gear, furnishings

tact   grace, diplomacy, taste, finesse, sensitivity, sensibility
TACTFUL

tactics   procedures, operations, methods, strategy, maneuvers

tag 1. label, brand, name, call, designate, 2. follow, shadow, pursue, trail, heel (*Slang* — tail)

tail 1. back, rear, end, tip, 2. follow, pursue, shadow, trail, heel (*Slang* — tag)

taint stain, spot, spoil, discolor, tarnish, mark, soil

take 1. seize, capture, get, receive, gain, obtain, procure give, 2. need, require, involve, entail, implicate, 3. choose, select, pick out, 4. bring, carry, convey, 5. suppose, assume, infer, understand, gather, guess, 6. hire, lease, engage, 7. tolerate, endure, bear, stand, suffer, swallow, stomach

tale 1. story, yarn, account, narrative, epic, saga, 2. falsehood, lie, untruth, fib truth

talent ability, skill, gift, endowment, genius, capability, capacity, forte, aptitude

talk 1. speak, converse, discuss (*Slang* — gab, yap), 2. gossip, rumor, report

tall 1. high, big, long, lengthy short, 2. exaggerated, magnified, enlarged, overstated, excessive, extreme true

tally 1. count, score, calculate, compute, estimate, reckon, figure, list, 2. agree, correspond, coincide, match, check

tame gentle, obedient, temperate, mild, domesticated wild

tamper meddle, pry, busybody, interfere, intrude

tang flavor, taste

tangible 1. real, actual, definite, substantial, concrete vague, 2. touchable

tangle twist, confuse, mess, complicate, knot, snarl, involve

tantalize torment, tease, molest, bother, harass, badger, worry, pester, torture

tantrum fit, outburst, scene, rage, fury, conniption, flare-up

tap 1. rap, pat, 2. faucet, valve, spigot

tape   1. wrap, fasten, bind, tie, bandage, 2. record

taper   lessen, diminish, narrow, contract   increase

tardy   late, overdue, delayed

target   object, goal, aim, end, mark, point

tariff   tax, duty, toll, assessment, levy

tarnish   dull, dim, fade, discolor, stain, soil

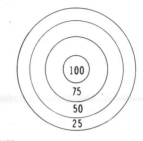

tarry   remain, stay, linger, wait, delay, loiter, dawdle, dilly-dally

tart   sour, sharp, bitter, pungent

task   work, duty, job, chore, stint, assignment, function

taste   savor, sample, experiment, test, try, experience, sense, feel

tattered   torn, ragged, shabby, shoddy, frayed, frazzled, seedy, tacky

tattle   gossip, chatter, rumor, report (*Slang* — blab, snitch, squeal)   TATTLETALE

taunt   mock, jeer, reproach, scoff

taut   tight, tense, unrelaxed, firm, rigid, stiff   relaxed

tavern   inn, cabaret, bar, saloon, pub

tax   1. strain, burden, load, encumber, oppress, 2. duty, tariff, levy, toll, assessment

taxi   cab

teach   instruct, educate, show, enlighten, tutor, coach, direct, guide   TEACHER

team   band, company, group, party, gang, crew

tear   cut, sever, split, slash, slice, slit, rip

tearful   weeping, sad, sobbing, crying   TEAR

tease annoy, vex, pester, bother, joke, jest, banter, badger (*Slang* — kid, rib, razz)

tedious dull, dreary, slow, dry, tiring, boring, monotonous, humdrum, wearisome exhilarating, interesting

teem flow, abound, swarm

telecast televise, broadcast

televise telecast, broadcast

tell say, inform, utter, voice, express, communicate, convey, impart, state, declare, assert, relate, recite, remark, comment, note, mention

temerity boldness, rashness, brashness, indiscretion caution

temper disposition, condition, nature, character, constitution, tendency, mood TEMPERAMENT

temperamental moody, sensitive, touchy, thin-skinned

temperate moderate, mild, gentle, calm extreme

tempest storm, violence

temporary passing, momentary, transient, short-lived lasting, permanent TEMPORARILY

tempt invite, attract, interest, appeal, tantalize, titillate, entice, seduce, lure TEMPTATION

tenacious persevering, persistent, continuing, diligent, steadfast, constant, unswerving, untiring, obstinate, stubborn, willful, headstrong lax

tenant dweller, occupant, resident, inhabitant

tend 1. be apt, be likely, incline, lean, 2. attend, administer, care for, look after, mind, watch over, foster, nurse, serve, help

tendency inclination, leaning, bent, proclivity, disposition, aptitude

tender 1. soft, delicate, gentle, kind, affectionate, loving, sensitive harsh, rough, 2. offer, present, submit, extend

tense strained, stretched, tight, rigid, taut relaxed
TENSION

tepid lukewarm, mild

term 1. period, time, duration, 2. condition, premise, 3. name, call, designate, dub, title, label, tag

terminate end, finish, close, conclude, stop, cease, complete begin TERMINAL, TERMINATION

terrible dreadful, horrible, deplorable, outrageous, scandalous, vile, wretched, abominable, detestable, despicable, contemptible, shocking, appalling (*Slang* — awful, atrocious) wonderful, superb

terrific great, superb, magnificent, marvelous, wonderful, colossal, tremendous, glorious, divine, sensational (*Slang* — super)

terrify frighten, horrify, appall, shock, awe, petrify, paralyze, stupefy (*Slang* — scare stiff)
TERROR, TERRORIZE

territory land, region, area, zone, place, country, district, section

terse brief, concise, short, condensed, compressed, curt, succinct, laconic lengthy, long

test 1. examine, question, quiz, interrogate, query, grill, cross-examine, 2. experiment, try, prove, verify

testimony evidence, proof, statement, declaration
TESTIFY

testy impatient, irritated, cross, cranky, irritable, irascible, mean, ornery, ugly pleasant

text subject, topic, theme, issue, point, question, problem, thesis, proposition

textile cloth, material, fabric, goods

texture structure, construction, composition, make-up, finish, grain

thankful grateful, appreciative, obliged, indebted
thankless THANKS

thaw melt, defrost freeze

theater 1. playhouse, hall, stadium, 2. arena, battlefield

theft stealing, filching, pilfering (*Slang* — lifting, swiping)
THIEVE

GLOBE THEATRE

theme 1. subject, topic, text, question, problem, issue, point, proposition, 2. composition, paper, article, treatise, essay, dissertation, discourse, discussion, study, thesis, 3. motif

theory explanation, speculation, supposition, hypothesis, inference, opinion, impression, idea, thought, attitude, view, conception, judgment

therefore hence, consequently, accordingly, for that reason

thick 1. broad, massive, bulky, coarse narrow, 2. numerous, swarming, teeming, crowded empty, 3. stupid, dense, asinine, dull (*Slang* — dumb, numskulled) bright

thief robber, pilferer, filcher, burglar, crook THIEVE

thin 1. slender, lean, slim, svelte, slight, frail, skinny, gaunt, lanky fat, 2. scanty, sparse, meager plentiful

think 1. believe, expect, imagine, deem, fancy, presume, gather, deduce, judge, conclude, guess, suppose, assume, suspect, infer, understand, 2. consider, contemplate, reflect, study, ponder, deliberate, meditate, reason, concentrate, muse, theorize

thirsty 1. dry, arid, parched, dehydrated, 2. desirous, craving, hungering for (*Slang* — crazy for) satisfied
THIRST

thorough complete, intensive, sweeping, all-out, full
shallow, incomplete

thoroughfare passage, road, highway, street, avenue, boulevard, turnpike, expressway, thruway, freeway

though however, in any case, nevertheless, notwithstanding

thought 1. thinking, idea, notion, contemplation, reflection, consideration, reasoning, deliberation, meditation, 2. care, attention, regard, concern, indulgence thoughtlessness THOUGHTFUL, THOUGHTLESS

thrash 1. beat, pound, knock, rap, batter, spank, whip, lash (*Slang* — wallop, lick), 2. toss, move violently, flounder, tumble, pitch, rock, roll, reel, wallow

threaten 1. warn, caution, advise, admonish, alert, forebode, 2. menace, intimidate, bully, terrorize, harass, browbeat, bulldoze (*Slang* — buffalo) THREAT

threshold doorway, portal, gateway

thrifty economical, saving, frugal, prudent, careful, economizing, sparing wasteful THRIFT

thrill tingle, excite, titillate, delight, enrapture, enthrall, enchant, charm bore

thrive prosper, grow, develop, increase, sprout, flourish, mushroom, boom, bloom shrivel, fade, fail

throb beat, pulsate, palpitate, pound, thump

throng crowd, cluster, congregate, gather, assemble, collect, meet

throw toss, cast, furl, fling, pitch, heave, chuck, flip, sling

thrust push, shove, press, bear, ram, drive, prod, goad, propel

thump strike, blow, pound, beat, knock, hit, jab, poke, punch, rap, bang, bat, clout (*Slang* — slug, belt, bash, sock, paste, swat, wallop)

thunderstruck astonished, amazed, surprised, astounded, bewildered, dumbfounded, aghast, awed, spellbound, flabbergasted

thus therefore, hence, consequently, accordingly, so

thwart frustrate, foil, oppose, defeat, balk, spoil, ruin, hinder, inhibit, obstruct, hamper, impede, prevent, prohibit, forbid, deter (*Slang* — foul up, gum up, louse up)
help, assist, encourage

ticket 1. label, stamp, sticker, seal, tag, 2. pass, certificate, token, credential, voucher, 3. ballot, slate, 4. summons, subpoena, citation

tickle amuse, delight, titillate, entertain, charm, thrill, excite

tidings news, information, word, advice

tidy 1. neat, orderly, trim, well-kept, shipshape sloppy, 2. considerable, large, sizable, grand, big, goodly, substantial
TIDINESS

tie fasten, bind, lash, wrap, strap untie, open

tier row, line, layer, level, story, deck

tight 1. firm, rigid, stiff, taut, tense relaxed, 2. snug, compact, close loose, 3. scarce, hard to get, sparse, rare, skimpy plentiful, 4. stingy, ungenerous, closefisted, miserly (*Slang* — penny-pinching) generous

till 1. cultivate, plow, work, 2. money drawer, cash register, moneybox, vault, safe, depository

tilt tip, slope, slant, incline, lean, list

timber wood, lumber, logs

time 1. duration, period, interval, spell, term, age, generation, era, epoch (*Slang* — hitch, stretch), 2. occasion, opportunity, chance, opening, 3. rhythm, tempo, meter, measure

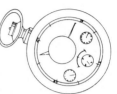

timepiece clock, watch

timetable schedule, list, program

timid shy, bashful, coy, demure, reserved, restrained, retiring, meek, sheepish, fearful, cowardly, shrinking bold
TIMIDITY

tinge color, tint, stain, dye

tingle sting, prickle

tinker mend, repair, fix, service, condition, patch up

tinkle ring, sound, toll, peal, chime, jingle

tint color, tinge, dye, stain, shade

tiny small, minute, undersized, little, slight, puny, wee large

tip 1. end, extremity, limit, tail, point, 2. slope, slant, tilt, list, leaning, inclination, 3. gratuity, premium, bonus, 4. advice, warning, information, pointer

tiptop excellent, first-rate, superior, high-class, topnotch inferior

tired weary, exhausted, fatigued, weak, run-down rested
TIRE, TIRELESS, TIRESOME

title name, label, tag, designation, caption, headline

toast drink to

together collectively, simultaneously, concurrently, jointly, cooperatively alone

toil labor, work

token 1. proof, sign, indication, evidence, clue, mark, symptom, 2. memento, remembrance, trophy, souvenir, keepsake, relic, 3. ticket, certificate, voucher, coupon, check

tolerate allow, permit, bear, endure, suffer, stand, abide, accept prohibit, forbid
TOLERABLE, TOLERANCE, TOLERANT

toll 1. ring, peal, chime, tinkle, jingle, 2. charge, fee, due, dues, fare, tax, duty, tariff, assessment, revenue, levy, tithe

tomb grave, vault, crypt, shrine, mausoleum

tone 1. sound, pitch, key, note, intonation, 2. spirit, character, style, nature, quality, mood, 3. condition, vigor, shape, 4. color, shade, hue, tint, tinge, stain, complexion

tongue language, speech, talk

tonic medicine, stimulant, bracer

too 1. also, besides, additionally, as well, furthermore, 2. very, exceedingly, overly, excessively

tool implement, instrument, utensil, apparatus, device, gadget, appliance

top head, highest, summit, peak, crown, tip, apex, acme, zenith, maximum   bottom

topic subject, theme, text, question, problem, issue, point, plot

topmost highest, uppermost, maximum, head, supreme

topple tumble, fall, overturn, sprawl, stumble

topsy-turvy upside-down, inverted, reversed, confused, jumbled, chaotic, mixed up (*Slang* — fouled up, haywire, snafu, balled up, screwed up)   orderly

torch light, lantern, lamp

torment pain, distress, torture, agonize, harrow, irritate, inflame, persecute, harass, molest, bother, trouble, harry, heckle, badger, pester, worry, tease, plague (*Slang* — pick on, ride)

tornado whirlwind, windstorm, tempest, blizzard, squall, gale, hurricane

torrent flood, burst, eruption, stream, outbreak, deluge

torrid   hot, sweltering, burning, scorching, blistering, roasting, broiling, scalding, seething, sizzling   cold

torture   pain, distress, torment, agonize, harrow, inflame, persecute, plague

toss   throw, cast, fling, pitch, hurl, sling, heave, chuck, flip (*Slang* — peg, fire)

tot   child, little one (*Slang* — kid)

total   1. whole, entire, complete partial, 2. add, sum up, figure up, count

touch   1. feel, contact, finger, handle, manipulate, 2. graze, brush, reach, scrape, skim, 3. affect, move, stir, impress, strike, 4. borrow, ask for, beg (*Slang* — mooch, bum, panhandle, hit up)

touching   tender, provoking, affecting, moving, pathetic

tough   1. hardy, strong, firm, sturdy, durable weak, 2. hard, difficult, complicated, obscure, unclear, vague easy

tour   journey, travel, voyage TOURIST

tournament   contest, tourney, game, sport, play

tow   pull, heave, haul, tug, draw, drag

towering   huge, lofty, high, elevated, soaring, immense, monumental, gigantic TOWER

town   metropolis, city, municipality

toxic   poisonous, venomous, noxious, deadly, malignant

toy   plaything, trinket, bauble

trace   1. copy, reproduce, duplicate, transcribe, draw, sketch, outline, delineate, 2. seek, track, trail, follow, smell out, 3. bit, small amount, touch, dash

track   1. path, trail, road, 2. mark, trace, sign, clue, evidence

tract   area, field, sphere, expanse, space, extent, measure, dimension

traction   friction, pulling, drawing, tugging, hauling

trade   1. exchange, barter, bargain, deal, switch, reciprocate, traffic, swap, 2. vocation, occupation, business, work, line, calling, profession, practice, pursuit, career, craft

tradition   custom, long usage, folklore   TRADITIONAL

traffic   1. buy or sell, exchange, trade, bargain, barter, deal, 2. vehicle movement

tragic   disastrous, dreadful, sad, catastrophic, grievous   TRAGEDY

trail   1. follow, pursue, go after, shadow, heel, tail, tag along, 2. track, hunt, trace, run down, 3. path, road, line

train   1. teach, rear, bring up, direct, drill, exercise, practice, prepare, condition, cultivate, discipline, nurture, foster, educate, groom, 2. series, succession, line, sequence, file, string, row, procession, column, 3. railroad cars

trait   characteristic, feature, peculiarity, earmark, type, quality, property, attribute, idiosyncracy, habit, pattern

traitor   betrayer, informer, tattler, blab, spy, undercover man (*Slang* — squealer, stool pigeon, rat, double-crosser, snitch, stoolie, fink)   TRAITOROUS

tramp   1. march, parade, hike, 2. vagabond, vagrant, hobo (*Slang* — bum)

trance   spell, ecstasy, rapture, hypnosis

tranquil   calm, peaceful, quiet, serene, untroubled noisy, tumultuous   TRANQUILIZE, TRANQUILITY

transact   execute, perform, discharge, dispatch, enact, carry out   TRANSACTION

transfer   hand over, deliver, pass, sign over, change hands

transform   change, convert, alter   TRANSFORMATION

transgress   overstep, trespass, encroach, infringe   TRANSGRESSION

transient fleeting, passing, migratory, vagrant, straying, drifting, wandering, roaming, roving, rambling, meandering, temporary, transitory, short-lived   permanent

transition change, conversion, transformation, transfer TRANSIT

translate interpret   TRANSLATION

transmit send over, pass along, dispatch, forward, transfer TRANSMISSION

transplant transfer, transpose, shift, change, move, reset

transportation conveyance, carrying, carriage TRANSPORT

trap catch, snare, hook

trash rubbish, rubble, scrap, debris, litter, junk

travel journey, go, proceed, move, pass, progress, traverse

treacherous deceiving, unreliable, two-faced, fraudulent, shifty, tricky, underhanded, insidious, shady TREACHERY

tread walk, step, pace

treason betrayal, double-dealing   (*Slang* — double-cross, sellout)

treasure 1. cherish, value highly, hold dear, adore, idolize, worship, prize, appreciate, 2. store, assets, accumulation, collection, funds, resources, abundance, fortune, wealth

treat 1. deal with, think of, consider, regard, handle, behave toward, 2. doctor, minister to, attend, nurse, 3. delight, pleasure, thrill, enjoyment

treatise study, thesis, article, paper, essay, dissertation, discourse, discussion

treaty agreement, compact, alliance, settlement, arrangement, truce, armistice

trek   travel, journey, voyage, migration

tremble   shake, quake, vibrate, shiver, quiver, quaver, shudder

tremendous   1. enormous, great, huge, immense, vast, titanic, colossal, gigantic, giant   small, minute, 2. superb, exquisite, magnificent, marvelous, glorious, divine, terrific, sensational   awful

tremor   trembling, shaking, quiver, quake, shiver

trench   ditch, moat, dugout, foxhole, channel

trend   direction, course, tendency, drift, current, movement

trespass   intrude, transgress, encroach, infringe, overstep

trial   1. test, experiment, tryout (*Slang* — workout), 2. trouble, hardship, tribulation, ordeal, 3. court case

tribe   group, class, set, kind, people, family, sect, breed, clan, folk, culture   TRIBAL

tribunal   court, forum, board, council

tribute   1. contribution, donation, subscription, 2. compliment, praise, glorification, eulogy, laudation

trick   deceive, cheat, hoax, dupe, delude, betray, fool, hoodwink (*Slang* — kid, spoof)   TRICKY

trickle   leak, drip, dribble, drop

tried   tested, proved

trifle   small amount, little bit   abundance, lots.
TRIFLING

trigger   begin, start, touch off, spark, fire, kindle   conclude

trim   1. cut, shave, pare, reduce, lower, 2. decorate, ornament, adorn, dress, garnish, deck, beautify, embellish, furbish, tidy, straighten up, clean, fix up, spruce up

trinket   trifle, bauble, knickknack, toy, plaything

trip 1. stumble, tumble, topple, fall, 2. journey, voyage, trek, tour, expedition, pilgrimage, excursion, jaunt, junket, outing

triumph victory, success, conquest, winning defeat
TRIUMPHANT

trivial unimportant, petty, trifling, slight, superficial, shallow, frivolous, light, foolish, silly, inane important

troop group, band, unit, company, party, gang, crew, body, bunch, crowd, mob

trophy prize, award, laurels, reward, memento, souvenir, remembrance, keepsake

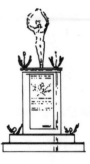

trot run, sprint, bound, trip

trouble distress, worry, disturb, agitate, perturb, disquiet, stir, bother, upset, discomfort, vex, plague calm, soothe
TROUBLESOME

troupe band, company, group, party, gang, crew

truant absentee

truce pause, rest, respite, break, recess, intermission, interruption, interval, armistice, peace

trudge plod, lumber

true real, actual, unmistaken, veritable, certain, valid, genuine, authentic, natural, legitimate, bona fide, right, proper, correct, exact, accurate false TRULY, TRUTH

trust believe, credit, accept, rely on, depend on distrust
TRUSTWORTHY

try 1. attempt, test, experiment, prove, verify, essay, undertake (*Slang* — take a fling at, have a go at, give it a whirl, make a stab at), 2. judge, prosecute, hear

trying annoying, distressing, difficult, troublesome, bothersome, burdensome

tube pipe, hose, reed

tuck   fold, crease, bend, gather

tuft   clump, bunch, cluster, group

tug   pull, jerk, wrench, draw, tow, haul, yank

tuition   teaching, instruction, education, schooling

tumble   fall, toss, sprawl, topple, stumble, wallow, flounder, pitch, plunge, lurch

tumult   noise, uproar, disorder, disturbance, commotion, turmoil, hubbub, racket, fracas, fuss, pandemonium, turbulence, excitement, rumpus, to-do, row   quiet, peace TUMULTUOUS

tune   melody, music, harmony, song

tunnel   underground passage, cave, grotto, cavern

turbulent   violent, disorderly, unruly, tumultuous, storming, frenzied, wild, blustering, furious, frantic, excited, riotous   calm, peaceful

turf   grass, sod

turmoil   commotion, disturbance, tumult, noise, uproar, disorder, hubbub, racket, fracas, fuss, pandemonium, turbulence, excitement, rumpus, to-do, row   quiet, peace

turn   1. rotate, pivot, swivel, wheel, twist, gyrate, go around, shift, swerve, veer, curve, circle, 2. change, alter, vary, 3. spoil, sour

tussle   struggle, wrestle, scuffle, contend, fight, battle (*Slang* — scrap)

tutor   teach, instruct, coach, prime, educate, school, enlighten, direct, guide, show, train, drill, prepare, condition

twig   branch, limb, sprig, sprout, shoot

twine   rope, cord, string

twinge   pain, pang

twinkle   sparkle, gleam, glitter, glisten, glimmer, shimmer, blink, shine

twirl   spin, rotate, whirl, turn, wind, swivel, wheel, pivot, gyrate

twist   1. turn, wind, curve, rotate, swivel, pivot, wheel, gyrate, circle, 2. change, falsify, misrepresent, distort, color, disguise, camouflage, alter

twitch   jerk, jiggle, fidget

type   kind, class, group, sort, ilk, variety, species, nature, make, brand, character, genus

typhoon   storm, hurricane, whirlwind, cyclone, tornado, twister

typical   representative, symbolic, characteristic, distinctive

tyrant   dictator, slave driver, despot, oppressor, martinet, taskmaster, disciplinarian   TYRANNICAL, TYRANNY

U

ugly   1. unattractive, unsightly, homely, plain, hideous pretty, 2. cross, cranky, bad-tempered, disagreeable, unpleasant, quarrelsome, irritable, testy, perverse, mean, ornery   pleasant

ultimate   last, final, terminal, conclusive, eventual

umpire   judge, referee, moderator, arbitrator, mediator

unable   incapable, incompetent, unfit, unqualified   able

unaccountable   unexplainable, inexplicable

unaccustomed   unusual, unfamiliar, strange, unused to accustomed, used to

unanimous   agreed, solid, concurrent, in complete accord

unarmed unprotected, defenseless, unshielded, unequipped
armed

unassuming modest, meek, humble, unpretentious, natural, genuine, sincere, honest boastful, arrogant

unattended alone, unaccompanied

unavoidable inevitable, certain, sure, inescapable
uncertain

unaware ignorant, unknowing, unconscious, unmindful,
unsuspecting aware

unbearable intolerable, insufferable tolerable

unbecoming inappropriate, inapt, unfit, unsuitable, improper, indecent suitable, proper

unbelievable incredible, doubtful, questionable, unconvincing, suspicious believable

unbend straighten, relax, loosen, slacken, let up, ease up
bend

unbiased impartial, fair, unprejudiced prejudiced

unbounded free, unconfined, unrestricted, wide-open

unbroken continuous, uninterrupted, constant, even,
regular, steady, perpetual, whole broken

uncanny strange, mysterious, weird, creepy, eerie

unceasing continual, constant, incessant, endless, interminable, perpetual, everlasting

uncertain doubtful, unsure, speculative, changeable, unpre-
dictable, insecure, precarious certain, sure

unchain free, release, unshackle, extricate chain, bind

unchanged same, permanent, unaltered, regular, constant,
steady changed, irregular

uncivilized barbarous, savage, bestial, wild, brutal, unrefined, uncouth, uncultured civilized, refined

unclean 1. dirty, filthy, soiled, grimy, smutty, slimy, polluted, contaminated, infected, 2. evil, obscene, lewd, foul, pornographic, indecent
clean

uncomfortable distressing, painful, disturbed, bothered, troubled, upset, uneasy comfortable

uncommon rare, unusual, unique, novel, different, original, infrequent, scarce common

uncompromising firm, unyielding, obstinate, stiff, rigid, adamant, unbending, inflexible, strict, relentless
compromising, flexible

unconcerned uninterested, indifferent, blasé, nonchalant, apathetic, easygoing concerned, interested

unconditional unqualified, absolute, unlimited, positive, complete, total, perfect, entire, utter, explicit, express
conditional, limited

unconscious 1. senseless, out cold, 2. unaware, unintentional, unthinking, preoccupied, absent-minded, oblivious
conscious, aware

unconstitutional illegal, unlawful, illegitimate, unauthorized legal

uncouth awkward, clumsy, crude, ungainly, vulgar, coarse, gross, rude, crass, boorish, unrefined, unpolished, uncultured, uncivilized, barbarous, common, base
genteel, courteous, suave

uncover reveal, expose, disclose, open, unmask
cover, conceal

uncultivated wild, undeveloped, rough, crude, fallow
cultivated, refined

undaunted fearless, unafraid, daring, bold, brave, courageous, confident, persevering, untiring meek, fearful

undecided uncertain, unsettled, pending, vague, indefinite, undetermined certain, settled

under below, beneath, lower *above*

underfed undernourished, starved

undergo experience, go through, meet, have, feel, encounter, endure, suffer

underhanded secret, sly, shifty, surreptitious, deceitful, dishonest, fraudulent, crooked, unscrupulous (*Slang —* shady) *open, honest*

undermine weaken, sabotage, destroy

underneath below, beneath, under *above*

underrate minimize, underestimate, belittle *overrate*

understand comprehend, follow, grasp, conceive, realize, know, appreciate

undertake 1. try, attempt, essay, pursue (*Slang —* have a go at), 2. promise, contract, agree UNDERTAKING

undertone murmur, whisper

undesirable objectionable, disagreeable, unpleasant, distasteful, offensive, repulsive, intolerable, loathsome, unsatisfactory, unacceptable, unsuitable *desirable*

undisputed unquestioned, uncontested, doubtless, accepted, believed *questionable*

undisturbed untroubled, calm, tranquil *disturbed*

undo 1. unfasten, untie, disassemble, take apart, dismantle *assemble*, 2. destroy, spoil, abolish, wreck *build*

undress disrobe, unclothe, strip *dress*

undying eternal, immortal, unfading, imperishable, everlasting, indestructible *fading, perishable*

unearth dig up, discover, extract, withdraw, remove, uncover, disclose, turn up *bury, hide*

unearthly strange, weird, ghostly, wild, supernatural, odd, queer, peculiar, spooky, uncanny, eerie

uneasy   restless, disturbed, anxious, uncomfortable, fidgety, impatient, distressed, troubled, bothered, agitated, perturbed (*Slang* — in a stew)   calm, comfortable
UNEASINESS

unemployed   idle, jobless, unoccupied, out of work
employed   UNEMPLOYMENT

unending   continuous, endless, uninterrupted, ceaseless, incessant, interminable, perpetual, infinite, everlasting, permanent

unequal   uneven, irregular, disparate   equal

uneven   unequal, irregular, disparate   even

unexpected   unforeseen, unanticipated, chance, accidental, sudden   foreseen, expected

unfailing   faithful, loyal, sure, true, constant, reliable, dependable, sound, firm, secure, stable, substantial, steadfast   undependable, unreliable

unfair   unjust   fair

unfaithful   untrue, unloyal, false, fickle   faithful

unfamiliar   unusual, strange, uncommon, rare, unique, novel, new, different   familiar, common

unfasten   undo, loosen, open, untie, unhook   fasten, close

unfavorable   unsatisfactory, harmful, detrimental, adverse, contrary, uncomplimentary, disapproving   favorable

unfeeling   hard-hearted, cruel, heartless, cold, callous
sensitive, compassionate

unfinished   incomplete, rough, undone, crude
finished, completed

unfit   unsuitable, inappropriate, incapable, incompetent, unqualified   fit, suitable

unfold   1. reveal, show, open, disclose, uncover, unmask, spread, unfurl hide, conceal, 2. explain, show, clarify, demonstrate, illuminate

unforeseen unexpected, unanticipated, sudden expected

unforgettable memorable, notable, noteworthy, remarkable, extraordinary, exceptional ordinary

unfortunate unlucky, ill-fated (*Slang* — jinxed) lucky, fortunate

unfriendly unsociable, aloof, standoffish, distant, remote, cool, uncordial, inhospitable friendly

ungainly awkward, clumsy, bungling, unhandy, ungraceful, gawky graceful

ungracious impolite, rude, discourteous, uncivil, ungallant, unkind gracious, polite

ungrateful unappreciative, unthankful grateful, thankful

unguarded unprotected, defenseless, unshielded, unsheltered guarded, protected

unhappy sad, sorrowful, uncheerful, displeased, discontented, wretched, miserable, dejected, depressed, downcast, disheartened, despondent, melancholy, blue, wistful, unsatisfied happy, cheerful

unhealthy sickly, infirm, unwholesome, unsound, weak, feeble, frail, run-down, ill, ailing, unwell, indisposed healthy

unheeded disregarded, unnoticed, unobserved, unseen heeded

uniform 1. even, alike, unvaried, constant, steady, regular, consistent, symmetrical, balanced uneven, irregular, 2. outfit, costume

unify combine, unite, consolidate, join, mix, merge, blend, fuse separate UNITE, UNITY

unimportant insignificant, trifling, inconsequential, trivial, petty important

uninhabited unoccupied, deserted, abandoned, vacant occupied

unnecessary needless, uncalled-for, unessential, superfluous, excess necessary, essential

unnerve upset, frighten, scare, alarm, startle

unnoticed unobserved, unheeded, unseen noticed, seen

unobserved unnoticed, unheeded, unseen noticed, seen

unoccupied vacant, idle, deserted, open, available, uninhabited occupied

unpack unload, discharge, dump pack

unpaid owing, due, outstanding paid

unparalleled unequaled, matchless, unsurpassed, unexcelled, unbeatable, incomparable, extraordinary, exceptional, remarkable

unpleasant disagreeable, distasteful, unsavory, undesirable, unlikable, offensive, odious, repulsive, repugnant, obnoxious pleasant

unpopular unappreciated, unloved, unwanted, unlikable, unwelcome, disliked popular, well-liked

unprecedented unduplicated, uncopied, unimitated, extraordinary, exceptional

unprepared unready, unwary ready

unprincipled dishonest, crooked, corrupt, criminal, fraudulent, unscrupulous (*Slang* — shady, fishy) honest

unprofitable unrewarding, fruitless profitable, rewarding

unquestionable certain, positive, undeniable, indisputable, questionable, dubious

unravel 1. unsnarl, untwist, disentangle tangle, 2. solve, explain, answer, resolve, figure out, unriddle, decipher, decode, crack

unreal 1. imaginary, fanciful, fictitious, 2. counterfeit, make-believe, false, mock, imitation, simulated, ungenuine, unauthentic, artificial, synthetic, pseudo, fake (*Slang* — phony) real

unreasonable extreme, excessive, outrageous, preposterous, extravagant, impractical, illogical, senseless, inconsistent, irrational, unsound reasonable, moderate UNREASONABLY

unrest restlessness, agitation, disquiet, stir, disturbance, commotion, turmoil, tumult, excitement calm, peacefulness

unrestrained unchecked, free, uncurbed, uncontrolled restrained

unrivaled unmatched, unequaled, incomparable

unruly disorderly, riotous, wild, rampant, lawless orderly

unsafe dangerous, unsound, precarious, imperiled, risky, perilous, hazardous safe

unsatisfactory ungratifying, inadequate, insufficient, inferior, second-rate, low-grade satisfactory

unscramble solve, explain, resolve, clear up, figure out, decipher, decode, crack scramble, confuse

unscrupulous dishonest, unprincipled, unethical, corrupt, crooked, criminal, fraudulent honest, moral

unseat displace, dislodge, depose, remove, dismiss, overthrow

unseemly improper, unsuitable, vulgar, indecent, offensive, coarse, crude, objectionable, wrong, unbecoming proper, suitable

unselfish generous, liberal, free, unsparing, lavish, open-handed, bighearted, magnanimous selfish

unsettle disturb, shake, upset, startle, shock (*Slang* — jar, jolt)

unshaken firm, resolute, staunch, solid, fixed, unyielding, steady shaken

unsightly ugly, unattractive, homely, plain pretty, attractive

unskilled untrained, untalented, inexperienced, raw, green, amateurish skilled, talented

unsophisticated simple, natural, artless, naive, green sophisticated

unsound unwise, ill-advised, unreasonable, illogical, unreliable, hazardous, risky, unsafe, unsure sound, reliable

unstable unsteady, weak, unsound, unreliable, unsure, unsafe stable, reliable

unsteady unstable, weak, unsound, unreliable, unsure, unsafe steady, reliable

unsuccessful failing, unfortunate, abortive, fruitless successful

unsuitable unfit, inappropriate, unbecoming, improper, unsatisfactory, objectionable, unacceptable suitable, proper

unthinkable unbelievable, incredible, impossible, inconceivable, absurd, ridiculous, preposterous, outlandish, unheard-of believable

untidy neglected, slovenly, shabby, frowzy, messy, sloppy, seedy (*Slang* — mussy) tidy, neat

untie loosen, unfasten, undo tie

untrained unskilled, unprepared, untalented, inexperienced, amateurish, raw, green trained, skilled

untried new, unused, untouched, unproved tried, tested

untrue 1. false, wrong, faulty, erroneous, fallacious true, right, 2. unfaithful, disloyal, fickle faithful, loyal

unused 1. new, fresh, firsthand, original, untouched used, 2. unaccustomed, unfamiliar with used to

unusual uncommon, rare, unique, out of the ordinary, novel, queer, odd, different usual, ordinary

unveil uncover, disclose, reveal, show, expose, open, unmask, divulge cover, hide

unwelcome unwanted, uninvited welcome

unwell ailing, ill, sick, indisposed well, healthy

unwholesome unhealthy, unsound wholesome

unwieldy unmanageable, unhandy, awkward, clumsy, cumbersome, bulky manageable

unwilling reluctant, forced, involuntary, disinclined willing

unwise foolish, unreasonable, unsound, senseless, irrational wise

unwittingly unknowingly, unconsciously, unintentionally, unmindfully aware

unyielding firm, stubborn, immovable, inflexible, unpliable, unbending, adamant, rigid flexible

upbraid reprove, blame, reprimand, scold, rebuke, chide, lecture (*Slang* — dress down, tell off, bawl out, chew out)

uphold support, confirm, sustain, maintain, bolster, substantiate, corroborate UPHELD

upkeep maintenance, support, backing, provision

uplift raise, elevate, erect, lift, hoist, improve lower

upper higher, superior, greater lower UPPERMOST

upright 1. standing, erect, vertical prone, 2. honorable, upstanding, reputable, respectable, moral, law-abiding

uprising revolt, rebellion, mutiny, insurrection, riot, revolution

uproar noise, disturbance, commotion, hubbub, tumult, clamor, turmoil, racket, fracas, ado, fuss, pandemonium, rumpus, to-do, row peace, quiet

uproot extract, withdraw, remove, pull out

upset 1. overturn, tip over, unsettle, capsize, 2. disturb, perturb, trouble, agitate, confuse, shake, fluster, ruffle, bother, unnerve soothe, calm, 3. overthrow, defeat, revolution, overwhelm

upshot conclusion, result, effect, consequence, outcome, fruit, development

up-to-date modern, contemporary, advanced, current, fashionable old-fashioned, outdated

urban metropolitan, civic, municipal, citified suburban

urge push, force, drive, plead, advise, incite, press, pressure, coax, goad, prod, spur, agitate, provoke, prompt discourage

urgent pressing, important, imperative, compelling, crucial, essential, vital, necessary, moving, motivating, driving unimportant

usage method, practice, way, use, procedure, treatment, handling

use 1. utilize, employ, practice, exercise, handle, manage, 2. exploit, take advantage of

useful helpful, beneficial, profitable, serviceable, advantageous, practical, functional, handy, valuable useless

useless worthless, ineffectual, fruitless useful

usher escort, conduct, guide, lead, squire, chaperon, accompany, attend

usual customary, ordinary, normal, regular, common, everyday, typical unusual USUALLY

usurp take command, take charge, take over, assume control, overthrow, seize command

utensil implement, tool, instrument, apparatus, device, appliance

utilize use, employ

utmost greatest, farthest, highest, extreme, most

utter 1. complete, total, absolute, thorough, downright, outright, pure, plain, sheer, unqualified, positive   partial, 2. speak, express, say, voice, sound

V

vacant unoccupied, empty, void, barren, desolate   occupied, filled   VACANCY

vacation rest, holiday, leave, recess, furlough, liberty, sabbatical

vaccinate inoculate, immunize   VACCINE

vacuum 1. void, 2. sweep, clean

vagabond wanderer, tramp, vagrant, hobo (*Slang* — bum)

vague unclear, indistinct, indefinite, dim, faint, shadowy, obscure, blurred, fuzzy, hazy, misty   clear, definite

vain 1. unsuccessful, ineffectual, futile, fruitless   successful, 2. proud, conceited, boastful, egotistical, egocentric, haughty, lofty, self-centered (*Slang* — stuck-up, cocky, uppish)   humble

valiant brave, courageous, bold, gallant, heroic, chivalrous, daring, unafraid, dauntless   cowardly

valid sound, true, good, effective, proven, established, well-grounded, cogent, legal, lawful, adequate, authorized   invalid, false

valor bravery, courage, boldness, gallantry, prowess, heroism   cowardice

value worth, excellence, usefulness, importance, significance, weight, merit, quality   VALUABLE

vandal destroyer, wrecker, demolisher   VANDALIZE

vanish   disappear, fade, go away, perish, cease to be   appear

vanquish   conquer, defeat, overcome, subdue, crush

vapor   steam, fog, mist, gas, fume, smoke

various   different, several, many, diverse

varnish   1. paint, coat, lacquer, shellac, 2. distort, falsify, misrepresent, color, disguise, camouflage

vary   change, differ, alter, deviate
VARIABLE, VARIATION, VARIED, VARIETY

vast   large, immense, great, enormous, huge, stupendous, colossal, monumental, mammoth, gigantic   tiny

vault   1. jump, leap, spring, hop, bound, hurdle, 2. storehouse, compartment, depository, safe, coffer, 3. burial place, crypt, tomb

veer   shift, turn, swerve, change

vegetation   plants, flora, growth

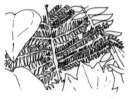

vehement   forceful, violent, fierce, furious, severe, intense, ardent, zealous   VEHEMENCE

vehicle   conveyance, carriage

veil   cover, screen, hide, conceal, cloak, mask, disguise, camouflage, eclipse, obscure   unveil, uncover

velocity   speed, swiftness, quickness

vend   sell, peddle   buy   VENDOR

venerable   revered, dignified, stately, grand, majestic, imposing, honorable, important

vengeance   revenge, retaliation, reprisal, avengement

venom   1. spite, malice, animosity, bitterness, rancor, 2. poison   VENOMOUS

vent   hole, opening, outlet, passage, duct

ventilate 1. air, aerate, refresh, cool, 2. discuss, reason, talk over, deliberate, consider, treat, examine, study
VENTILATION

venture undertaking, enterprise, project, attempt, adventure, experiment

verbal oral, spoken, uttered, said, vocalized, voiced, pronounced, sounded, articulated, enunciated written

verdict decision, judgment, finding, determination, decree, ruling, pronouncement

verge 1. tend, incline, lean, border, 2. edge, rim, brink, border

verify confirm, prove, certify, validate, substantiate, authenticate, corroborate, support, document, double-check

versatile skilled, talented, competent, capable, many-sided, adaptable, all-around

verse 1. poetry, rhyme, jingle, 2. section, chapter, passage, part, division, measure

versed experienced, practiced, skilled, educated

version rendition, account, interpretation

vertical standing, upright, perpendicular, erect

very greatly, extremely, much, exceedingly, quite, pretty, intensely

vessel 1. container, receptacle, 2. ship, boat

veteran 1. experienced, practiced, worldly-wise, sophisticated, 2. ex-soldier

veto refuse, deny (*Slang* — kill) accept

vex annoy, disturb, trouble, provoke, irk, irritate, aggravate

viaduct bridge, span

vibrate shake, quiver, quake, tremble, quaver, wobble, bob, bounce

vice fault, bad habit, weakness, failing, foible, shortcoming, wrongdoing, malpractice, sin, crime

vicinity 1. region, area, zone, territory, place, district, quarter, section, neighborhood, 2. nearness, closeness, proximity

vicious evil, wicked, spiteful, malicious, bad, naughty, wrong, sinful, base, low, vile, cruel, ruthless, brutal, barbarous, savage, ferocious, inhumane   kind, good

victim prey, dupe, loser, underdog, sufferer (*Slang* — sucker, sap, pigeon, pushover, butt, goat, easy mark)

victory success, triumph, conquest, winning, win, knockout   defeat   VICTOR, VICTORIOUS

vie compete, rival, compare with, match

view 1. see, sight, look at, behold, observe, perceive, watch, regard, 2. opinion, belief, attitude, sentiment, feeling, impression, notion, idea, thought, conception, theory, judgment, outlook

vigilant watchful, alert, wide-awake, cautious, careful   VIGIL, VIGILANCE

vigorous strong, energetic, potent, powerful, mighty, forceful, rugged, hearty, robust, dynamic, intense, active, lively, animated, spirited, vivacious   weak   VIGOR

vile foul, disgusting, bad, terrible, dreadful, horrible, deplorable, outrageous, wretched, base, odious, obnoxious, abominable, detestable, despicable, contemptible (*Slang* — awful, atrocious)

villain rascal, scoundrel, rogue, knave, scamp, devil

vim force, energy, vigor, verve, punch, dash, drive, snap, push (*Slang* — pep, kick, zip)

vindicate justify, uphold, defend successfully, pardon, excuse, forgive, acquit   VINDICATION

vindictive   revengeful, avenging

violate   break, trespass, infringe   VIOLATION

violence   anger, rage, passion, fury, force, intensity, vehemence   VIOLENT

virgin   pure, spotless, unused, new, firsthand, original, fresh, green   used, old

virtual   real, actual, basic, essential, fundamental   VIRTUALLY

virtuous   good, moral, righteous, angelic, saintly, chaste, pure, innocent, faultless, sinless   sinful, wicked   VIRTUE

visible   apparent, manifest, noticeable, open, exposed, perceptible, evident, obvious, plain, clear   concealed

vision   1. sight, perception, 2. apparition, image, illusion, phantom, fantasy, dream, specter, ghost   VISUAL

visit   attend, go to, call on, drop in   VISITOR

vista   view, scene, sight, outlook, perspective, scenery

vital   1. necessary, important, essential, fundamental, needed, required   unimportant, 2. living, alive, animate

vitality   strength, vigor, might, potency, power, energy, stamina (*Slang* — guts)

vivacious   lively, sprightly, animated, gay, spirited, exuberant, active, spry, brisk, dynamic, energetic (*Slang* — snappy, peppy)   lethargic, dull

vivid   bright, brilliant, strong, clear, distinct, splendid, flamboyant, glaring, dazzling, rich, colorful   dull

vocal   spoken, uttered, said, voiced, pronounced, sounded, oral, verbal, articulated, enunciated

vocation   occupation, business, profession, trade, work, line, calling, craft

vociferous   noisy, loud, shouting, clamoring, boisterous, blatant   quiet, hushed

vogue   fashion, style, mode, popularity

voice   express, utter, verbalize, say, articulate, enunciate, pronounce, communicate, tell

void   1. empty, vacant, bare, blank, barren, desolate, unoccupied, deserted, open, available   filled, 2. invalid   valid

volume   1. amount, quantity, capacity, content, proportion, measure, extent, 2. book, publication, writing, work

voluminous   generous, ample, extensive, bulky
skimpy, slight

volunteer   offer, come forward   VOLUNTARY

vomit   retch, heave, regurgitate, spew, throw up (*Slang* — upchuck, puke)

voracious   ravenous, greedy, piggish, hoggish, gluttonous

vote   ballot, choice, voice, poll, referendum, designation, selection, decision, determination

vouch   testify, bear witness, swear, promise, assure, guarantee, vow, pledge

vow   swear, promise, assure, guarantee, vouch, pledge

voyage   journey, travel, sail, cruise, navigate   VOYAGER

vulgar   coarse, common, unrefined, indecent, improper, offensive, crude, crass, obscene, uncouth, foul, filthy, nasty
refined   VULGARITY

vulnerable   sensitive, exposed, open, susceptible, unprotected, defenseless

vying   competitive, rival

W

wad   lump, mass, hunk, chunk

wag   wave, flap, flutter, wobble, bob, sway, swing

wage   1. pay, payment, salary, remuneration, compensation, 2. pursue, conduct, carry on, practice, exercise, follow, engage in

wager   bet, gamble, hazard, stake

wagon   carriage, vehicle

waif   stray, vagabond, gamin

wail   cry, screech, shriek, scream, squeal, howl, bawl, moan

wait   delay, postpone, defer, put off, shelve, table, procrastinate, stay, tarry, linger

wake   awake, arise, get up, rouse, arouse, stir (*Slang* — rise and shine, roll out)

walk   step, tread, pace, ambulate, stroll, hike

wallet   billfold, purse

wallop   hit, thrash, beat, strike, knock, jab, smack, whack, slug, rap, whip, spank, flog, bat, crack, clout, lick (*Slang* — belt, clobber, paste, clip, swat, sock)

wallow   roll, flounder, rock, reel, toss, tumble, pitch, lurch, swing, sway

wan   pale, faint, weak, pallid, sallow, pasty, ashen, haggard, ghastly   ruddy, robust

wand   rod, staff, scepter

wander   stray, meander, roam, rove, gad, drift, ramble WANDERER

wane   decrease, diminish, lessen, decline, subside, recede increase, wax

want   1. desire, wish for, like, long for, fancy, 2. need, lack, require

wanton   1. reckless, careless, hasty, impetuous, wild careful, 2. erratic, whimsical, uncontrolled, unreasonable steady, 3. immoral, unchaste, wayward, loose   moral

war fight, conflict, strife, battle, combat, engagement, encounter, clash, struggle, hostilities, campaign
WARFARE

warehouse storehouse, depository, depot

warm 1. hot, tepid, 2. friendly, enthusiastic, cordial, congenial cold WARMTH

warn 1. inform, give notice, notify, caution, forebode, advise, alert, 2. threaten, menace WARNING

warp bend, twist, distort, contort

warrant 1. authority, right, sanction, authorization, certificate, justification, reason, voucher, writ, mandate, 2. guarantee, pledge, promise, vow, word, assurance, oath

warrior soldier, fighter

wary cautious, careful, guarded, suspicious, distrustful (*Slang* — cagey, leery) WARILY, WARINESS

wash clean, scrub, launder, bathe, rinse, scour

waste 1. spend, squander, consume, use up, exhaust save, 2. garbage, refuse, scraps, dregs, rubbish

watch 1. look at, view, observe, regard, 2. guard, protect, mind, tend, shield, care for

waterway channel, river, canal, passageway

wave 1. sway, move, flap, flutter, swing, 2. signal, gesture

wax 1. increase, gain, grow, rise, swell, heighten, intensify, enlarge, develop, sprout, flourish decrease, wane, 2. polish, burnish, furbish, glaze, shine

way 1. manner, style, custom, mode, fashion, usage, practice, 2. means, method, procedure, process, 3. point, feature, detail, respect, 4. direction, line, course, 5. distance, reach, remoteness, length, extent, 6. will, nature, character, constitution, temperament, disposition, mood, humor

waylay ambush, attack, lie in wait

wayward 1. disobedient, lawless, undisciplined, troublesome, loose, immoral, difficult, perverse, contrary, wanton   obedient, 2. irregular, unsteady, changeable, unsettled, erratic, wavering   steady, settled

weak feeble, powerless, impotent, debilitated, fragile   strong, sturdy   WEAKEN, WEAKLING

wealth riches, affluence, prosperity, abundance, opulence, possessions, fortune, treasure, resources, assets   poverty   WEALTHY

wean cure, break of, turn away from

weapon arms, munition

wear 1. dress in, have on, don (*Slang* — sport), 2. deteriorate, corrode, decay

weary tired, fatigued, weak, faint, listless, lethargic, sluggish   lively, energetic   WEARILY, WEARINESS, WEARISOME

weather climate, the elements

weave braid, intertwine, lace

wed marry, join, unite (*Slang* — get hitched)   WEDDING

wedge jam, push, lodge, squeeze

wedlock marriage, matrimony

weep cry, shed tears, sob, bawl, blubber, snivel

weigh measure, gauge, assess, estimate, rate, appraise, size up   WEIGHT

weighty 1. heavy, hefty   light, 2. burdensome, oppressive, onerous, 3. important, influential, powerful, effective, serious   trivial

weird strange, mysterious, odd, fantastic, queer, creepy, peculiar, spooky, eerie, ghostly   normal

welcome   greet, receive

weld   join, unite, cement, bind, solder

welfare   well-being,   good,   benefit,   interest,   advantage, behalf,   prosperity,   success,   comfort

welt   sore, swelling

whack   strike, blow, hit, jab, smack, slug, bat, crack, clout, lick (*Slang* — belt, clobber, paste, clip, swat, sock, wallop)

wharf   pier, dock, port, harbor

wheedle   coax, persuade, urge, press, goad, prod

whet   sharpen, edge, intensify, stimulate

whether   if, provided, on condition

whiff   odor, smell, scent, fume

whim   fancy, notion, caprice, fad, phase   WHIMSICAL

whimper   cry, whine

whine   cry, whimper

whip   strike, beat, thrash, spank, flog, pummel, lash, lace, strap, paddle (*Slang* — lick, wallop)

whirl   spin, turn, wheel, twirl, reel, swirl, rotate, pivot, swivel, gyrate

whisk   1. sweep, brush, 2. rush, speed, hurry, hasten

whisper   murmur, mutter, mumble

whole   complete, total, entire, one, solid, undivided   partial WHOLLY

wholehearted   earnest, sincere, hearty, cordial, gracious insincere

wholesome   healthful, beneficial, salutary, sound

wicked   1. bad, evil, sinful, vicious, naughty, wrong, base, low, vile   good, saintly, 2. difficult, rough, hard, unpleasant, severe, rugged, tough   easy, pleasant

wide   broad, extensive, expansive, roomy, ample, spacious, far-reaching   narrow   WIDTH

wield   hold, wave, handle, manipulate, use, employ, manage, control

wife   spouse, mate, married woman

wig   hairpiece, toupee

wiggle   wriggle, squirm, writhe, twist, fidget, jerk, twitch, toss

wild   1. untamed, uncivilized, savage, unchecked, unrestrained, violent, barbarous, brutal, rampant, fierce, ferocious, bestial   tame, 2. rash, crazy, reckless, impetuous, furious, mad, wanton, frantic, frenzied, rabid, delirious, hysterical, overwrought   calm

wilderness   wasteland

will   1. wish, desire, pleasure, fancy, hope, urge, inclination, volition, 2. resolution, determination, decision, resolve, purpose, choice, selection, election, intention, design, plan, contemplation, 3. bequest, legacy, testament

willful   1. stubborn, obstinate, headstrong, bullheaded, firm, adamant, uncompromising, 2. intended, intentional, designed, meant, deliberate, conscious, calculated, voluntary, purposeful   involuntary, chance

willing   ready, consenting, agreeable, inclined, compliant, eager (*Slang* — game)   unwilling

wilt   wither, deteriorate, pine, droop, fade, shrivel, dry up, languish   flourish

wily   tricky, cunning, crafty, sly, artful, shifty, smooth, slippery, foxy, canny, shrewd, clever (*Slang* — cagey, slick)

win   gain, capture, carry, succeed, triumph, be victorious, prevail   lose   WINNER

wince   recoil, draw back, flinch, shrink, cringe

1. wind   1. air, draft, breeze, gust, 2. breath, respiration

2. wind   turn, bend, twist, roll, coil, spiral, pivot, swivel

wink   blink, squint

winning   charming, attractive, alluring, fascinating, captivating, lovely, enchanting, enthralling, intriguing, bewitching, interesting, delightful, appealing, enticing, inviting, tantalizing, provocative, fetching (*Slang* — come-hither)   repulsive

wipe   rub, stroke

wire   1. telegraph, cable, 2. fasten, tie, bind, 3. electrify

wiry   1. lean, stringy   stout, 2. strong, tough, muscular, athletic, brawny   weak

wise   bright, smart, knowledgeable, sage, knowing, learned, profound, educated, cultured, scholarly   dull, uneducated   WISDOM

wish   want, desire, long for, like, fancy, request

wistful   longing, yearning, desirous, pining, hankering, nostalgic, homesick, melancholy, pensive

wit   humor, intelligence, understanding, sense

witch   hag, vixen, shrew, sorceress

withdraw   1. retreat, recede, retire, fall back, reverse, quit, vacate, abandon   advance, 2. remove, subtract, deduct, extract   deposit   WITHDRAWAL

wither   fade, shrivel, dry up, shrink, wane, deteriorate, droop, wilt, languish, pine   flourish

withhold   1. reserve, keep, save, preserve   spend, 2. refuse, deny, disallow   give

within   inside, in   outside

without   lacking, wanting, needing, missing, short of, minus, less   with

withstand   endure, resist, oppose, repel   succumb, give in

witness   1. testify, vouch, swear, 2. see, observe, behold, view, perceive, discern, glimpse, spy, sight

witty   clever, amusing, humorous, funny, whimsical, droll   dull

wizard   1. sorcerer, conjuror, 2. expert, master, genius (*Slang* — champ)

wobbly   unsteady, shaky, wavering, rickety, trembling   steady

woe   grief, trouble, distress, misery, anguish, agony, heartache, desolation, oppression, sorrow   happiness WOEFUL

woman   female, lady, matron

wonder   1. marvel, gape, stare, 2. doubt, question, be uncertain, not know

wonderful   marvelous, remarkable, striking, astonishing, incredible, extraordinary, exceptional, superb, magnificent, miraculous, splendid, fabulous   ordinary, plain

woo   court, pursue, bid for

woods   forest, bush

word   phrase, say, express, put, voice, tell, communicate WORDING

work   1. labor, toil, accomplish, achieve, effect, make, busy, occupy, engage, employ, 2. operate, run, manage, conduct, handle, manipulate, maneuver

workout   1. exercise, practice, drill, 2. trial, test, rehearsal, dry run, tryout

world   universe, earth, globe

worn   1. damaged, old, secondhand, used, impaired, ragged new, 2. tired, wearied, fatigued, weak, faint   energetic

worry   bother, trouble, torment, molest, harass, harry, badger, plague, vex   soothe, console

worse   deteriorated, impaired, aggravated

worship   respect, honor, idolize, adore, revere, admire, cherish

worth   merit, usefulness, importance, value, benefit, significance, weight   WORTHLESS

wound   1. harm, hurt, injure, damage, bruise   heal, 2. irritate, provoke, sting, infuriate, madden, pain, grieve, offend   soothe

wrangle   argue, quarrel, dispute, bicker, contend, disagree, spat, differ, squabble, row (*Slang* — hassle)

wrap   cover, envelop, sheathe, surround, encompass, bind   uncover

wrath   anger, rage, ire   WRATHFUL

wreath   garland, coronet, festoon

wreck   destroy, ruin, devastate, ravage, demolish, dismantle, disassemble

wrench   1. pull, twist, jerk, tear from, wrest, yank, 2. sprain, injure, hurt, strain

wrestle   struggle, battle, fight, tussle   WRESTLER

wretch   1. beggar, sufferer, poor devil, derelict, 2. scoundrel, villain, knave, rogue, shrew

wriggle   twist, turn, wiggle, squirm, writhe

wring   twist, squeeze, press out, wrest

wrinkle   1. fold, ridge, crease, corrugate, furrow, pucker, crinkle, 2. age, grow old, decrease, decline

writ   notice, order, warrant

write   record, inscribe, mark, note, post, pen, scribe   WRITER, WRITING

writhe 1. twist, turn, squirm, wiggle, 2. suffer, hurt, ache, wince, anguish, moan, agonize

wrong 1. incorrect, improper, unfit, unsuitable, untrue, false, mistaken right, 2. bad, evil, ill good

wry twisted, crooked, askew, contorted, distorted

X

x-ray photograph

Y

yacht boat

yank jerk, pull, wrench, wrest, tug, draw, heave, haul (*Slang* — lug)

yap bark, yelp, howl

yard 1. court, pen, enclosure, confine, 2. three feet

yarn 1. thread, wool, 2. story, tale, account, narrative, anecdote, spiel

yearn desire, long for, wish for, hope for, pine for, crave YEARNING

yell shout, cry out, call, howl, scream, shriek, whoop, roar, bellow, wail, squall, bawl (*Slang* — holler)

yelp bark, yap, howl

yield 1. produce, give, grant, bear, provide, supply, furnish, 2. surrender, give up, relinquish, waive, forego, part with, sacrifice keep, retain

yoke harness, shackle, bridle

young youthful, juvenile old

youngster child, minor, youth, kid

youthful young, fresh, juvenile, childish, kiddish, callow
mature, old YOUTH

yowl cry, howl, yell, whoop, shriek, scream, wail

Z

zany foolish, clownish, scatterbrained, comical, silly, crazy

zeal enthusiasm, eagerness, sincerity, ardor, fervor, passion
indifference, apathy ZEALOUS

zenith peak, summit, crown, top, tip, crest, apex, acme,
pinnacle bottom, base

zero nothing, naught, nil, none

zest relish, enjoyment, gusto, savor, delight, eagerness,
pleasure, satisfaction

zone region, area, territory, place, district, quarter, section,
division, part, department, compartment, vicinity,
neighborhood

zoo menagerie, animal enclosure

zoom speed, zip, whiz, fly